S0-BMT-171

HUSTLER DAYS

HUSTLER DAYS

MINNESOTA FATS
WIMPY LASSITER
JERSEY RED
AND AMERICA'S
GREAT AGE
OF POOL

R.A. DYER

THE LYONS PRESS
GUILFORD, CONNECTICUT

AN IMPRINT OF THE GLOBE PEQUOT PRESS

Copyright © 2003 by R. A. Dyer

ALL RIGHTS RESERVED. No part of this book may be reproduced or transmitted in any form by any means, electronic or mechanical, including photocopying and recording, or by any information storage and retrieval system, except as may be expressly permitted in writing from the publisher. Requests for permission should be addressed to The Lyons Press, Attn: Rights and Permissions Department, P.O. Box 480, Guilford, CT 06437.

The Lyons Press is an imprint of The Globe Pequot Press.

10 9 8 7 6 5 4 3 2 1

Printed in the United States of America
Designed by LeAnna Weller Smith

Library of Congress Cataloging-in-Publication Data

Dyer, R. A. (Richard A.)
  Hustler days : Minnesota Fats, Wimpy Lassiter, Jersey Red, and
America's great age of pool / by R.A. Dyer.
      p. cm.
Includes bibliographical references (p.   ).
  ISBN 1-59228-104-4 (HC : alk. paper)
  1. Minnesota Fats, 1913- 2. Lassiter, Luther. 3. Breit, Jack. 4.
Billiard players—United States—Biography. I. Title.
  GV892.D94 2003
  794.73'3'0922—dc22

                        2003017753

FOR GRETTEL, ALEC, AND SOPHIA

CONTENTS

HUSTLER DAYS

INTRODUCTION

"That's what the game's all about."

—*Minnesota Fats, as portrayed by actor Jackie Gleason,* The Hustler.

THE HEAVY WOODEN DOORS OF AMES POOL HALL SWING WIDE. The round clock, tick-tocking just above, strikes eight. And there stands Minnesota Fats, the lion. With a rose in his lapel and a fedora atop his head, Fats regally strides forth. A shiny diamond adorns a plump finger.

"Is your name Felson, Eddie Felson?" Fats offers the young man a smile, a broad gleeful one—but there's cruelty there too. And deceit. *"I hear you been looking for me."*

"You're Minnesota Fats, ain't you?" says Eddie. *"They say Minnesota Fats is the best in the country where I come from. They say that ol' Fats shoots the eyes right off them balls…"*

Thus it begins: this, the single most important display of pool prowess in American pool history. Played out by actors Jackie Gleason and Paul Newman, the famous scene took less than twenty minutes of the first reel in Robert Rossen's 1961 film *The Hustler.* Time enough, though, to launch careers and create fortunes. Time enough to spark new table sales, create new pool halls. *The Hustler* inspired millions of Americans to take up pool; it literally sparked a renaissance.

Although I came to pool after *The Hustler,* I must still indirectly credit this film for my eventual arrival. In 1986 Hollywood produced a sequel, *The Color of Money.*

I then lived in Costa Rica, was just out of college, and had more than a little time on my hands. So I saw the film once, a second time, and then saw it again. The film led me to the local pool halls, and there, living my own bachelor days, I first discovered the true possibilities of this, the most roguish of sports.

That I first came to pool in Costa Rica—and not the United States—is not without its own significance. There one can behold a poolroom culture that no longer exists in northern climes, but which *The Hustler* nonetheless describes perfectly. Men argue over missed balls, or hurl crumpled bills across green felt, or make unmakable shots at ten before midnight. But other than my friend and fellow expatriate Kathleen, few women ventured inside.

Neither could I discern any of the typical socioeconomic hierarchies that govern all other aspects of human existence. All class distinctions had curiously vanished. I perceived a pecking order, certainly—but one based on an ability to gamble and pocket balls, not one based on wealth and education. It didn't seem to matter whether a man earned twenty colones a day or twenty thousand—but rather whether he could *win* it.

Although I didn't realize it then, what I had stumbled across in Costa Rica was the culture of the *permanent bachelor*. This culture once flourished in the United States and permeates *The Hustler* like the sweet stench of cheap cigars. It is an integral part of the story of American pool and it serves as a backdrop for this book. I came to understand it only after some friends handed me a yellowing dog-eared copy of *Hustlers, Beats and Others* by sociologist Ned Polsky.

"The poolroom," wrote Polsky, "blossomed as a kind of behind-the-lines or inner frontier, the new no-woman's land...[catering] to men who wanted to be able to curse and spit tobacco, fight freely, dress sloppily, gamble heavily, get roaring drunk, whore around." He writes that pool hustlers "comprise one of the last American occupational groups in which the majority of adults are non-homosexual bachelors." They virtually live in the poolroom. They build their careers around life there.

I spent several more years in San José, and then continued watching pool players upon my return to Texas in 1989. In the early 1990s I met Jack Breit, the legendary pool hustler also known as Jersey Red. Although then an old man, Red would still elicit reverent whispers from the regulars: *There's Jersey Red, man—best one-pocket player ever.* Red's vision was failing; he was graying and dead broke. He wore dress slacks with his white sneakers, a Hawaiian shirt, a gimme cap. But it didn't matter. To the regulars in the Cue & Cushion, his favorite room in downtown Houston, Red remained king.

Ain't seen nothing like it, man. Never.

Red reminded me a lot of what I had encountered in Costa Rica, and—although married—he reminded me of the culture described by Ned Polsky. The two other principal subjects of this book—world champion Wimpy Lassiter and the charlatan known as Minnesota Fats—also fit this mold. Like Red, each came from working-class backgrounds, each went childless,[1] and each was drawn early to the danger and mystery of pocket billiards. They forsook what most of us take for granted: sometimes a wife, sometimes a home, always a job.

Against all of society's dictates, Red, Wimpy, and Fats made an honest living doing absolutely fucking nothing. They never worked, at least as most Americans understand the word.

----

[1] Rather, the pool hustlers *admit* to no children. R&B legend Etta James, in her autobiography, provides evidence that she was the product of an out-of-wedlock union between her mother and Minnesota Fats. James and Fats—legendary entertainers both—also bear a striking resemblance in photographs.

BUT I, LIKE MOST OTHER AMERICAN ADULTS, CANNOT LIVE SUCH A LIFE. In fact, one of my deepest concerns during the years I spent researching and writing *Hustler Days* was how it led to long hours away from my family. But the book alone was not to blame: my newspaper job often required me to work ten or twelve hours per day, sometimes I sacrificed weekends, and worst of all, I often *worried* about work. And for what? So I could pay the mortgage and utility bills? So I could get cable service? I work, and I work, and I work— and yet I *still* fret about the kids' college fund and whether I have enough socked away for retirement.

In this regard, my life is like that of any other American adult with a family to feed. We live lives fraught with seemingly ridiculous worries, unending vague anxieties. We live lives overcome by the mundane. Deny it if you like, but how else to explain midlife crises, petty addictions, the purchase of cherry-red sports cars? How else to explain bad men and bad marriages? What many Americans really want, if they pause a moment to think about it, is *escape*. This is the unpleasant secret of suburbia, and explains the romance of pool. The danger of the sport is not so much that it corrupts, but rather that it offers an alternative.

Consider this: Rudolf Wanderone, the man who would become Minnesota Fats, once said that he enjoyed nothing more than driving into the country to look at wheat fields. He would gather his friends together and they'd motor about in the afternoon sun. After an hour or more of searching the horizon they'd head back home—but not before stopping at a roadside fruit stand, where Fats would eat a whole red watermelon, making his face sloppy with juice.

For much of his life, Wanderone slept whenever he felt like it, ate when- ever he felt like it, played poker and one-pocket when he could get games.

And this, for Wanderone, constituted "work." Like Red and Lassiter, Fats lived a vampiric life, a life without clocks, but one interrupted by sudden acts of larceny. This life comes by necessity to the professional hustler—for one who dares to gamble for a living must embrace cheap hotels and sleeping until 2 p.m., and must reject home mortgages and nine-to-five responsibilities. To mix the straight life with the gambling life invariably leads to failure at both. There is no middle ground.

LIKE THE EBB AND FLOW OF A STORM'S TIDE, POOL THROUGH THE YEARS HAS ALTERNATELY CAPTURED THE IMAGINATION OF AMER-ICANS AND LEFT THEM INDIFFERENT. Its origins predate the nation's founding, as it was popular in the Old World among the English and probably invented during the fifteenth century by the French.[2] The European aristocracy often built billiard rooms as adjuncts to their posh country estates, and from there the game spread downward to the working man.

Pool's moral stigmatization also began before its arrival in America. In England, for example, Polsky finds evidence in 1674 of the nobility seeking to distinguish itself from the hoi polloi, then overrunning the "gentlemen's game." By 1744 the government of Dublin even attempted a crackdown on public rooms. This stigmatization would lead to pool's reputation for moral deviancy—a stigmatization that would cling to the sport throughout its history—and would become the rock on which a distinct poolroom culture could form.

----

[2] However, the game was *not* played by the ancient Egyptians, as has been supposed by some fanciful writers. A reference to billiards by Shakespeare (he has Cleopatra saying "Let's to billiards") is probably responsible for this misconception.

The English and French upper classes exported the game to their colonial holdings. In the United States, one of the earliest references to the game comes from the diaries of colonial explorer William Byrd. In 1710, Byrd notes the purchase of a pool table...and then using it to lay his wife. "It is to be observed that the flourish was performed on the billiard table," wrote Byrd on July 30 of that year. George Washington also enjoyed a game or two and was said to have won a pool match in 1748.

Pool then died off in the Colonies for some years (apparently stricken by the lack of hardwood maples necessary for the construction of billiards equipment) but would reemerge with a vengeance during the first half of the nineteenth century. In 1828 President John Quincy Adams came under fire for the installation of a pool table in the White House. In 1859 *Frank Leslie's Illustrated Newspaper*, a popular publication of the time, began a regular column on the sport. A few months later Michael Phelan, the father of American billiards, won $15,000 in one of the first-ever national competitions.

From there, a full-on boom carried pool through the 1920s, when legend Ralph Greenleaf earned $2,000 per week just performing trick shots, and continued nearly unabated through the Depression and World War II. But then its popularity fell off precipitously and the game nearly disappeared during the 1950s.

I think a brief note explaining why I selected the subjects of this book is necessary. Although Fats, Jersey Red, and Wimpy were among the finest pool players of their age, there were others who could match them. Fats himself was nowhere near as great as his legend and was surely inferior to both Jersey Red and Wimpy Lassiter. But Fats was the most colorful player of the era and the most famous ever to wield a cue. Wimpy was the world's all-time finest nine-ball player, and Jack "Jersey Red" Breit was both colorful and one of the era's best one-pocket and all-around players. Jack Breit was also a friend of mine.

Throughout this work, other players will be highlighted: Cornbread Red from Detroit; Daddy Warbucks, a close friend of Fats; Cicero Murphy, the nation's first African-American champion; Eddie "Knoxville Bear" Taylor; Bill "Weenie Beenie" Staton; Boston Shorty; Handsome Danny Jones; Cowboy Jimmy Moore; and another of Fats's friends, Marshall "Tuscaloosa Squirrel" Carpenter.

Their glory days came in the 1960s, during a new renaissance of blue-chalk poolrooms, televised tournaments, all-night gambling. A pool sensation washed across America then, a Hula Hoop™ fad of suckers and stolen money. It came as a result of a Hollywood film, two actors, and a pool game in which Fast Eddie feels tight, tight but good, and Minnesota Fats could shoot the eyes right off them balls.

"It was pure, raw...*real*," said one eyewitness of that magnificent age. "After *The Hustler* there came a moment in time, a freeze frame, and, oh my God—it was awesome."

1

SHOOTING DOWN THE COWBOY

"Back in the '20s, every living human was making what they called whoopee from morning to night." —*Minnesota Fats*

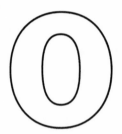**N JANUARY 19, 1913, AT AN HOUR UNCER-TAIN, THE CHILD WHO WOULD BECOME MINNESOTA FATS TOOK HIS FIRST GASPING BREATH IN THIS WORLD.** This birth came not in Minnesota—in fact, nowhere near Minnesota—but in New York City, specifically Manhattan, the neighborhood of Washington Heights, 167th Street and Amsterdam Avenue. He received the Christian name of Rudolf Walter Wanderone Jr. (after his dad), but his family called him "Roodle." He had three half sisters: Rosie, Julie, and Jerry.

Fats probably did not enter this world fat, although he certainly wasted no time becoming so. At age five, Fats later boasted, he was as big as a pony. At age eight, "on account of I was so enormous," Fats started wearing long pants. At age ten he stood five feet, five inches tall and weighed 150 pounds. Such titanic girth he inherited from his father, whom Fats remembered as a whale of a man, a hulking behemoth who stood six feet, two inches tall, weighed 275 pounds, and could pull boxcars like a mule. Fats also inherited his father's face, fleshy and somewhat flat, as well as his father's wide-set blue eyes, his dark hair, his tiny tulip of a mouth.

Rudolf Sr. (one of sixteen brothers and sisters) had spent his childhood on a farm in Suhr, Switzerland—a farm that Fats later described as containing one million storks. Fats said his father, as a young man, served as a mercenary fighter in several South American wars: "He was a professional soldier, a gun for hire. But he wasn't what you called a reactionary or a zealot or a fanatical partisan. He always fought for whatever side offered the best proposition." Fats's father also supposedly fought in the Russian-Japanese War of 1906— but for which side and for what pay remains a mystery.

The tanking of the Swiss economy sent Rudolf Sr. sailing for New York, where he took a $1.50-a-week job as a blacksmith's apprentice. Fats said his father probably waited no more than two or three of these $1.50 weeks to request a twenty-five-cent raise. *Vot about this I hear of opportunity in America? I am a good blacksmith, yah? I am strong like an ox, yah? I deserve more money.* The blacksmith's answer was emphatic: yes, Rudolf Sr. had come to a land of opportunity—but if this hulking Swiss beast didn't like the pay, he could find opportunity *elsewhere.* The temerity of Rudolf's request shocked and disgusted the blacksmith. His new employee, after all, had practically just fallen off the boat.

And so Rudolf Sr., the 275-pound monster immigrant, dejectedly returned to his iron block anvil and figured his options. He furled his flat face, he squinted his far-flung blue eyes, he thought and he muttered. And then, after five minutes of very deep rumination, Rudolf Sr. "picked up that anvil with one arm like it was a suitcase, carried it about 100 yards into an open field and dropped it in a big hole.

"The old blacksmith," said Fats, "screamed like he was getting deported… It took ten men to lift that anvil out of the hole."

The lesson Fats took from this tale, and from the example of his father's life, was that one should never work too hard. Or at least, hard work should never interrupt happiness. Fats's father did work—he later created a heating and plumbing business—but he also remained particular about which jobs he would accept. And more than work, Rudolf Sr. preferred the life of bars, saloons, pool halls: the sporting life. "Never do anything that makes you unhappy," the father told the son. "An unhappy man will not live long. Ah, but if you are happy, then already you are a rich man. If a man has health and a roof over his head and good food and good friends, what else does he need? What else? He is already wealthy beyond compare."

Right then and there, Fats devoted his life to doing nothing. "And that's all I've ever done."

Fats's mother, by contrast, was a fanatically hard worker, a diligent, rosary-praying Roman Catholic, the keystone of the House of Wanderone. One of eighteen children born to a family in Basel, Switzerland, Rosa came to America to escape a bad man and a bad marriage, bringing Fats's three half sisters with her.

Rosa believed in the sanctity of work—literally, the sanctity of it—and Fats recalled that she sometimes would sic the parish priests on the idle stumblebum drunks of the neighborhood. But Rosa could never get little Fats to lift a finger. Despite her best efforts, Fats lived in a perpetual state of transcendent idleness, a sublime childhood in which he did nothing strenuous or worthwhile. He became a victim of his own precociousness, eventually growing into a gigantic, ham-eating, fleshy pink lump. Fats, forever the Giant Baby. Even at age fifty, Fats somehow remained perversely cute.

"I had a mother and three sisters who worshipped me," Fats said. "And when I was two years old they used to plop me in a bed on a jillion satin pillows and spray me with exotic perfumes and lilac water and then they would shoot me the grapes. When my old man walked in, he would laugh and say, 'Ah, my son, the sultan.' He would tell my mother and the sisters: 'More pillows! More grapes!'

"Then he would jump in the bed with me and we would wallow in those pillows and belt out the grapes until it was time for dinner."

FATS BLAMED A WHITE GOOSE NAMED GANS FOR HIS INTRODUCTION TO POCKET BILLIARDS. Fats was a four-year-old child, Gans his ill-tempered pet. The bird and boy were inseparable. But sometime around 1917, while Fats and his goose were strolling together through a New York amusement park, Gans somehow slipped from his tin collar and fled honking and flapping into a big pavilion. And like Alice down the Rabbit Hole, little Fats gave chase inside.

"It was an enormous place with bowling lanes and card tables and a bar that looked like a distillery and right near the bar, they had these pool tables," Fats recalled in his autobiography. "It was the first time I ever saw one. So I held Gans in my lap and watched the games. When I got to watching those balls rolling I was like in a trance and I would sit there for hours and hours.

"One day, two fellows quit a table, so I tied Gans to the table leg and started rolling the balls. At first I tried to shoot them like they were marbles, but after awhile, I started sneaking a cue stick and stroking the balls.

"Kids my age weren't supposed to play pool in a bar. But when I was five years old, I was as big as a pony. I weighed over 100 pounds. Anyway, I had won the bartender a zillion hams and turkeys at the raffle wheels, so he would let me play anytime a table was open. And that's how it all started."

By age six, Fats supposedly could run a rack of balls. By age eight he was throwing dice "in the back of ball diamonds, in cellars and in tenement houses, where the ice men and the delivery men came." And at age ten, during a vacation to the old country with his father, little Fats matched up with a verifiable champion.

It was 1923, and Rudolf Sr. had recently made the acquaintance of Erich Hagenlocher, then the German king of balkline pool.[3] Hagenlocher reportedly went just crazy agog over Rudolf's prodigy son—"Little Pink Cheeks" he called him—and gave the boy tips regarding caroms and angles. Hagenlocher also instilled in the boy a true love for pool. After that vacation, young Fats thought of little else.

In 1926 a local automobile association hired Fats to play an exhibition against Cowboy Weston, a former nine-ball champ. At the time Fats was just thirteen; Weston was in his mid-fifties. The association promoted the event as a sort of "May and December proposition," Fats recalled, and sent boys all over town with posters. The build-up lasted nearly a month.

New cars—polished, shiny, and ready for quick sale—paraded down Washington Heights. Auto dealers brought their Templars. They brought Maxwells and open-topped Lexingtons. Atop the lead convertible sat Cowboy Weston, resplendent in his white chaps, his ten-gallon Stetson, his impossible pointy boots that went right up to his knees. Crowds cheered at his passing.

But if all the bombast and screaming in any way robbed Fats of his confidence, the reality of Cowboy Weston—up close, and in the poolroom— restored it. "He was all gray and weather-beaten," recalled Fats. "He looked so old I figured he came over from the Mayflower." Fats forever claimed utter and absolute courage; he vowed to never, ever allow fear to consume his confidence. It was then, after the gathered boys took their chairs and Weston removed his hat and six-shooters, that Fats came into his own. The game was

---

[3]A variation of billiards, played on a pocketless chalk-marked table.

call-shot straights—any ball, any pocket—to 125. Besides a little rotation, it was all Fats could play.

Perhaps Weston lost that day because he came to entertain the crowd. Perhaps he attempted foolhardy shots, ridiculous shots—and when those shots failed, he left an open table. Perhaps Weston simply neglected to take young Rudolf Wanderone seriously. But whatever the reason, Fats said the former champion found himself defenseless.

Imagine the scene: A young boy wipes his brow, licks his lips, surveys the table. Guided by the gentle touch of plump fingers, colored balls drift quietly into pockets, one after another, with thuds barely perceptible in a hushed room. And when Fats misses, he does so with purpose. He delivers whitey to the far rail, or snuggles it in tight against the rack, and he leaves poor old Cowboy with no shot, no safety, no shelter.

"It was brutal," Fats recalled. "I mean, I really whacked him out cold."

A GLORIOUS TIME, THE 1920S, WITH LONG-HAIRED WOMEN AND RISING HEMLINES. The Wobblies had become an object of hate, Sacco and Vanzetti were put to their wrongful deaths, and young Rudolf Wanderone Jr.—then becoming Broadway Fats, and Double-Smart and Triple-Smart Fats (but not yet *Minnesota* Fats)—had become a bona fide gambler. Fats learned during those years that all men hustled…and that a sweet payoff awaits those who hustle without fear. In the 1920s Fats learned that vice paid.

Fats spent much of the decade at Cranfield's, a second-floor pool hall at 146th and Broadway, just a half mile from Yankee Stadium. By age sixteen he was scaling those stairs daily. He would emerge puffing and sweating into the bright fluorescence, the white linoleum, the green felt. Cranfield's had twenty-six tables, a three-stool lunch counter, a Chinaman's restaurant next door. It reeked of spent cigarettes and hollow curses. Gorgeous colored girls marked points on green slate.

At the lunch counter, Fats would order his usual soda and then begin noisily scarfing steam-table hot dogs: old, nasty, but delicious beyond belief. Incredibly, Fats probably loved eating more than he loved playing pool. Eating, after all, entailed much less effort. The downside, of course, was that the calories made Fats fat. But he couldn't care less. "I wouldn't know a calorie from a chrysanthemum," he once said.

On many such occasions, Fats would watch as the door separating Cranfield's from an adjoining greasy-spoon restaurant swung wide. From it would emerge a man somewhat older than the hustler, but only slightly slimmer. He wore an expensive dark suit, thin lapels, fat tie. The man's belly may have been full of chow mein, his famous mug pasted with a tiny bit of yellow noodle. Players would stand in midstroke. The incessant chatter would cease.

Babe Ruth, the Yankee home run king, the Sultan of Swat, had come to Cranfield's. And following close behind, joining him from the Chinese joint, were a handful of other ball players who took two tables and began running balls, jabbering loudly. It would be a Monday or a Tuesday, an off day for the Yankees, because it was then that Ruth and his cronies often frequented Cranfield's.

Arthur Cranfield, former world champion and only son of the room owner, remembers those visits. Nicknamed "Babe" because of his association with the famous slugger, the boy was just ten years old when Ruth first came around. Blond-headed, lithe, skinny like a deer, Babe Cranfield in 1925 would have been the youngest person in the room—younger even than Fats. Hardly big enough to hold a cue and small, even for his age. But Babe

Cranfield was precocious too, and he would set upon the giant Sultan of Swat, challenging the hot dog-chewing legend to a friendly game of odd-ball, which is like rotation except only every other ball counts.

Cranfield remembers crawling on the table—he was so little, it was easy—and he got to the shots like some sort of trained monkey. And Babe Ruth would laugh and shout and point, and slap his knee. A good guy, Ruth, friendly, and one to share a drink or two and cut up with the other regulars, down in the street, during the New York days of Prohibition.

Fats, gulping down five-hour-old hot dogs from the steamer, would also see other celebrities at Cranfield's. Among them was Ralph Greenleaf, perhaps the greatest pool player ever to hold a cue, even greater perhaps than his pupil, Willie Mosconi. Greenleaf was a handsome man—everybody remembers that—like a Hollywood actor, or some Madison Avenue model. His dark hair was gelled and pushed back, parted in the middle, as was the style during those days. His nose was delicately chiseled; parting his chin was the cleft of a movie star. And Greenleaf smiled easily: a comforting sort of smile, like that of a child.

In that day and age Ralph Greenleaf was a monster, an absolute monster, with a fame rivaling that of Babe Ruth himself. Competing in the world pool tournament of 1919, held in December at Philadelphia's Parkway Building, Greenleaf won every game. He had just turned twenty and still managed to plow through all the elder champions: Bennie Allen, Jerome Keogh (the inventor of straight pool), Johnny Layton, Edward Ralph. Greenleaf then continued winning, over and over again, taking first place at every tournament—for the next *five years*. Nobody could touch him.

It's hard to overestimate the popularity of pool when Fats hustled for dollars at Cranfield's and Ralph Greenleaf reigned as king. Greenleaf parlayed fame into a gig on Broadway, shooting banks and combo trick shots at the Palace Theater for $2,000 a week. Beneath a backdrop of giant mirrors he would appear—elegant beyond belief in a dark tuxedo, flashing a million-dollar smile beneath the big spotlight.

Still other giants could be found, on occasion, around Cranfield's. Fats befriended Titanic Thompson, one of the greatest gamblers who ever lived and the man who gave Fats his first nickname. (According to legend, Thompson had just witnessed Fats's victory over a Coney Island hustler by the name of Smart Henry. The victory, in Thompson's eyes, made Fats "Double Smart.") Fats also befriended Jimmy Castras, also known as Jimmy the Greek, and Arthur Rothstein, who helped rig the 1919 World Series, and who reportedly bet $6 million on the outcome of the 1928 presidential election. These gamblers, said Fats, "were the faculty deans of my alma mater."

PROHIBITION LEFT AN INDELIBLE MARK ON THE PSYCHE OF AMERICA, JUST AS IT MARKED FATS AND BILLIARDS IN GENERAL. Ned Polsky, author of *Hustlers, Beats and Others*, said the rising divorce rate during Prohibition likely drove bachelor men into the poolroom. The multitude of World War I veterans, many of them farm raised, learned city ways during their stateside training for the war—and during R&R overseas. These men likewise came to pool halls.

"Pool was enormous then," said Polsky. "There were more than 10 times as many pool halls per capita as there are now. And they were bigger, and had more tables on average…The war introduced a lot of the rural population to cities and that had as much influence [on the rising popularity of pool] as anything else."

Fats attributed pool's rising popularity during those years to the Volstead Act, adopted by Congress to enforce Prohibition. The act was broken with abandon, he said, and millions of otherwise hardworking, decent Americans— suckers, he called them—found a sort of release through lawbreaking. The suckers frequented the speakeasies and the secret gambling joints, and government agents, few in number but with over 18,700 miles of coast and border to guard, did little to stop it. Decadence descended upon America. Under such conditions, reasoned Fats, could pool halls do anything but thrive?

"Back in the 20s," Fats wrote in his autobiography, "every living human was making what they called whoopee from morning to night. The big proposition was the Volstead Act, which said any sucker found belting the booze was a public enemy. So what happened was all the suckers wanted to be public enemies. They guzzled the bathtub gin like it was lemonade and cut up in those all-night speakeasy joints until the sun came up, even though that kind of action was against the law."

During Prohibition, wrote Fats, the nation's adults went "crazy doing ridiculous things they never would have dreamed of doing if the generals in Washington hadn't put a contraband on the refreshments." And the nation's children, barred from pool halls, stood witness to this wanton lawbreaking.

Under Prohibition, children saw drinking and drunkenness...*everywhere*.

"They knew it was against the law to drink, but everywhere they went they saw people guzzling the juice," wrote Fats. "And when they got home at night, there was the old man sneaking in with a couple more pints. Junior knew the old man wasn't obeying the law, so when Papa told Junior the pool room was out of bounds, the kid almost broke a leg getting there."

Marketing also emerged as a separate industry during Prohibition. Fats witnessed this phenomenon firsthand through the tall boots and six-guns of

Cowboy Weston—and through the glittery hype surrounding Ralph Greenleaf. Fats loved the attention, the fanfare, the razzle-dazzle. And he would emerge from the decade not just as a hustler, but as a *showman*.

And somewhere in there he abandoned PS 132, and he purchased first a Stutz Bearcat and then a Caddy. He played Cranfield's and he played Heights Recreation, and he beat poor old Cowboy Weston. And finally, just as America's magical twenties gave way to its sad thirties, Fats steered clear of Manhattan altogether. He drove his fat Caddy right off Broadway, right out of New York City, right into the big time.

Like the changing of seasons, the wintry blanket of the Great Depression had descended upon America. And Rudolf Wanderone—possessed by some panicky joy, even as dread overtook the nation—went on the road.

His fire burned hot. He was... *invincible*.

UNDER THE
LEMONADE SUN

"Those well-dressed strangers with their slick hair and clean finger-
nails began to drift into town from all around and try and get me.
All the good old boys at City Billiards thought that was pretty
funny. I could always get up plenty of local money to back me, and
we would shoot those strangers loopy-legged and leave them just
enough to catch the bus out of town and split the winnings."

—*Wimpy Lassiter, speaking to* Sports Illustrated, *1967*

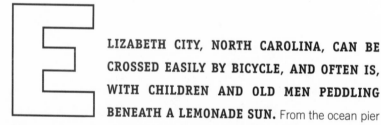

LIZABETH CITY, NORTH CAROLINA, CAN BE
CROSSED EASILY BY BICYCLE, AND OFTEN IS,
WITH CHILDREN AND OLD MEN PEDDLING
BENEATH A LEMONADE SUN. From the ocean pier
to the far side of the tracks (where the black folks live), Elizabeth City has but
one library, one high school, a handful of stores. It seems small in every
respect—smaller, in fact, than its population of thirty-three thousand might
dictate.

Above all, Elizabeth City feels *settled*. But it has not always been so. For bor-
dering the city to the north lies a great stinking chocolate swamp—the Great
Dismal Swamp—with its spindly, grasping vines; its mud red shoals; its stag-
nant, shit-colored canal. It is a place of buzzing, festering malevolence. It is, as
Colonel William Byrd once described it, "a vast body of dirt and nastiness."

If the fate of Elizabeth City has been tied to the Atlantic Ocean, then it also has been tied to the Great Dismal Swamp, which Byrd first explored in 1728 and which General George Washington[4] began draining and dredging in 1764. In 1793 (with those operations still incomplete) Elizabeth City received its charter. And then, in 1805, nearly eighty years after Byrd first explored the swamp, successors to Washington used slave labor to complete a twenty-two-mile waterway.

That waterway, with its flat-bottomed barges drifting quietly like ghosts on a green pond, brought not just travelers and boatmen to the area. It also brought highwaymen and thieves. To the Great Dismal Swamp Roadhouse, built two and a half miles south of the Virginia border, came desperate and wild-eyed fugitives. The Lake Drummond Hotel,[5] built in 1826, became a place of ruinous romance and furious, bloody duels. And from the sea, just to the west, came pirates. Blackbeard was said to have used an Elizabeth City home as a hiding place, and Gentleman Stede Bonnet and Calico Jack Rackham hid their ships in the tidal rivers and sounds up and down the North Carolina coast.

Perhaps the nearby Swamp, and the area's long history of violence and mystery, kept too oppressive a grip on the town. Notwithstanding its proximity to the ocean—despite its intrinsic *pleasantness*—Elizabeth City can lack the jubilation, the irresistible and irresponsible flavor of a vacation resort. The people of Elizabeth City have an undeniable cautiousness about them, the cautiousness of practical people before the unknown, before the wild-eyed and

----

[4] As noted in the introduction, both Byrd and Washington were billiards enthusiasts.

[5] It was also at the hotel that the desolate and sickly Edgar Allen Poe penned "The Raven," one of the most macabre examples of American poetry.

the dangerous. If that mysterious, beautiful, horrible, languid brown pond to the north has left any mark on the character of Elizabeth City, perhaps this is it.

And yet wildness would return to Elizabeth City. For it is here, on November 5, 1918, that the pool hustler Luther Clement Lassiter Jr. was born.

LASSITER'S GRANDFATHER, HENRY E., ONE OF THE FIRST IN THE POOL PLAYER'S FAMILY LINE FOR WHOM RECORDS CAN BE FOUND, FOUGHT IN THE CIVIL WAR. But unlike other North Carolinians, Henry E. did not serve under the Confederate flag. Rather, he became a member of the First North Carolina Infantry, a Union outfit, and records show he made a piss-poor soldier. Copies of the muster roll for the First North Carolina Infantry indicate that Henry E. enlisted in the Union Army at age twenty-five at Mintonville, which then wasn't more than a cross in the road and appears on no modern maps. He possessed blue eyes, black hair, and a complexion described only as "light." The army showed his residence as Gates County, about twenty-five miles from Elizabeth City, and listed his profession as farmer. The last record of Henry Lassiter from the company muster rolls of Company E, First Regiment, North Carolina Infantry, shows him at Beaufort, North Carolina, where he went in May 1864 to recuperate from an unspecified illness.

But between his enlistment on August 4, 1862, and that last known record, Lassiter spent six months in the stockades. The reason remains unclear, but the general muster rolls unequivocally show that Lassiter was "confined by sentence of general court martial" from July 6, 1863, to January 26, 1864, at Fort Macon, North Carolina. The court martial cost him his rank: Lassiter made sergeant on May 1, 1863, but got busted back to private two months later. He recovered part of his rank after his release, getting promoted to corporal in August 1864.

After the war years, Henry E. returned to Gates County, where he farmed potatoes, cabbage, wheat…and sired Luther Clement Lassiter Sr. After the death of his wife, Henry sent young Luther to live with relations—effectively orphaning the boy. Perhaps as a result of that upbringing, Luther Clement Sr. grew up quiet and retiring. And yet there may also have been some wildness about Luther, as none of his relations would keep him for more than a year or two. They constantly shuffled him back and forth.

Florence Stowe, the woman Luther would eventually marry, lived in a big house on Hatteras, one of the islands along North Carolina's Outer Banks. Her father owned several large ships, including schooners. "The only way to get from Cape Hatteras was to catch the ferry and so Mom would come down on a fishing boat with her father to visit relatives in Elizabeth City," recalled Clarence Lassiter, her youngest son. "She would come to visit people and shop, because there was nothing out at Hatteras, except a sandbar. And that's how she became acquainted with my father. That's how it evolved into a relationship."

In 1915, sometime after their marriage, Luther Sr. and Florence Stowe purchased a new home at 406 Pearl Street, in the heart of downtown Elizabeth City, the county seat of Pasquotank. With two floors, a flat-faced exterior, and white-trimmed windows, the house appeared like others on the block. It had a steep, green-painted roof. A porch ran along its perimeter. In the backyard grew a giant cypress, from which hung a children's swing. The house was constructed of wood, painted yellow, and sat along a brick-paved street, once cobblestone but later asphalt.

And it was here, tended by a family physician in a second-story bedroom, that Florence gave birth to the future pool hustler. He would inherit his father's name, including the middle name, Clement, which means calm or sedate.

"Ain't that a laugh?" the pool hustler would later remark. The irony is this: Luther Clement Jr. *did* grow up calm and sedate. He grew up with all the quiet reserve of his father—and then some. He became a living ghost, a dispassionate observer to his own wagers, to his eighteen world titles. He even appeared to sleep through matches.

But while "Clement" accurately described the tranquility of his nature, it utterly failed to capture the chaos of his life. With unnerving placidness, Lassiter dived into a frenzied world of smashed cars and poolroom hustles, of petty arrests and big money.

FOR YOUNG LUTHER, THE GAME BEGAN ON THE HOMEMADE, FOUR-POCKET CONTRAPTION OWNED BY HIS CHILDHOOD CHUM, JACK WEEKS. A tire's inner tube served a double purpose: it held the table together and served as rails. The table came with small cue sticks, but no leather tips, no chalk. Jack, who lived on nearby Martin Street, set up the table in his back-yard, and there the two—Luther, then of medium build and slouching about, and Jack, lanky and thin with dark hair—spent their afternoons. The table played like shit; it was crooked and uneven, with balls veering off to one side or the other. It was a toy, and at first Luther hated it. But even then he had a great stamina, a great tolerance for repetition, and so he quickly became the game's master.

As pool was then near the height of its popularity, it's not surprising that Luther's father also purchased a table. This one required checkers instead of pool balls. The checkers slid about on a hard, wooden surface, and car-omed off one another much like shuffleboard disks. The table came with tiny child-sized cues, which were constructed cheaply and warped quickly.

Clarence, Luther's younger brother, recalled that the game had some qualities of pool—although one could never quite impart English to the disks. "It was a Christmas present, a child's game," said Clarence. "It had four pockets in the corners—drop pockets—and it came with two cue sticks. Short sticks. You'd shoot checkers in those four holes, and you could also play checkers on the thing. I think he started with that, and he pursued it right strong."

The Lassiter boys—Luther ("Bud" to his siblings), Charles, and young Clarence—amused themselves in other ways as well. They constructed small toys using wood scraps and tools from their father's shed. A popular item was the slingshot, particularly useful for downing squirrels and possums. They hung forward, backward, and sideways from the backyard swing, which was attached with long ropes to the tall cypress. They played baseball.

Jack Weeks always joined in. And there was Walter Davis, a boy about Luther's age, who later became Elizabeth City's most famous millionaire. From about age ten to age fifteen, Walter, Jack, and Luther were nearly inseparable—playing ball, running around, swinging like monkeys in the backyard. Walter once broke both arms on the swing—he said he was playing Tarzan, lost his grip, and ended up in twin casts. Luther would pick up a few extra pennies selling candy after school and share what he made with Jack and Walter. He became their benefactor.

Years later, after Luther lost it all, the multimillionaire Walter Davis repaid that early generosity. "[Lassiter's] family was considered more or less middle income," recalled Walter, remembering those early years. "His father was a working man, but he was making as much as anybody, running that mill. But my family, they were really poor farmers. And he [Wimpy] would always give me some money. He would sell candy in the back of the schoolyard, and he would always give me a couple of dollars—and that was a lot of money to me in those days. We didn't have anything and he was always generous."

The Lassiters were a tight-knit family, and the parents expected the children to help with the chores—even Luther, whose aversion to work held throughout his life. The Lassiter social life revolved largely around the dinner table. "Everybody had to be there," recalled Clarence. Typical fare included beef roast, baked chicken, potato salad, creamed potatoes, peas, squash, and collard greens. Clarence said his family "had three meals a day, at home, and that was our big social hour." Florence did the cooking; Luther Sr. ensured that each child washed up and helped clean the dishes. "We lived good," said Clarence. "We had it all."

Florence, like many of the good people of Hatteras, was a tough woman—a disciplinarian. And while she doted on young Luther, she also rode him, moving him to work harder, to help out more. But Luther refused to work. Beyond his schoolyard salesmanship, Lassiter would hold few jobs during his lifetime—and his first came around age thirteen, when he delivered groceries on his bicycle, picking up bags from the Poindexter market half a block from his home. For this, the grocer paid Luther precisely eight and one-third cents an hour.

It was also then that young Luther began bicycling over to Elizabeth City Billiards, where he brushed the tables and swept floors. There he beheld the real wonders of pool: the blue smoke, the crack of ivory against ivory, the muttered curses from sailors and farmers hunched over run-down tables. There he found heroes: gunfighters from the movies, men who could shoot with unnerving straightness, men without fear, men who risked their money and that of others for the promise of more.

"Long time ago, I used to stand there and peek over the latticework into that cool-looking darkness of the old City Billiards in Elizabeth City, North

Carolina," Lassiter later told *Sports Illustrated*. "And I heard the sound of those old ivory balls going 'pock!' Man, there is no other sound in the world nice as a ball dropping into a pocket.

"It seemed as though the place had a special sort of smell to it that you could breathe. Like old green-felt tables and brass spittoons and those dark, polished woods. Then a bluish haze of smoke and sweet pool chalk and, strongest of all, a kind of manliness. All through me, I could feel something else, I didn't know what, but it seemed like a fine, lazy tension in the air. I was thirteen. And that did it."

WIMPY REMAINED IN SCHOOL A WHILE LONGER, ALTHOUGH YEAR-BOOKS OFFER LITTLE EVIDENCE THAT HE MADE ANY IMPRESSION AT ELIZABETH CITY HIGH. "School," Wimpy said later, "was in my way." Neither, during those years, did Wimpy enjoy much success with girls. He was a handsome youth: slender, with curly hair, intense eyes, high cheekbones. But Wimpy was shy. Walter Davis recalled that young Wimpy could hardly speak to girls, although they often pursued him. He would become paralyzed, frozen. He was incapable of making that first contact, and although he longed his entire life for the lasting companionship of a good woman, he would never find it.

Dating was disastrous. On one occasion, recalled Davis, Wimpy took his father's car over to the house of Florence Woodley, a local girl. They may have gone out to dinner, or perhaps to the movies. Florence likely initiated this excursion, as there was nothing about Wimpy's character to indicate that he would embark on such madness. And Florence, perhaps, was the sort of girl with whom Wimpy should have ended up—he needed someone exactly his polar opposite, somebody who didn't fear the first move, someone not afraid of the opposite sex. And such a girl was Florence Woodley, a pretty girl, a sweet girl, a precocious girl.

The date did not go well. Sometime during the course of the evening young Florence insisted on a kiss, just a little kiss—and at that moment, of course, everything fell to shit. She was leaning over, right there in the car, with pursed lips and closed eyes and swooning breath, and it was just... too...much.

"He said no," recalled Davis. Wimpy refused to kiss her, wouldn't do it, couldn't do it—for what reason, who knew? And so Florence just got out of the car and sat on the curb. If Wimpy wouldn't kiss her, she would walk home. "And Wimpy said, 'I'm going to go home and tell your mom,' and that's what he did," said Davis. "He got up and went home, and told her mom, and that's where he left her, on that curb."

If Wimpy had any personal success during those years—outside the glory he began earning on the green felt—it came not as the result of good grades or heady romance, but for the precision with which he could hurl a baseball. Kids love baseball and Wimpy was no exception. He became a strike-out king, a coveted player for sandlot games. An ace. He would get up on that mound, stretch his periwinkle gaze across ninety feet, wind up—arms and legs flailing—and *throw!* Like all great pool players, Wimpy possessed uncanny coordination. His pitches were nearly always on the mark, smacking into the catcher's glove with a *splat* and a *"Steerike!"* He could out-duel any of the sandlot pitchers, and the high school coach, recognizing this, felt that baseball might hold more promise for young Wimpy than pocket billiards.

"Coach was always trying to sign him up," said Clarence, Wimpy's younger brother. "You know, Bud could *pitch* a ball. But by then, pool had caught him and he didn't care about the athletic end of things. The coach pestered him and pestered him and tried to get him to play, because he had a natural talent for baseball. But he didn't use it; he was trapped by pool."

"Oh, sure, I played some baseball," Luther recalled. "In fact, it was at some little old ball game that I once ate twelve hot dogs and drank thirteen Cokes and Orange Crushes, and everybody fell to calling me Wimpy. But still I began playing pool in my old plaid knickers that buckled right below my knees, and I had a slingshot hanging out of my back pocket...

"Mama always wanted me to study and become a doctor. Daddy mostly wanted me to do the chores and grow up to be a *something*. Neither one of them ever wanted me to shoot pool. But by the time I was fifteen years old, I was shooting maybe seven, eight hours a day and people had already started to back away from me. I had a little bit of money in my pocket, and the game had me up tight."

This odd passion that gripped Wimpy, this craziness, broke his parents' hearts—especially his father's. Their relationship grew difficult. And the two men, never great communicators to begin with, spoke less and less to one another. Wimpy had taken a tough course, no doubt about that, one which Wimpy's father could never really approve...or understand.

"My father was a Christian man, and he tried to raise his family the best he could," Clarence recalled. "And in those days, you didn't just hang around the poolroom if you were a fifteen-year-old child. But Bud couldn't stay away. It wasn't that he was rowdy—he just had a thing about pool. And Father, all he did was work all the time. And he'd have to go out and search for him.

"I remember Father stomping out for him, worried. He never raised his hand. There wasn't any belt swinging. But he'd give him a guilt trip. He never screamed, or hollered. He'd talk. And I really remember those search-and-rescue missions, and him coming back, and saying, 'I got him' or 'I found him.' It was worrying him right good.

"My parents didn't think it was right what Bud was doing; they thought he needed to get in school, that he needed to get an education and he needed to prepare himself for life. It was about the same that parents think now. And Bud would go back to school. But after a while, he'd play hooky again."

THE OWNER OF THE OLD CITY BILLIARDS, SPEEDY IVES, EXCHANGED TABLE TIME FOR ELBOW GREASE. He let the underage Wimpy in the back door—he got him to sweep the floors and brush the tables—and then let the boy practice. And practice. And practice. On the back table, shot after shot: cuts, banks, rail-first kicks. Over and over again he lined up a mind-numbing succession of shots that trained his eye and built muscle memory. And then, leaning over the tables, Wimpy began beating his friends. And he began beating older men. And soon, by the time he was sixteen years old, Luther "Wimpy" Lassiter could beat everyone in Elizabeth City.

It was then that Wimpy Lassiter's true education began. The stock market crash four years earlier had pushed unemployment to unheard-of levels. Wimpy's dad kept working—the Foreman Blades Mill remained open—but the Depression idled other men. And idle men, of course, surge like lifeblood into poolrooms.

Elizabeth City, a town of less than thirty-five thousand residents, supported five pool halls during the Great Depression. There was the Hurdle Brothers' room, City Billiards, Brock's Billiards, and two other rooms across the railroad tracks where black folks played banks and rotation. Wimpy went to each—an Elizabeth City poolroom circuit—learning from all the top players.

No jobs. No money. A great and horrible depression had descended upon the land, and here appeared a child who could *play*—play like no one had ever seen. He could put together three- or four-rack runs of nine-ball; he could pocket seventy balls in straight pool. *A boy!* Here, in Wimpy Lassiter, the Orange Crush-drinking, knicker shorts-wearing child of a millwright, one could find easy money.

Sweep the floors and brush the tables, Speedy Ives told the boy, and then play to your heart's content. "And you know what happened?" recalled Wimpy. "Wasn't long before I was hanging around down at City Billiards…It finally got so I looked like a piece of furniture down there, and nobody ever noticed I was underage."

The boy should have been at home. He should have been in school. But Speedy gave Wimpy the *opportunity* to brush those tables, to sweep those floors. And because of that opportunity, Wimpy met Bill McMullen, an older player, a poolroom bum, a man feared for his ability to run balls. Like Speedy, Bill McMullen tended to the boy's education.

McMullen gambled day and night with Wimpy. He showed the child how to get position, how to kick out of tight spots, how to make the tough cross-table banks. At first McMullen took the boy's money—but only at first. With strange and beautiful shots, never-before-seen shots, the pupil quickly surpassed the teacher. But his education was not complete.

Beefy Laden, a mean son-of-bitch, was Wimpy's next instructor. Beefy was big; he was imposing. He had thick arms and a barrel chest. He could cuss a blue streak in his North Carolina drawl; he smoked and spat and gambled. And Beefy Laden brooked no shit from no man, so all men handled Beefy with great care. Beefy played Wimpy too, and lost a bit of money to the boy. But not much. Because Beefy didn't have much to lose, and besides, he could see what this boy could do; he could see there was no point in playing him.

Instead, Beefy looked into Wimpy's blue eyes, still bright with the innocence of youth, and saw there—dollar signs. *Opportunity! Oh, glorious opportunity!* So Beefy tended to the education of Wimpy Lassiter—even though the poor boy should have been in school, and not hanging out with a bunch of old poolroom bums and worrying his mother sick.

Beefy, Speedy, and Bill McMullen stakehorsed Wimpy Lassiter. They showed him how to gamble, how to match up, when to press, when to slow down. They became jockeys, he their Thoroughbred. Like a bolt of lightning he came, like a biblical Red Sea flood, moving balls, *bam! bam! bam!,* breaking nine-ball racks, colors exploding across green felt, table after table, room after room, down in Charlotte, up in D.C., across to Nashville, and in Norfolk—especially in Norfolk—downstairs at the old Tuxedo poolroom, upstairs at St. Elmo's. *A bit of nine-ball, suh? Twenty dolluhs a rack, suh? Yessuh, I play some pool, I surely do, but perhaps I can interest yew in thuh sevuhn and thuh break, suh, jes to make the propuh-sition more to yer liking...*

Always polite, Wimpy Lassiter, always the southern gentleman, with the North Carolina drawl, the Bible references, the tranquil eyes, the broad smile that said *Trust me!* Pushing up and down the Eastern Seaboard he went, roaring up U.S. Highway 17 in a beat-up Oldsmobile, jabbering and laughing and making games. Good God Almighty, *a pool hustler!* Wimpy Lassiter! Watch him go, watch him go—unstoppable, unbeatable, *one two three*—Wimpy Lassiter, just sixteen, still an unknown: and action, action *everywhere!*

For a while there Wimpy took to wearing glasses, round wire rims with little egg-shaped lenses that exactly framed his face: his basset hound jowly cheeks, his thick lips, his big smile. The gray hair had not yet arrived—not then, not in the late 1930s, when Wimpy was yet new to the world of big-time pool. Rather, a shock of wavy darkness crept unkempt over a tall forehead. And a sort of doughy softness engulfed him—a baby's fat from which Wimpy would never emerge—and so the pool hustler seemed even less substantial than his five feet, nine inches and 138 pounds might otherwise suggest.

Wimpy would don his old filling station outfit—before that face became known, before the unwary recognized those giant cheeks, those periwinkle blues. He came on in the cheap suit, with the thin lapels and the pinstripes and the two buttons high up on his chest. So likable, this boy. So friendly. *Jes in for the day, jes passing through, yew understand...but perhaps we could play a little nine-ball? Say, five dolluhs a rack?* It was stealing, really. Just stealing. Because nobody could beat him—*nobody!*—especially not these dumb-as-dick pigeons taking offers from bankrolled out-of-towners.

Oh, Glory Day.

Thievery. Pure and simple.

Wimpy Lassiter lived in a different world then, during those tired days of the Great Depression. The whole nation suffered. Soup lines. Working for food. Apples for a nickel. But Lassiter and his backers cut through the poverty, through the hunger and sadness. Tooling around in the car—bought with Wimpy's sweat and talent—they cut through the twilight years of America's first great age of pool.

The game continued to thrive. It drew sustenance not from the exuberance of men, but from their woe-begotten misery. The Depression and pool ran together, a grand confluence of streams. When the stock market plummeted, and the bank panics began, and men suddenly found themselves without work, these walking dead huddled together in old rooms like the Tuxedo and St. Elmo's and warmed their tired souls. Pool saved men from layoffs, family bankruptcy, hungry children. Pool saved men from the indignity of real life, from the reality of failure.

Back then, back during those troubled days of the Works Progress Administration, FDR, and the Lindberghs, pool had no respect. There was a word for men who wasted days in pool halls: bums. But the broken economy had created countless bums, in every city and on every street corner, and these jobless millions would gather in the poolrooms, in Manhattan or Philly or at the smaller three-table joints all across America. The Great Depression had robbed great numbers of great men of their very spirit, and so they came to the poolroom searching for the solace of each other's company...

Lassiter, however, came searching for neither solace nor succor, but for *freedom*. Money remained in the American poolroom, money enough to escape despicable poverty—if only one could tame that shrew of a sport. Money came easy, yes, if one possessed the strength and disposition to conquer others. To *use* pool during those dreadful days, men became hustlers.

Shuffling around in old trousers, never saying too much, always polite, Wimpy made gelt for his backers. *I believe I've made the nine off the break, suh. A bit of luck, there, suh, but pay up all the same. Pay now, if you pulease.* And Wimpy made a little for himself. Not much, but a little. *My gracious, another bit of luck there, suh. I declare.*

Wimpy crisscrossed the highways, stopping in D.C., Roanoke, Charleston. Everywhere. Anywhere. Searching for action and sleeping in motels, Wimpy stalked his quarry northward and southward...and then returned home to Elizabeth City after twenty-four, thirty-six, forty-eight hours, after one week, after two. His backers drove the old Oldsmobile and Wimpy slept passed-out sore, sometimes half drunk, in the big backseat. Colored balls cascaded through black-and-white dreams...the happy explosion of misspent youth. A life somehow both worthless and priceless, all at once and every day.

Wimpy related that his father never saw him play—"not even when I was world champion"—and instead concealed his pain in dark brooding. This was not the path he had envisioned. The taciturn father never expected to wait helplessly, night after night, while the boy ran around with a bunch of no-account poolroom bums, common hoodlums who cared little for his son or the Lassiter clan. He never expected to spend night after night searching for a lost boy while a hysterically worried wife paced the floors at home.

Lectures replaced any real communication, but still Wimpy could not stop wandering away. Speedy Ives and Beefy Laden had trapped Wimpy. Pool had trapped Wimpy. By then, school was in the way. And dinner at home was in the way. And baseball was in the way, and swinging from that old cypress tree with Jack Weeks and Walter Davis beneath the beautiful lemonade sun of Elizabeth City—all that was in the way. Because Wimpy Lassiter could think only of pool.

At age sixteen Wimpy Lassiter became a professional road player, a boy with no permanent address. He left behind Elizabeth City, North Carolina, and a happy youth.

But he also kept Elizabeth City inside him. For Wimpy, like all great pool players, had lost part of his childhood, and so he could never really grow up.

WRITING IN HIS AUTOBIOGRAPHY, *THE BANK SHOT AND OTHER GREAT ROBBERIES,* MINNESOTA FATS RECALLED HIS FIRST, EARLY ENCOUNTER WITH THE FUTURE KING OF NINE-BALL. The Great Depression was winding down and Fats was running a poolroom for a friend, a fellow by the name of Jimmy Jones, who had taken ill. Fats was about five years Wimpy's senior—

and probably then possessed about three times the younger man's playing experience. Fats's room was in Anacostia, a suburb of Washington, D.C.

Fats boasted, "Wimpy would come up to Washington from his home in Elizabeth City, North Carolina all the time and after a while he got so good with the cue he was breaking every living human in the District of Columbia, only when me and Luther got on the table the currency always changed hands. I sent him home penniless so many times that I almost needed a lobbyist to get him to play me."

Pool hustlers, by nature, are liars. And by this measure, Minnesota Fats was just a very, very good pool hustler. For no one in their right mind—no one who ever studied the progression of these two fine players—would argue that Minnesota Fats shot straighter pool than Wimpy Lassiter. Fats could certainly boast more. Fats could argue more. Fats may even have been the smarter gambler. But Fats, definitely, could not play better pool.

Back during the mid-1930s, however, Wimpy had but two or three years' playing experience under his belt. Fats, by contrast, was near his prime. So it's quite plausible—indeed, evidence even suggests—that during those Great Depression years Minnesota Fats consistently beat Wimpy Lassiter at straight pool. A radical notion, perhaps, but Ed Tarkington, a trusted friend of Lassiter, confirmed as much: "Fats could beat people playing one-pocket and straight pool, and he could beat Wimpy playing straight pool, to begin with..."

And remember this: after his months on the road, Wimpy Lassiter would have begun feeling a reckless confidence. The desperate chill of poverty drove him. The fiery exuberance of youth drove him. In Fats's room, he would have begun with lesser players, with the hoary old men venturing inside from the cold and sloshing crap snow. These men looked there for warmth and succor. Instead they found Wimpy Lassiter, the winter predator.

The sevuhn and the break, suh? The sevuhn, five, and the break, suh? Wimpy went through them all, one by one, a wolf devouring the lame. The first bloody law of the jungle: Conquer weakness.

Lassiter gloried in that cruelty. Good God, he was something to behold. And behind the rising wall of suffocating dust and lights flickering incandescent, the Fatman would watch the devastation, and slyly calculate his odds. There was no fear in the Fatman's eyes. Just amusement. And greed.

Like Speedy and Beefy and Bill McMullen, Fats could see opportunity. Before him stood a boy hustler drunk with his own imagined invincibility. This, Fats could exploit. First he would search for signs of fatigue—the almost imperceptible slackening of stroke, the missed shots, the errant cue balls—and then issue his challenge. He would invest in the boy's inexperience.

And when he finally issued the challenge—*Let's go, boy, you and me*—it made Lassiter take a quick breath. This here was something different. This was something new. He'd *heard* about Fats. He'd been told how the Fatman gambled high, how he attracted OPM—Other People's Money. All hustlers love it. Fats, it was said, had OPM to burn. Lassiter knew of the Fatman's reputation, his prowess. He watched as a spreading twitch contorted Fats's face, a startling tick that sent ripples across Lake Placid. Fats was no stumble-drunk redneck down from Nixonton. No pimple-faced know-nothing kid from the local school.

This here was something else altogether.

Yes, indeed.

Months on the road—scorching up and down Highway 117, in those rooms along the East Coast, in Roanoke and Edenton—Wimpy never understood he had begun a quest. No glory—not now—from beating drunken bums down at Speedy's. No glory won from imbecilic school kids and sailors. This was New York Fats, Chicago Fats, Double-Smart Fats. This was big time.

The hair stood up on the back of his neck; his palms went cold and wet. Suddenly Lassiter became aware of *himself*. He was alone now, his beloved Elizabeth City far away. But deep inside himself, amid all the fear and loneliness, Wimpy began to understand what he had been looking for—what every person looks for, but seldom finds. This boy hustler, this child prodigy, somehow had become a ball-running *machine!* Wimpy felt fear—yes, fear right down to his toes—but he also felt his heart fairly exploding from his chest.

Win, lose, or draw, he had found himself. Alive, like never before, nerves tingling, Wimpy Lassiter had finally arrived.

3
THE RING GAME

"Young as I was, I could move that cue ball without touching any other ball, unless I wanted to. I moved it from shot to shot and I knew three, four, five ahead what I would shoot next."

—Jersey Red, 1961

N EXCHANGE FOR GUNPOWDER, LEAD, AXES, COATS, GUNS, SWORDS, KETTLES, BLANKETS, KNIVES, HOES, "10 PAIRS OF BREECHES...AND 3 TROOPER COATS," NEWARK, NEW JERSEY, WAS ACQUIRED FROM HACKENSACK INDIANS. The year: 1666. The buyers: fundamentalist Christians. The settlers divided their town with two main thoroughfares—Broad and Market Streets—and allotted six acres to each family. They named their town in honor of their first pastor, the Reverend Abraham Pierson, who received ordination in Newark-on-Trent in England. And so Newark, New Jersey—the birthplace and ancestral home of Jersey Red, America's finest Jewish pool hustler—began as a Christian theocracy.

Louis Jacob Breitkopf, the first of Jersey Red's line in America, arrived in 1887, some fifty years after the formal incorporation of Newark. His wife, Eda Weinstein, and eight-year-old son Max accompanied him from Austria-Hungary, where Louis Jacob purportedly served as both a tobacco smuggler and personal bodyguard to the emperor. In Newark Louis Jacob worked at a Derby hat factory and later at a soda business. Bearded, bald, standing over six feet tall, and in possession of considerable strength, Louis Jacob cut an intimidating figure. But he was also friendly, gregarious; he enjoyed drinking and supposedly died—at age 104—smoking cigars.

Eda, by contrast, was a tiny little woman—but she had a temper. According to Eda's granddaughter, "When she got angry, he [Louis Jacob] would pick her up in his arms and carry her around." Jersey Red eventually inherited something of his great-grandfather's strength and size, as well as Eda's red temper.

Their son Max, Jersey Red's grandfather, married Hungarian Pauline Ziegler, who in America received the nickname "Peppie." Always, it seemed, was Pauline Ziegler flying about, jabbering and moving like a hummingbird, exhausting others with her blinding peppiness. According to Arthur Breitkopf, Jersey Red's cousin, their grandmother possessed a fantastic intelligence, speaking six or seven languages fluently. She became the first interpreter for the City of Newark.

Peppie and Max spent their entire lives in Newark, where they grounded each of their children in the Jewish faith. Their second son, Jake, the man who would father Jersey Red, made deliveries (probably fruits, vegetables, and other produce) through the streets of Newark in a horse-drawn carriage. This was how he met his wife-to-be, Rachel (Ray) Cohn. "One time my mother was walking down Walnut Street, going to the candy store, and my father saw her," said Marty, Jersey Red's brother. "He was driving that team of horses and he must have parked those horses and went inside."

Ray's family then possessed great sums of money. And so with white gloves and parasol, her gaze fixed forward, would Ray have walked down Walnut Street. Her expensive patterned dress sashayed about her ankles; her auburn hair moved not a whit in its tightly wound bun. And behind her eyes one could detect the pride of wealth. No clear record of that first encounter exists; but Jake, if he did not speak directly of his affection, probably wasted no time in charming Ray with quick words. That is the Breitkopf way.

Jake eventually graduated from horses to an old Mack truck, in which he delivered fruit for the Woll Brothers fruit company. But Ray's family—half Irish Catholic, half Jewish—went broke. The Great Depression wiped them out. And so in the course of a few short years, Rachel Cohn went from pampered debutante to the working-class wife of a truck driver.

At 4:35 a.m. on July 29, 1934, Ray gave birth to her third child, Jacob Jerome Jr., the future prince of one-pocket. The birth record indicates that the Breitkopfs then resided at 100 Ingram, in the suburb of Irvington. Ray, thirty-two, was identified as a housewife; Jerome, thirty-three, a chauffeur. The birth certificate shows a full-term birth for Jack (as he later became known), although it doesn't note his size or weight. Those that remember say Jack quickly grew coarse, curly, reddish hair. He had green eyes, a slightly pointed nose, high cheekbones, and a mouth that formed a perfect 'O' when he was startled or amused.

The Breitkopf family regularly changed homes during the child's early years. Jack's mother, apparently possessed by some secret longing, ordered the moves. She never felt settled. "She was a little wacky," recalled Arthur Breitkopf, Jersey Red's cousin. "He [Jersey Red's father] would go to work in the morning, and she had moved…He'd come home and nobody was there." Was Rachel longing for old wealth? The reason for the moves never became clear, although Marty confirmed they occurred with bewildering frequency. "My mother and father would move around quite a bit. For no reason, my mother would get tired of one place, and we would move somewhere else. She just didn't want to stay in one place."

This impatience, this dissatisfaction with the way things *are*, Ray passed to her hustler son, who from the beginning seemed slightly nervous, slightly frenetic. Her insistence on moving from house to house served as a model for his later life, when Jersey Red would live for two decades without a permanent address. And from grandfather Max, who was said to have been gripped by some strange lethargy, Jack inherited that other famous pool hustler trait: a disdain for hard work.

Chores he left to his older brother Marty or his sister Ella. Those who knew Red (just as those who knew Wimpy and Fats) said he could spend sixteen hours a day playing pool. He interrupted backbreaking one-pocket sessions with gin rummy and poker. Frantic talking, nonstop jabbering, quick movements of the arms and upper body, laughter—these traits marked Jersey Red. But not work.

Jack's singular intelligence became apparent early in life. One could see it behind his green eyes, hear it in his quick wit, which came in bursts of quick one-liners. There's a story about Jack, about when he was a kid sneaking into poolrooms. Father Jake, with whom Jack would always have differences, was none too pleased that his youngest son sometimes disappeared for days at a time, only to come back haggard and dirty. And so they fought, the father and the son, and then Jack got sent off to have his head examined. The final report on the state of Jack Breitkopf's head has been lost to time, although friends insist it uncovered something obvious to anyone who ever knew the pool hustler: If the boy was not a genius, he was very nearly so.

Even at a young age, Jack possessed a startling, bedazzling, truly remarkable memory. Facts. Statistics. Who led the American League in homeruns in 1942? Ted Williams. Who had the most stolen bases that year? George Case, with 44. Jack turned that keen mind to things that interested him, such as baseball and boxing, and built a body of knowledge about sports and players and stats. This knowledge grew within him, like a stack of musty old newspapers, and kept getting bigger and bigger throughout his life. He remembered so *much*—it seemed like he would never stop accumulating more trivia—and it was not until he was sixty-two years old, sleeping in medicated dreams and waiting to die, that he put it all to rest. With the doggedness of a professional researcher—reading newspapers, reviewing the tip sheets, watching the games—Jack pursued his sports education. It became his *job* to know the players, the games, the odds—and later, as a gambler, to know when to bet, and how much.

While Jack loved boxing (he loved the fighters), his favorite sport was baseball. The game possessed a secret poetry that spoke directly to Jack's soul, and as a boy he would play it for hours, hitting left-handed fly balls and running bases in the afternoon sun. His father eventually opened a diner (after years of driving trucks) within a mile or so from a minor league stadium. Jack and his buddies would walk there almost every week; and Jack, glad-handing and smiling, likely met some of the players, to whom he recited their own stats.

He possessed such brilliance, this boy, such innate smarts. But here's the irony: Jack couldn't give a rat's ass about school. He never liked it, never liked the structure; he just wanted to be outside, spending time with friends.He *hated* school. And besides, he had gotten to playing pool with his older brother, Marty, and his brother-in-law, Nic Nicola, even though they were all grown up and Jack was just a kid—maybe thirteen, maybe younger.

At first, Nic and Marty and young Jack strolled to a poolroom they called The Chinese. Located four blocks from the Breitkopf house, the room had three or four beat-up tables and an Asian attendant—hence the name. At first Jack could hardly fold his long fingers to make a bridge, but he watched Marty and Nic, and they told him about aiming, about keeping his cue stick level, about making shots. They explained how simply smashing balls into pockets, although satisfying, seldom brought victory.

It wouldn't be long, of course, before Jack walked the four blocks by himself. There at The Chinese he would play for an hour or so, sometimes more, just knocking balls around. He eventually taught himself how to make the cue ball fly backward. Nothing to it, really: just stroke the cue a bit below center, hit it smooth, and after making contact that cue ball will zip back every time—just like a yo-yo on a string.

And then, after Jack got to practicing all this, he began to see *it*. An ancient knowledge, a heart-pounding epiphany—this was the *it*. Tough to fathom for those who didn't know, like Jack's parents, but the *it* was like an invisible line connecting ball to pocket, as if the green of the felt were of a different hue, brighter, diffuse with all the energy Jack had stored up in his big brain. He directed all that mental power onto the object ball, and then— *wow, wow*—he could see the future. He could *see*, really literally, no-bullshit *see* the line. And so Jack began to know where the balls would go—and when they did something different, and he would miss, it became as startling as two plus two equals five.

Jack, who by this time had grown old enough to help out at the diner, instead spent his days goofing at the pool halls. He had already quit school, and he'd happily leave home for a day or so, sometimes longer, to run wild with his friends. "He was a like a street kid," said one old acquaintance. And Jack's old man, working like a dog at the diner, got pissed; and they fought. Their relationship soured further as a result of the father's fondness for liquor. It wasn't that the older man became abusive, or belligerent, or prone to jabbering loud nonsense in the front yard—but he was an alcoholic.

Jack eventually began taking up residence somewhere other than the family's broken-down, cramped home at 75 Walnut Street. Just a boy, this wild-eyed jabbering Jack, but he seemed never to sleep in his own bed.

Never. He had become intoxicated by the crazy exhilaration of wild eight-and-outs in one-pocket, of runs of twenty and thirty and forty in straight pool. The wild life of pool halls seemed so much better than that other life waiting at home, with the old man always on his back and his family hassling him about school. Some said pool became a prison from which Jack could never escape. To Jack, however, it seemed a refuge.

"They really didn't like it that much that he was playing like that—that he'd go out and, like, play pool all the time," recalled brother Marty, speaking in that familiar gravelly New Jersey honk-honk of all the Breitkopfs. "Like, he would go into the poolrooms, and I would be the person who would have to work, but he would stay away for two or three days, and come back, and then stay away for a couple more days, and come back again. You know, kids are wild, and you can't keep track of them. My folks didn't like it, but what could they do?"

JACK SKIPPED OUT THE FRONT DOOR, TRUDGED DOWN SNOW-BLOCKED SIDEWALKS, TURNED A CORNER, AND THERE JUST A FEW BLOCKS FROM HIS WALNUT STREET HOME WAS THE BARE-WALLED AND CRUD-FLOORED POOLROOM OF JERRY STOKES, A SLOW-MOVING, SLOW-TALKING BLACK MAN AND JACK'S FIRST MENTOR. A quick survey of the room revealed no player much younger than sixteen (except Jack, who then was fourteen) and no other white player. The future pool hustler, just beginning to feel that dumb cockiness that comes with adolescence, experienced a jolt upon entering the room, a slight quickening of the pulse. Jack admired old man Stokes—after all, he'd let Jack through the front door even though the boy was far too young and far too white—and Jack admired the other players, who cursed and gambled and drank whisky from brown paper bags. Stokes, his poolroom, and its gambling denizens represented life's exhilarating possibilities.

"They called him Straw Hat," Jack later said of Stokes. "He was a nice guy and a good player, and he let me hang around the poolroom. He liked me a lot and let me work racking balls and stuff...It was 1946 or 1947, and I wasn't supposed to be playing. I wasn't old enough. But he liked me and pretty soon, I was playing all the guys. I was the only white guy in the room, but all the guys liked me—they were all real nice—and so I got to playing pretty good."

Jack, who back then possessed a Jersey growl that sounded more like a Jersey squeak, had the body of a growing boy: long and lean like a snake and composed entirely of lanky legs and arms. His hands ended in long, tapered fingers that moved with a magician's grace. The rest of his body moved in long, flowing movements, like those of a dancer. And every day spent at Stokes' place made Jack seem less like a child. His willful cockiness was fueled by his natural athleticism; his daily proximity to gamblers gave him street smarts and a rough edge to his personality.

At age fourteen, Jack robbed his first sucker. This coming of age—for what else can one call a hustler's first sucker?—freed him from one life, imprisoned him in another

As with many first things, Jack's first score started quite small. Another young man had walked into Stokes' poolroom—a kid not much older than Jack—and was knocking balls across a worn-felt nine-footer. Jack watched for a while, regarding the kid as a young lion regards a wildebeest, and got to thinking. *I can beat this kid. Beat him easy. No sweat.* Problem was, Jack had almost no money. Just eleven cents in his pocket—no wallet, just eleven cents—and so Jack's first wager would *have* to be small. Maybe that would make the challenge easier, make it more like playacting than real gambling.

So Jack walks up to the kid, kind of slow, but with that smile, and he offers the challenge. "Hey kid," growls Jack, but all friendly-like, "let's play for a soda."

The first game goes by pretty quickly. Jack crawls all over the table, like some damned lizard, making a few shots, lucking in others. The game was probably nine-ball, one-through-nine, all in order, and after a bit, Jack wins. But now Jack decides he doesn't want that soda. "Why don't you just give me the money," he says. This is the bait and switch, part of any con man's repertoire, and something that Jack appeared to know instinctively.

And so within a few moments, Jack turned his dime and penny into a quarter. Jack, all squeaky-voiced and lanky-long, then lost a few games—not many, but a few—and so when he upped the bet the other child thought he stood a chance. Jack's winning smile and infectious laughter kept the boy at the table. The boy did not yet realize what he had stepped into. He didn't realize that a quarter wagered on nine-ball, a game that could end on the break or a quick combination, might quickly become very expensive. Especially in 1945.

Jack, of course, kept winning; the kid became his three-cherried, one-armed bandit. *Ding ding DING!* Another quarter for Jack. *Ding ding DING!* Another quarter for Jack. And Jack, just fourteen years old, just a boy, had never seen so much money. It was like stealing—the exhilaration was the same—but without much guilt.

And so the opium flowed into Jack's veins, the tingly pleasure of any gambler on a roll. And this new thrill fueled his arrogance and pride. Within the other boy, by contrast, a different sort of feeling began to grow. It was like a horrible tightness in the stomach, it was the opposite of a winner's exhilaration: it was the dispiriting realization that money would not be gained for nothing, but rather squandered without cause. Like the savage irony of rape: it's gambling's victims who become most tortured by guilt.

And so, dejected, the other kid walked away. And Jack, with several dollars that seemed to have magically appeared in his pocket, wanted more. He wanted more! He jumped into a ring game—more nine-ball, or maybe Kelly pool. He played not a single opponent, but several, and the pots become very large indeed. A single quarter wagered could become four quarters won. And more often than not—whether through luck, fate, or the seeds of coming greatness—Jack would sink the winning ball. Money fell into Jack's pocket like an avalanche—quarters, quarters, *quarters*. He felt his pockets heavy with them, and as he walked, he heard a happy jangling.

And so these players quit him too—all of them—and then a real murmuring began. It was then that the men down at Stokes' began to take note, and started eyeing Jack with something approaching respect. He was just a boy, after all, and he seemed to be winning an *awful* lot. Some of the guys pulled up chairs to watch—Jack's first railbirds—as he got himself into another game. Nine-ball again, but at two dollars a game. Real money. Fast money. Especially for a boy, just fourteen years old, a kid without education, running wild and dirt-haggard. Practically a street kid.

But for Jack, the money didn't seem to really exist, for only a few hours earlier it had not weighed so heavily in his pockets. It had lost its meaning and so lost its power. Unburdened by its tyranny, Jack came at the other fellow ferociously, with blinding aggression, his young lion heart pounding with every soft thud of the nine-ball.

And so after that day, a day in which he began with eleven cents and ended with seventy dollars, the black guys down at Stokes' place began to treat Jack differently. In the egalitarian subculture of billiards, race, wealth, and class count for little. What matters most is an ability to run balls and to win big. Jack, as anyone could see, had such abilities. He had won respect through victory, and so the boys bestowed upon him a special status. They gave him his first nickname and made him a friend. "And you know," said Red, who then possessed tightly curled auburn hair and a ruddy complexion, "they like figured I was a black guy."

Jack learned there how to make money, and how to conquer fear, and he began to see that which was hidden to others. Victorious and defiant, laughing and gambling and making friends, Jack became a man. This was the Jewish pool hustler's only bar mitzvah. He became Jersey Red.

4

THE BIG LIE OF LITTLE EGYPT

"You're trying to write a book and you're trying to establish what's true and not true? Are you kidding me? I hate to say this, but about eighty percent of what Fats said was bullshit. If you listened to him, he'd make you believe he built the Empire State Building."

—Dowell mayor Luciano Lencini, March 18, 2000

THE STORY BEGINS WITH FATS AND FRIEND JIMMY CASTRAS DRIVING SOUTH THROUGH ILLINOIS ON TREACHEROUS WINTER ROADS. It was 1941, only a few years after Fats's Washington D.C. match-up match with Wimpy Lassiter. The hustler carried in his pocket a thick bankroll, the result of a big score at the World's Pool Tournament[6] a few days earlier. Fats, or course, had not competed in the Chicago event (he almost never played tournaments), but rather had won 154 of 156 side bets. The result: a lavish payday, a new LaSalle, a road trip to Hot Springs, Arkansas, to the south, away from the foul Illinois winter.

Fats babbled as he drove. It was nonstop bullshit, just a stream of mind-numbing claptrap, and he would have made road partner Jimmy Castras fucking nuts. Not much snow fell, but neither was there much sunlight, and so Jimmy found no relief in the sort of gone-gray pallor outside the

---

[6] Won by Willie Mosconi.

passenger-side window. The failing light had a dead-man's grip on the land, and it brought desperation everywhere: to the dirt roads, to the simple wood frame houses, to the weird towering mounds of dirt scattered across the countryside. Through this gloom streaked Fats's money-green automobile, an unexpected flash of color in dour surroundings.

Little Egypt was the informal name given to a dozen or so Illinois counties spanning southward from Mount Vernon and bordered on either side by the mighty Mississippi and Ohio Rivers. There one could find Cairo, Thebes, and Karnak—small towns with Egyptian place names—and Goshen too, named by Baptist missionary John Badgley in 1799 for Egypt's most fertile place. Many said these Egyptian place names gave southern Illinois its nickname, while others attributed the name to the area's role in supplying grain to the north during the particularly harsh winter of 1830.

But to men of keen eye and little education—to men like Fats—the name Little Egypt came from those weird mounds, those odd dirt hills, the ones he spied all up and down Highway 51. They looked exactly like pyramids, Fats told Jimmy Castras, exactly like what you'd find in Egypt, with all them Arabs and camels. As he motored southward beneath gray skies and dirt-snow-covered pastures, Fats seemed unable to keep quiet about the damn things.

In fact, Fats likely commented on just about everything, always jabbering like a damned parrot, and he could never, ever, it seemed, shut the fuck up. He probably had not the slightest notion of what the mounds were (they were upturned earth, the result of coal mining), but that would not keep him from proffering expert explanations about the mounds and their long and varied history, or from making scatological jokes about them, all the while breathing heavily through his nose, his big stomach pushed uncomfortably behind the steering wheel. And Jimmy Castras, the one they called Jimmy the Greek, would have been smoking cigarettes one after another, staring desperately out the window at the doleful hills and only half listening to his friend, the world's most annoying road partner.

And it was then—at a moment when death itself might have brought sweet relief for the long-suffering Jimmy—that Fats was supposedly touched by Fate. It came in the form of a patch of ice along Highway 51, which, according to The Story, sent the car into a terrifying skid. And then, of course, came the *ohshitohshitohSHIT* from Fats, and his car fishtailed from one side of Highway 51 to the other, crossing over the yellow line and then back. *Bang!* A mailbox would have exploded. *Bang!* Another mailbox. There would have been the sickening sound of scraping metal, and the car would have skated clear off the roadway, settling in a patch of dirty grass and black snow.

Jimmy the Greek, who had braced himself with locked elbows and gritted teeth, then cast a panicked gaze at Fats; and his stricken friend, wide-eyed but uninjured, returned the gaze. There they sat for a moment, neither speaking nor moving. But that lasted for just a moment—just a moment—for then all at once and at high volume, Fats unleashed a machine gun blast of *unholy shits* and *goddamn fucks* and *dirty son of a bitches*, because this was the brand fucking new LaSalle, *for crissakes!* And when the two men emerged from the car with Fats spewing curses that echoed through the hills, he would have spied the damage: those fucking mailboxes had dinged up the front bumper, but good. The mailboxes had torn the damn thing nearly completely off. This wouldn't do. No, not at all.

And that was The Story—at least as told by Fats, and repeated in various news articles, and retold by official Minnesota Fats historians down in southern Illinois. It was a car wreck that brought the gamblers down to Little Egypt, just a vague region not even marked on most maps, just a confluence of hills and roads and abandoned mines. And from here, Fats would tell certain important lies, and befriend certain important people, and promote what became the most celebrated tournaments of an age. He would get married, build a life. He would help fuel a decade-long renaissance in American pool.

Not yet, not now, not in 1941. But eventually.

And it all began in Little Egypt, supposedly because of a car accident and a dark patch of ice.

IN THE 1940S, DU QUOIN WAS A BOOMTOWN. It may have been small—no more than twelve thousand residents then—but it was a principal destination for the rowdy airmen of Scotts Field, and for the hard-living workers from coal mines still operating in the area. All those mines have long since shut down, and the airmen from Scotts Field were eventually barred from Du Quoin. But for a while, at least, the town was wide open territory for a professional hustler. Five or six whorehouses—at least—lined the main thoroughfare. There were slot machines and poker at every bar. Sidewalks got so congested that children walked in the gutters.

And the same could be said for nearby Dowell, a town of three hundred but with six taverns, and Johnston City, no larger than Du Quoin, which would eventually host the most celebrated pool tournaments in American history. The entire patch of land between the mighty Ohio and Mississippi Rivers—Little Egypt—had become a promised land of sin and vice.

"Back in the forties and fifties, there was all kind of action here," recalled Jess Kennedy, a longtime Du Quoin resident. "All kinds of action. At every place in town you gambled: crap tables, pool tables, card tables, slot machines—everywhere. Gambling was illegal, but nobody bothered anybody, you know, if the gamblers took care of the place, took care of the mayor, took care of the sheriff. It was like some of those backwoods places down south where you got the sheriff paid off and he don't bother nobody. That was the way it was here. Gambling was so common that people just accepted it."

Another longtime resident, Ronnie Stroud, gave testimony as well: "All these stores on the main street were open back then, and people walked elbow to elbow. You couldn't find a parking spot anywhere on the street. If you wanted liquor, there was liquor. If you wanted women, there was women. Whatever you wanted, they had."

And so The Story had it that an unfortunate accident brought Minnesota Fats to Little Egypt. Their car was in the body shop, they insisted. They were *stuck* in the town; it was Fate that brought them to this promised land of whores and crap tables and late-night card games and cussing drunks. But this explanation of what must now be considered a seminal moment in pool history—of how Fats came to Little Egypt—was, as longtime confidant Joe Scoffic would say, pure Minnesota Fats bullshit. There was no car accident— no skidding tires or exploding mailboxes. Those who really knew Fats, those who knew the whole story, knew it was a con and a lie. Fate did not bring Fats and Castras to Little Egypt. It was Greed.

"He didn't have no car accident," said Scoffic, Fats's very first acquaintance in Du Quoin. "He was just traveling around here. They were hustling. That's bullshit about the accident. He was telling people he was in town getting his car fixed, and then he ended up staying with me. They were just hustlers, and there would have been plenty of miners to play."

But the locals would repeat the lie, over and over, feeding it until it grew into official Little Egypt history. Fats himself devoted nearly a chapter to The Story in his own autobiography, *The Bank Shot and Other Great Robberies.*

Supposedly, the *car mechanic* directed Fats and the Greek to The Beanery, a restaurant then owned by Scoffic. In reality, Scoffic himself sent them there, just as he told them about the all-night card games on the outskirts of town. "Hell, Fats came to me looking for a game," said Scoffic.

And once at The Beanery, of course, Fats's bullshit machine would have gone nonstop. *Jes passin' through,* he would have said. *Got the car in the shop for a few days, ya understand.* And Fats marveled at The Beanery's home-cooked meals, said Scoffic, and marveled even more at the pool tables out back. *What the hell? A pool table? Well, shit, mister—how 'bout you and me play a game or two?* And then, of course, the bloodbath would begin. Fats said "you could get more action in that little four-table room right smack in the middle of nowhere than you could get on Broadway at times." There was action, down in Du Quoin, Illinois, beyond *belief.*

"Pretty soon, word got around about this Fat Man from Chicago whacking every living human behind The Beanery, so every day there were more and more miners in the room," recalled Fats. "They came in packs and they followed me around...I had to spot a ball and then two balls just to get the action—but the odds didn't matter."

Fats and the Greek took rooms at the St. Nicholas, then owned by Joe Scoffic. Located just outside downtown, the hotel possessed a reputation for action both fast and high. Guns, poker, cash, all-night money games: this was the essence of the St. Nick. And Scoffic presided over it all, profiting from the slots that lined one wall, the card games in the back, the pool tables for the crossroading hustlers. "Miners, gamblers, they all congregated here, see, and you could have played *anybody*," he said.

The hotel had always had the slots. These attracted blank-faced, dull-eyed men who would sit for hours on tall barstools, dropping piles of coins down the insatiable machines. The slots, like the ponies, were for suckers. The real action, the games that brought the seasoned crossroaders, were the regular gin games, the five-card knock rummy games, and the poker, back in the kitchen. These were not friendly games—these were big-money serious games, with giant green C notes passing through the blue cigar smoke and the scurvy-orange light of flickering tungsten. Unforgiving men like Hubert "Daddy Warbucks" Cokes, the gun-toting oilman down from Evansville, wagered thousands. And Titanic Thompson, a killer of five men, a known card cheat and golf hustler—he came too.

Scoffic said it was not unusual for the combined bankroll of those gathered to total over $100,000. In the kitchen of the St. Nick hotel the crossroaders and alligators and eyeballers would gather, going snug, playing jammed up or jelly tight, herking and jerking, anchored to chairs, tens of thousands moving north and south. Tens of thousands! A combined total of more than *$100,000!*

For a while, the gloriously sinful St. Nicholas became home for Fats and the Greek, who ventured from their upstairs rooms only at night, lured by the siren call of craps and knock rummy and nine-ball. Fats slept whenever he felt like it, ate whenever he felt like it, played poker or one-pocket whenever he could get a game. He would eat entire cakes and watermelons at single sittings, sometimes several times a day. He ate, in fact, whenever he felt the slightest twinge of hunger, which was pretty much always.

Sometimes Fats even ate in his room, with its heat-knocking iron radiator and thick dusty curtains. There he would sit, barefoot and in giant boxer shorts, his hands and face covered in grease, quietly or loudly consuming horrible quantities of meat and sweets. Fats took pride in this revolting behavior, and often boasted of his transcendent gluttony—to belt out the calories, as he was wont to say—and for once, it seemed, he did not exaggerate. Scoffic recalled how Fats would order an entire turkey with all the trimmings, take it up to his room, and eat the whole thing by himself.

"Sometimes he'd come into the restaurant and tell us to put on two chickens," recalled Scoffic. "We guessed he had three or four people with him, so we set up a table for four. But he would eat it all by himself. And he'd do that three times a day. I don't think he ever ate a chicken until he got here. But at our place, he'd order enough chicken for four people."

As night descended upon Little Egypt, Fats and the Greek would appear magically at The Beanery, and mark time there with jokes and more soft drinks and more food. Sometimes this went on for hours—Fats and the Greek sitting on high stools in the back room, or propped with an elbow against the wall— doing absolutely fucking nothing. But they'd be friendly, of course, always real friendly, and they laid on the short con like Aunt Jemimah syrup. *Hey, buddy, wanna play some? How 'bout a little one-pocket, friend?* And then, with a nod and a fifteen-ball rack, the Fatman and the Greek would pounce. They were nocturnal predators hiding in tall grass, heart-pounding intense, suddenly alive.

NOT LONG AFTER HIS ARRIVAL IN DU QUOIN, FATS ACCEPTED A ONE-POCKET CHALLENGE FROM A LOCAL HIGH ROLLER BY THE NAME OF MUZZ RIGGIO, SCOFFIC'S BUSINESS PARTNER. The date was March 7, 1941. Muzz would have stridden into The Beanery with a custom cue looking like a twig beneath his ham-hock arm. He may have worn a fedora, as was then the style, and southern Illinois remained cool in March. Like Fats, Muzz was big—very big. And like Fats, Muzz was a gregarious man, friendly to a fault, a known jokester.

At first, Muzz tried to play Fats even—the game was one-pocket—and Fats beat him mercilessly. And so Muzz demanded balls and break. And Fats beat him some more. And then he wanted Fats to play one-handed. And Muzz kept losing. It was hopeless for Muzz Riggio, but acceptance was a long time coming. Instead of seeing he was outmatched, instead of under-standing he would never win and that he should just quit—instead of *sanity*—Muzz Riggio opted to play and play and keep playing, fishing around in his pockets for money after each loss like some damn fool kid trying to win the stuffed bear. And no matter what the spot, no matter how much Fats gave away, the result remained the same: the pair traded safeties and then Muzz would make a slight error, and Fats ran four or five; and then Muzz would make another error, and Fats would suddenly be out.

And it went like that for the whole exhausting afternoon.

During his early years in Little Egypt, Fats remained close to his playing prime. He shot wide open and aggressive, assaulting his opponents with ball after ball, a veritable barrage, and he seemed always to look for the run-out. Fats, then in his late twenties, would ignore the obvious defensive shot—and defense, remember, is the heart and soul of one-pocket. Instead, the fat gambler would opt for the tough cut shot, the cross-table bank, the three-railer. Jersey Red, then about six years old, later witnessed this unorthodox playing style—and copied it. "Fats could play some pool," said Jersey Red. "I don't care what anybody says. He could play some pool."

Fats's contribution was to turn one-pocket on its head. A relatively new game at the time (it was said to have been invented by Jack Hill, a pool shooter from Oklahoma), one-pocket typically involves both shotmaking and an ability to hide, with players looking to make tight banks or cuts and then stranding the cue ball on the end rail. With no good offensive shot, an opponent might respond by sending whitey uptable, behind a difficult ball cluster. Shoot and duck, shoot and duck—like snipers—this is the essence of one-pocket.

But not for Fats. Fats played offensive. "He kind of invented the wide open game," said one old timer, "and he was damn good at it." Instead of looking for a place to hide, Fats attacked. He could go defensive if he needed, and show patience when necessary—but he knew that defense is useless when you're stuck in the chair. And Fats was also a natural banker—an indispensable skill in the game. So instead of becoming a one-pocket sniper, he became the machine gun-toting gangster of one-pocket. Instead of hiding from his opponents, he simply slaughtered them.

Now, such a drubbing might make a man angry, but as Muzz was a seasoned gambler, and fairly good-natured to boot, he took none of it to heart. Perhaps he found Fats entertaining. Perhaps he simply respected Fats's game. But instead of griping and moaning and cursing, Muzz managed a sheepish smile, patted Fats on the back, and a lifelong friendship was born.

It was also then, on the very day of that expensive one-pocket session, that Fats began another decades-long relationship. Hoping to recoup some of his lost money, Muzz sent Fats to The Evening Star, a restaurant located on the outskirts of town. Muzz owned The Evening Star (along with Joe Scoffic) and knew instinctively that its doe-eyed hostess, Evelyn Inez Grass, would enchant the out-of-town crossroader. "Tell Evelyn Inez that Muzz and Scoffie sent you," Muzz said, a knowing smile crossing his face.

"Me and Jimmy the Greek got in the LaSalle and drove over to The Evening Star and just as we're walking in the front door, I pulled out a $100 bill and stuck it in my handkerchief pocket. Now who is standing just inside the front door but the tomato called Evelyn Inez, who happened to be the hostess and head waitress. She was beautiful beyond compare, a gorgeous doll without a flaw. She was a tall, dark-eyed brunette, who went about 5-7, but she had padding in all the right places. And legs? Listen, Betty Grable never had legs like Evelyn Inez.

"'Why you must be the high rollers down from Chicago,' she said, and when she smiled, she had teeth like a whole tray of pearls. So I said, 'What makes you think we're high rollers?' and Evelyn Inez said, 'Well, nobody in these parts carries pictures of Benjamin Franklin in their handkerchief pockets.'"

Evelyn, who Fats preferred to call Eva-line, enjoyed the high life—adventure, drinking, fun—she made no pretense about that—and at the time of Fats's arrival in Little Egypt, she was happily carrying on with a bass player from the Evening Star house band. But Fats, crashing into town like an enraged moose, did everything imaginable to capture the heart of his sweet Eva-line and quickly wrecked her five-year relationship with the musician. Fats also fought off his own road partner, Jimmy the Greek, who had become similarly enraptured by Evelyn. For Fats, it was love at first sight, and he could hardly endure the thought of his young princess driving about town with the evil Greek, or eating ice cream sundaes with him, or even talking with him over steaks at The Evening Star. Oh, how the portly one suffered.

Fats would credit a back-room one-pocket game for his eventual success with Evelyn. He said the Greek had set up a date with Evelyn—they were to take a spin in the green LaSalle—but then he got detained in a big-money match at The Beanery. Knowing full well the true priorities of Jimmy the Greek—that is, that the Greek would never trade an easy pigeon for a fresh tomato—Fats wolfishly agreed to cover for him. And so Fats unexpectedly arrived at Evelyn's house, explaining that his friend Jimmy had become detained, but to come on out anyway and have some fun. Fats bought Evelyn an ice cream sundae that night, and drove her about town, and told her jokes. And all the while, Fats would have gleefully disparaged his friend—*the Greek is a great guy, you know, too bad he's such an imbecile*. And Fats would have jabbered constantly, making Eva-line laugh until her sides hurt. He could tell almost instinctively that Evelyn loved to laugh and that she shared a similar conviction about life, the conviction of all gamblers, which is sort of the opposite of conviction: that life, all of it, way down deep and up on the surface, is really quite absurd. Best just to enjoy it. Best to have fun, to laugh and dance. For our time on this earth is really quite short.

Evelyn Inez remembered the courtship—typically ungentlemanly on the part of Fats, "who had his hands all over me." Pointing to a place just above her heart, Evelyn said Fats "sometimes would start kissing me too, kissing me like you wouldn't believe." This is where Fats kissed her, the beast. She also remembered ditching the bass player, a fella by the name of Joe, in favor of this bigger-than-life pool hustler.

"I was working at The Evening Star as a hostess," said Evelyn. "It was an up-and-up place, you know—no crummy place. Community people went there, and they appreciated it. Fats and the Greek would come in as customers, and they kept coming in, because I was there. And you know, Fats would say all over that I was the prettiest girl in the world."

Fats's beloved sister Rosa died that summer—a devastating occurrence for the oddly sentimental gambler—and Evelyn accompanied him to Brooklyn for the funeral. The trip cemented the love affair and eventually led to Fats's down-on-one-knee marriage proposal, delivered in the kitchen of Evelyn's house. The couple drove down to Cape Girardeau, Missouri the next day, found a poolroom with an upstairs JP and married over the muffled thuds of break shots. The date: May 7, 1941—exactly two months after they first met. Evelyn paid for the ceremony. Fats moved into the house she shared with her mother.

But the marriage lasted nearly 40 years.

"Fats came in floating in like a breeze," said Evelyn, "and he was full of malarkey from the beginning."

DURING THE NEXT SIX MONTHS OR SO, FATS'S NECK EXPANDED TO 19 INCHES, HIS WAIST BALLOONED TO 55 INCHES; SOON HE TIPPED THE SCALES AT NEARLY 300 POUNDS. Fats blamed the home cooking of Evelyn's mother, Orbie, who worked at a public school cafeteria in Dowell. His favorite dish was fried chicken, which he sometimes ate for breakfast. A whole chicken, of course—along with about six Coca-Colas. Fats also tortured Evelyn and Orbie with his monstrous snoring. "With the neck gone, my snoring became so hideous that it was waking up the neighbors," Fats boasted in his autobiography. "In fact, one night I slept at the St. Nicholas Hotel in Du Quoin during a long cash match and I woke up every guest in the joint. When I came down the next morning for breakfast there was a traveling salesman sitting in the lobby waiting to see if I was human."

Fats and Evelyn stuck close to Little Egypt for the next year or so, where Fats pursued serious money games down at The Beanery, The Evening Star, and a third place known as Curly's. Fats also became a regular at Joe Scoffic's legendary poker games. The stakes soared into the thousands; the payoffs were astronomical. But big cash always attracts bad men, and down in the back room of the St. Nick, there was big cash to spare.

And so the bad men came.

"One time, they just came in, there was about seven of them, and they came in with machine guns," recalled Scoffic. "They were gangsters. They just happened to be coming through town, I guess, and they must have heard there was gambling, so they decided to rob us." The highwaymen rushed in like wildfire. They had angry eyes, faces masked with bandanas, automatic pistols. Fats, Muzz, Hubert Cokes—they were all there that day—"and they probably had $150,000 on them," said Scoffic. Each was made to strip naked, just bare-ass butt-naked, and ordered belly down on the ground. The highwaymen bound the players' hands, pulling them painfully behind their backs with rope, and then stole their watches, jewelry, pistols, and cash.

Fats, of course, seemed forever and always incapable of keeping his mouth shut. And getting nervous, with a gun poked in his face, the prospect of death and violence before him, would only exacerbate this most annoying personality defect. And so Fats immediately started bitching and moaning and breathing heavy, and he complained that he was *too* fat to lie on his stomach, that he would surely *die* if he had to lie ass-up on the tile floor, his hands tied behind his back like a damn hog. Please sirs, he asked, could he just stand up against the wall? *I can't lay here on my belly. I'm too FAT. My stomach is just too big. Look at me, for crissakes!* And shit, Fats kept going on and on like this, jabbering like a damned mental case, forcing the highwaymen to finally relent. And so they ordered him to get his ass off the ground and put his fucking hands on the wall and *shut the fuck up*. Either that, or they'd put a bullet through his head.

But, of course, it wouldn't end there. It never ended with Fats.

"Fatty owed Hubert Cokes a bunch of money, see, and so Fats sees them robbers coming in, and so he tells 'em, 'Just a minute, before you rob me, let me pay this guy the $5,000 I owe him; lemme pay my debt to Hubert

Cokes,'" recalled Scoffic. "But Cokes says, 'You ain't paying me now, you son of a bitch.' And that's a true story. Fats, you know, was a real comedian. And I don't care what was happening, or who they was, or where he was: Fats was going to talk. I guaran-tee it."

Fats frequently took to the road during those years and sometimes returned home with bags of cash—literally bags of it. He'd eagerly show it off to his friends. "You ain't never seen nothing like this," he'd boast, dumping the green stuff out in a heap. Sometimes Fats took Evelyn on the road trips and when they picked up a nail, he'd make her change the flat. "Fats never changed a flat tire in his life," she said. Fats wouldn't even leave the front seat.

But Evelyn didn't complain much. They drank. They danced. They made love. "It was good to have found someone who could share a laugh," she said. And while Fats always promised a Niagara Falls honeymoon—which he never delivered—the other road trips seemed more exciting. To Chicago they went. To D.C., to Philly. Fats took Evelyn to America's greatest action towns, searching, searching, always searching for quick money and good times.

"We visited a zillion different towns all over the country in 1941 and 1942," he said, and everywhere, it seemed, they heard the same story. Something special was happening in America. Something unforeseen. As the Great Depression melted away and the Allies fought the Axis overseas, a new, number one, King Kong headquarters for gambling and vice had emerged. Not New York. Not Las Vegas. Everywhere men whispered about *Norfolk*. Somehow, unexpectedly, this naval town on the Atlantic Coast had become a paradise of easy money and broken men.

And so late in 1942 the couple again took to the road. And it was the fun-loving wife, not the bullshitting husband, who suggested the next stop.

It was time to see if the tales were true.

5
THE KING OF NORFOLK

"And I wasn't an hour out [of the Coast Guard] than I was in Norfolk playing pool. No one beat me. No one. Hundred-dollar bills there then were like one-dollar bills now. That's when I knew I was going to play pool forever."

—*Wimpy Lassiter*

A **TERRIBLE PITCHING, JUST A TERRIBLE SWAYING.** It made of the world a giant seesaw. And blue everywhere: across the tumultuous mid-Atlantic, across the impossible sky with fat white clouds, and behind the fine sea mist that drops like a gossamer scrim before Coast Guard vessel 74307. Fourteen bare-chested sailors mop decks and tie ropes topside an eighty-three-foot cutter; the fine mist soothes their burnt-brown faces, the leathery napes of their necks, their tattooed sailor arms. And the mist electrifies the wood-paint reds and blues. It makes the vessel glow slick and bright in the afternoon sun.

But most of all, the fine mist dampens the curly black hair on the back of Wimpy Lassiter's head, which lolls rag doll-like over the starboard railing. His face is bulgy-eyed pale, his body convulsing and heaving, his hands and gut white-knuckle knots. Wimpy Lassiter the dog. Wimpy Lassiter the dog sick. Wimpy Lassiter desperately laps up the cool, damp air and affixes his bleary eyes on the horizon.

Just the horizon, he thinks.

Not the sea.

Not the boat.

Not hands, nor feet, nor churning stomach.

But his world seesaws with the waves, and the impossible blue devours him whole, and that cool mist seems to vanish altogether. All the air in the world has evaporated, and that god-awful sour bile rises in his stomach…up, up, up from some horrible hellish place…and then that taste comes to his mouth—the taste like mustard, the smell overwhelming. He squeezes his eyes shut. The spasms come, followed by the bile that fills his throat.

Sweet Lord Almighty.

And then bile spews over the starboard railing of the eighty-three-foot cutter; Lassiter's guts spill overboard into the near Atlantic.

Sweet Lord Almighty. Help me Jesus—I'm DYING!

The Japanese had bombed Pearl Harbor and the Germans had swept across Poland and France, and our boys were getting shot to shit overseas. The whole damn world had gone upside down. And into this fire and blood and blinding smoke staggered Wimpy Lassiter: the high-school dropout, the poolroom genius, the piss-poor sailor. Lassiter spent World War II in a Coast Guard cutter, cruising the Atlantic coast at 5.2 knots. He greased the diesels or stood lookout behind twin .30-caliber machine guns, and he *tried*—oh, how he tried—to keep vigilant for enemy U-boats and burning hulls.

The 1940s were years of extremes for Luther Clement Lassiter. He would never hold a straight job longer than the three years, ten months, and seven days he spent as a professional sailor—and he was an utter failure at it. But he also would never confront more high-rolling pool sharks than those in Norfolk during his sickly Coast Guard years. He eventually devoured them all.

The decade began for Luther with bile and stomach cramps and pail moaning. It ended at the cusp of a world championship.

AT AGE TWENTY-TWO, SOME SIX MONTHS BEFORE AMERICA WENT TO WAR, LUTHER LASSITER JOINED THE U.S. COAST GUARD. His reasoning was simple: he wanted to avoid getting drafted. Like most Americans, Wimpy figured war with Germany was only a matter of time. By enlisting in the Coast Guard early, Lassiter figured to avoid overseas combat later on.

But what Lassiter didn't figure on was German Admiral Karl Doenitz. His fleet of long-range U-boats came to within fifty miles of the mainland—very close, indeed, to Elizabeth City itself—and they bit like steel sharks into the very belly of U.S. shipping. Doenitz's U-boats caused more damage during those early months than all of Hirohito's planes at Pearl Harbor. With its fifty aircraft, two hundred ships, and First Classman Luther Lassiter, the U.S. Coast Guard was America's last line of defense.

Lassiter enlisted on April 2, 1941, at a Coast Guard station in Norfolk, Virginia. His special temporary contract described him as possessing a fair complexion, blue eyes, black hair. He stood five feet, ten inches and weighed just over 136 pounds. A doctor's physical conducted later reveals that Wimpy had 20-20 vision, no sign of color blindness, and normal hearing.

Enlistment papers show a wretched employment history and no known experience in any trade. The papers note that he left Elizabeth City High for Christmas vacation in 1935 (as a junior) and then never went back. What few job references Lassiter managed to dig up he probably should have left buried: like Minnesota Fats and Jersey Red, Lassiter would never impress others with his work ethic.

On one standard recruitment form, for instance, character reference A. Horitz noted that Lassiter was neither a committed employee nor an industrious person. The Coast Guard posed the following question: "What are his usual habits as regards to sticking to his job?" Horitz (who also noted a decade-long friendship with Lassiter) replied: "Not so good."

Another resident, local grocer J. C. Connery, grandly noted that he employed young Lassiter from "July, 1936 through April, 1941" at a wage of twelve dollars per week. At first glance, this appears to confirm a separate assertion that the boy abandoned public school for private employment. But Connery also noted that sometime after July 1936—probably within months of taking the grocer's job—Lassiter quit "for (a) better position and came back April 1941." No record exists of that "better position" because Lassiter never took it. His brief employment at the Connery grocery would be his *only* employment—other than those years in the Coast Guard and a few months managing a pool hall.

With such spotty references, Coast Guard recruiters may have thought they had signed another Depression-era bum. They could not have known, of course, that the recruitment bonus paid Lassiter—$112.75 on May 1, 1941—likely represented a pay cut for the boy. They could not have known that few recruits would master a skill so completely and transcendently as had the unskilled Wimpy Lassiter. And they could not have predicted that Lassiter's utter dominance on the green felt would earn him a small fortune during the war.

JUST AS FATS TOLD HIS LIES IN LITTLE EGYPT AND JACK "JERSEY RED" BREITKOPF HUSTLED SODAS IN NEWARK, WIMPY LASSITER BEGAN BOOT CAMP IN CURTIS BAY, MARYLAND. There he learned the importance of tight formations and taking orders. Six months later the Navy (which subsumed the Coast Guard during World War II) sent Luther to Norfolk, where he learned about internal combustion engines.

Records show the future hall-of-famer excelled at none of these endeavors. He did receive a special commendation for his marksmanship, which may come as no surprise given his ability with a cue stick. But Lassiter pretty much washed out in other regards. In Norfolk, for instance, Luther Clement graduated near the bottom of his forty-five-man internal combustion engine class.

For the next three years, Lassiter and his shipmates would hunt for enemy submarines and missing vessels. They plucked burned men from lifeboats. During that time, Lassiter would keep watch and manage the ship's engines. His discharge was honorable. But the record also reveals that seasickness, a kidney infection, and other maladies kept him from effectively discharging his duties.

On one particularly stormy outing, panicky crewmates thought surging waves had washed Wimpy overboard. They frantically searched the vessel top to bottom, but found him nowhere. "It was a terrible rough day and he had crawled into this box where they put all the life preservers," recalled Jane Thompson, wife of Lassiter's commanding officer. "And that's where he would stay. He said it was the nearest thing to a coffin he could find."

On August 12, 1941, Lassiter requested a transfer to the Coast Guard station in Elizabeth City. "My reason for this request is that my home is in Elizabeth City, and such a transfer would enable me to be closer to my relatives and friends," he wrote to the Norfolk commandant. Lassiter often said his only love was pool, but that wasn't quite true. Lassiter also loved his hometown, with its ocean pier, its brick-paved streets, its gray-haired Confederate grandsons shit-shooting down at Comstock's. By 1941, Lassiter had already spent six years burning up those yellow-striped freeways. Just twenty-two years old, and already he understood the loneliness of life.

But the commandant rejected the request, and so Lassiter spent most of his Coast Guard years off Moorehead, North Carolina. That didn't stop him, though, from returning home nearly every weekend. At 406 Pearl Street, Wimpy's mother would pamper the boy with home-cooked meals and laundry service. He slept till noon in his own soft bed and then loafed away the hours with pimply-faced boys and the old geezers down at Elizabeth City Billiards.

The only other town close to Lassiter's heart during the war was Norfolk, about forty miles to the north. Lassiter had played the town before, during his road time with Beefy Laden and Speedy Ives. Lassiter knew the town had action. But after 1941, after the outset of the war, the town became lousy with it. Everything changed. Tens of thousands of troops flooded into Norfolk, then a principal mustering point for World War II. So too came the shipbuilders, older and more experienced than the young recruits—but with more money.

Bachelorhood fuels poolrooms. And to Norfolk, during the 1940s, came the uber-bachelor. Facing the prospect of death overseas and with money-for-nothing recruitment bonuses weighing heavy in their pockets, the soldiers abandoned all caution. They came with heads filled with wine, pockets filled with cash, and a future uncertain. Like New York of the 1950s and Johnston City of the 1960s, Norfolk of the forties became one of the nation's great meccas of poolroom vice. It became home to hustlers and whores, card men and thieves.

And it was here—during his R&R from the Coast Guard, and for a few years afterward—that Wimpy Lassiter amassed a fortune. He won over $300,000 between 1942 and 1948, and frequently accepted astronomical $1,000 games. He pocketed $15,000 in a single week. He also built his game to championship levels. Lassiter would emerge from Norfolk confident, strong, and ready to challenge the greatest player that ever lived: the great and almighty Willie Mosconi himself.

"You had action, you know, once or twice a week," recalled Lassiter. "Greatest pool town that's ever been. You had five or six people there who were really gambling. People had lots of cash, and players from all over the country, anyone that played for money at all came to Norfolk."

Fats, who likewise settled there in 1942, described Norfolk as a wide open frontier town—the gold rush and oil boom all rolled into one. Soldiers lost to the local hustlers, who lost to the roadmen, who lost to the big boys like Lefty Lewis, Fats, and Wimpy Lassiter. "Every big action man in the country had converged on Norfolk," said Fats. "Wagering was nonstop, unlimited and gargantuan beyond compare."

Hustlers, hustlers everywhere, playing every hustle imaginable: playing the lemon, making the propositions, giving the weight. And when Lassiter wasn't stuck on that godforsaken Coast Guard cutter out in Torpedo Alley, plucking burned men from the sea or vomiting into it, he was in Norfolk.

"That's where he spent the war years," said Clarence Lassiter, Wimpy's younger brother. "And when he was on leave, he'd go off to the Norfolk area, and he'd hustle pool. He was probably one of the richest first classmen in the entire Coast Guard. But he'd always blow the money. It was always party time."

IF LASSITER MADE A PISS-POOR SOLDIER, FATS DID NOT EVEN MAKE THAT. Although he dutifully appeared before recruiters, Fats was ultimately rejected as unworthy. Fats's wife Evelyn later did not recall—or would not say—why recruiters gave her husband the thumbs-down. "He was just undesirable," said Evelyn, years afterward. "He was drafted and they went and examined him—not once, but two or three times—and finally they came to the conclusion that he wasn't desirable."

It may have been his weight, she said. Or it could have been his age—he would have been nearly thirty. Or recruiters simply may have pegged Fats (more or less accurately) as a shiftless degenerate. But whatever the reason, the rejection freed Fats to spend the war not in Europe, but at Norfolk's Monticello Hotel. And from there, every day, he would set forth for the Tuxedo pool hall, on City Hall Avenue, and then to St. Elmo's, with its flashing neon ball-and-stick above the door.

In Norfolk, Fats and Wimpy feasted upon the luckless and the hapless, the lame and the stupid. But Fats and Wimpy didn't feast upon each other. Despite all evidence to the contrary, Fats was no fool. If Fats had been able to whup Lassiter during the early years, he could do so no longer. Fats understood this basic fact. So instead of engaging Lassiter in battle, he partnered with him against their lessers in Norfolk, or against the real and true suckers during quick road trips in the Fatman's fat Caddy.

And then after days of this glorious blood-splattering cannibalization, the two kings would drive down to Virginia Beach, and there they'd put out the lawn chairs, and they'd prop dark glasses across pale faces. With Bermuda shorts and goofy grins, Luther "Wimpy" Lassiter and Rudy "Fats" Wanderone watched the pretty girls pass by.

Lassiter would also sometimes take a room at the Thomas Nelson Hotel, a short walk from the nearby Tuxedo, a favorite of both hustlers. There Lassiter would sink balls one after another—he sank them with maddening regularity, like a damned metronome. Some players get on high runs, get excited, and then up the pace. This typically leads to disaster. But not Wimpy. He was calm. Sedate. And so he could start with the nickel-and-dime games—the afternoon games—and start sinking balls. Click. Click. Click. If he had a pigeon, which was often, he'd lie low. He'd purposefully leave hangers—that is, those balls stuck right in the jaws of the pocket—and then strand whitey on the end rail. He'd curse his luck—just for effect, you understand—as he walked away from the table. And the pigeon would still have nothing, and would lose—lose a seemingly close game—and not understand he was beaten. And so the pigeon would just keep gambling.

In the evenings, Lassiter left the easy pigeons for the big money games, the hundred-dollar nine-ball freezeout, the heavy handicaps. Stinking and sweating in a dirty shirt, Wimpy would play all night long, his back and arms aching. His stomach—which never seemed quite the same after his life at sea—would grumble and complain. And as the sun came inching through the rectangular windows and the hardwood floors of the old Tuxedo, Wimpy would still be sinking balls. A night's worth of blue chalk and gray smoke lit the room in pixie dust. And that's when the rack boy would throw open the front doors and brush the tables and sweep the floors. The morning had come, but Lassiter would not stop pocketing balls.

"By the time I got to Norfolk, I was really shooting high and handsome," Wimpy recalled. "Gambling for big pots. I mean, you talk about discipline. Well, maybe milking a whole herd of cows every morning and keeping the woodbin full is good for your soul, but I swear, ain't no tougher builder of men than fifty-dollar freezeout. That is where each guy puts fifty dollars in the pot and you all take off your coats and settle down to shooting some serious, uninterrupted pool, and first guy gets ten games ahead takes it all. Ten games builds a lot of tension, I'll tell you. I can remember one time when it took me eighteen straight hours to get ten games ahead, and I was so disciplined I couldn't stand it."

On other occasions, Fats and Wimpy would motor down to a casino owned by Whitey Harris, a millionaire bookie fond of driving about town in a big ostentatious bus. Located fourteen miles from downtown Norfolk, the casino was filled with every game imaginable: craps, cards, roulette. A giant temple to the gods of vice, Whitey's became the place of worship for hundreds of high rollers then flocking to Norfolk.

"Whitey ran a very discriminating joint, on account he wouldn't allow a sucker near it," Fats recalled. "He always said suckers were good for one thing: trouble. So by word of mouth he let it be known that suckers were not welcome at his place, which was a tremendous arrangement because if you happened to break a guy down to his alligator-skin shoes you never had to worry that he needed the money to feed a wife and a half dozen kids. Whitey only skimmed his own kind. His joint was run like a high-class private club."

Wimpy and Fats and guys like Andrew Ponzi and Marcel Camp played cards there, and threw dice, and won and lost all night long: the doubles, the boxcars, the horrific, stinking snake eyes. At Whitey's, Fats and Wimpy could lose in ten horrible minutes everything gained over ten wondrous hours at the Tuxedo or St. Elmo's. The need to lose was like a craving, an undeniable hunger, and it could come at the craps table, or at cards, or over a game of pool.

Fats told of losing thousands there one night. "It was unbelievable," he said. "That quick, I was as busted as an ordinary sucker." Several witnesses said an errant nine-ball sent Fats home broke. Fats, who would never admit to losing at pool, blamed a pair of snake eyes. But whatever the truth, it appears certain that the unexpected loss quickly attracted a torrent of gleeful abuse from fellow hustlers.

"So now, all the mooches start heckling and berating me as mooches always do when a high roller has the horns on him real bad," Fats recalled. "And since I wasn't in the proper frame of mind to engage in a lot of verbal grief, I walked out of Whitey's joint into the snowstorm. I didn't even take my coat."

It was also at Whitey's—in a specially constructed billiards room where

Fats recalled "you could go broke in quiet and peace and with as little pain as possible"—that the casino owner and Lassiter went head-to-head for $5,000. Whitey Harris was a seasoned bookie and a top-rate player, but he was no Luther Lassiter. And since he owned the room, he set the ground rules.

First off: *No nine-ball*. Whitey figured to get Lassiter off his game. So Harris, a man who had been playing pool all his life, a man who could sink some balls, suggested straight pool. A race to one hundred balls, say, in no particular order, no particular pocket, no stripes or solids. Just sink balls and call them. One ball, one point. First to a hundred wins.

This was Whitey's game, a game he could win: but only if Lassiter would agree to give him an advantage. To make the game even, Whitey would demand a *spot*—that is, he'd play only if Lassiter gave him several balls free. Lassiter would start the game at zero, and Whitey would start at something ridiculous, something like fifteen or twenty points. Something to make his bet a sure thing, a lock.

But like any transaction, getting the good spot requires a bit of bartering. You're supposed to start high, then accept something lower. And so Whitey suggested a *forty*-ball spot. That is, Whitey would have to pocket just sixty balls to Lassiter's hundred. And to Harris's very enormous surprise, Lassiter agreed. No bartering. No whining. No nothing. Seven or eight railbirds then settled down on a long bench on the north wall, loosened their neckties, lit their cigars, and prepared for some serious sweating.

The two men lagged—that is, each floated a ball downtable. The one to bring the ball back, closest to the near rail, would make the other break, a disadvantage in straight pool. Harris won the lag, and made Wimpy break, which he did to near perfection, two balls softly rolling from the stack and then returning like repentant runaways, and the cue ball a catamaran around two rails and then returning downtable, only to stop near the short rail farthest from the stack. But there was just a bit of a shot showing. Just a wee bit of a ball peeking out from the stack. Just enough.

And so Whitey Harris got up and, almost without thinking, ran two racks. He ran twenty-eight balls. Such a run, on top of such an enormous spot, should have been enough to strike fear in the heart of any player. It put Harris only thirty-two balls from victory. Lassiter still needed a hundred—and had not yet shot at *anything*. But Lassiter didn't say a word, and he was grinning like a possum. He didn't seem concerned in the least.

Running more than fifteen balls in straight pool can be a very tricky thing, because no more than fifteen lie on the table at any one time (no more will fit into a rack). But good players can do it fairly often, and this is how: First, the player runs fourteen, going left, going right, connecting the dots. But before the player gets down on the last ball, the fifteenth ball, he stops, retrieves the fourteen balls already pocketed, and reracks them. And then *bang,* he shoots again—but not at the rack. Instead he targets the fifteenth ball, the one he stopped at earlier, the ball that wasn't reracked, and he sends that ball flying into a hole—and if his aim is true and right, the cue ball will divert from the fifteenth ball and bust the stack, sometimes sending balls flying every fucking way, or sometimes just shaving one or two from the pile...and then he keeps running.

It takes some skill and Harris managed it once. He ran fourteen, reracked, and then ran another fourteen before getting stuck. That is, twenty-eight in a row, no misses. And when he finished his work, he played a safety. He buried the cue ball against a rail, leaving no good shot. And so Wimpy, curly-haired Wimpy, a man who had spent the last ten minutes scratching his head and smiling, got to the table, and played a safety right back.

It went back and forth like that—with $5,000 on the line, and with the rail-birds coughing and sweating and exchanging glances. And then suddenly Harris saw an opening. Not much, but enough. There it was, the two ball peeking out of the stack. He began running balls—one, two, three, four, five. Thirty balls dropped for him. A big, horrifying, devastating run.

And now the score stood at 58-8. Wimpy had managed just eight balls, and Harris, remember, needed just sixty. He was two from victory. It was late, and Lassiter was tired, and his back ached, and he had hardly more than $5,000 in his pocket. A king's ransom, surely, but not enough to keep from going broke. Broke down to his shorts.

But Wimpy had not stopped smiling. He had not surrendered. And that maddening calmness never seemed to leave, and he seemed unconcerned about the money, the game, Whitey Harris, the railbirds. It was as if Wimpy was detached from *himself*. And so he surveyed the lay, and he circled the stack, and it was then that he saw that Whitey Harris had made a slight error. A ball frozen in the stack was dead-on for the corner pocket. That ball, sir, is *dead*.

Bang.

The cue ball smashed the stack, and the object ball became a streaking skyrocket to the corner pocket, and all the rest scattered in every direction. The table was open.

Bang.

Another ball found the side pocket

Bang.

Another.

And now Wimpy could shoot. He had some room to move. And Whitey Harris, the very rich Whitey Harris, settled down in his chair, and a frown crept across his face.

If the room was quiet before, now it was a tomb. Lassiter was now dropping balls one after another, sending each home quietly, and the cue ball glided effortlessly from point to point, never drifting more than a foot or so. Total control. Like magnets and power steering.

Lassiter completed one rack and then two and then three more. Now he needed fifty balls, Harris his two. But Wimpy controlled the table, and the angles had become clear to him, and he knew, intuitively, where that cue ball would be five, six, seven balls ahead. He knew, where the cue ball would go at the end of each rack.

Whitey Harris could only watch in horror. More railbirds had gathered to watch the devastation, and they began to whisper. For them, the air was electric, on fire. It was a bedazzling display. But for Harris, there was no air at all. Wimpy Lassiter had sucked all of it away, suffocating the hapless bookie under a torrent of sunken balls. The insolence of it.

"I went ninety-two and out," recalled Wimpy. "Ninety-two and out."

IN 1947, TWO YEARS AFTER HIS DISCHARGE FROM THE COAST GUARD, WIMPY BOUGHT HIMSELF A BRAND NEW BUICK. A beautiful car, a gleaming rival to any of Fats's fat Caddies. He wrecked it within months—got drunk, wrapped it around a tree—and with little more than a shrug and a smile, replaced it with a brand new Olds. All paid for with cash money, of course. And when Wimpy went home, he went with pockets filled with tens, twenties, hundreds, more. He'd give some to his brothers and sisters.

It was also about then that Lassiter took up with a local Elizabeth City woman—some remember her name as Frances—and for her, he considered the purchase of a home, a couch, and a refrigerator. Wimpy even agreed to work for a living—that's how bad it got. "It was serious, mighty serious," he recalled. But both the steady work and the steady girlfriend went awry. The marriage was canceled.

By then, Wimpy's almost comical haplessness with regards to the opposite sex had become the stuff of legend. One frequently repeated tale, for instance, involves the "swolls," a strange and esoteric affliction that reportedly first appeared in Norfolk. Overtaken by shyness and hypochondria, Lassiter would come vaulting across the poolroom, one hand over his mouth, his eyes wide with terror, and whisper urgently into Fats's ear, "Fatman, I got the *swolls!*" Fats had never seen anything like it.

"His lips would be all puffed up and at first I thought it was from wiping off the lipstick," said Fats. "But there was nothing he could do about it, so he finally gave up on tomatoes across the board by remaining a bachelor. Evelyn told Wimpy he should fall in love and get married, but Wimpy would always say, 'Bless you, Mrs. Wanderone, but I'm already in love—I'm in love with pool.' And he really was."

Luther became a prince among hustlers. The pressure, the high-stakes gambling, the Norfolk action made him so. Three hundred plodding straight-poolers, three hundred sharpshooting nine-ballers, and three hundred wily one-pocket men came to challenge Wimpy Lassiter. Rarely could they beat him. Not straight up, anyway. Lassiter became the number one hustler in the nation's number one town. He became the undisputed king.

IN 1953 LASSITER QUALIFIED FOR HIS FIRST MAJOR TOURNAMENT, THE WORLD'S STRAIGHT-POOL CHAMPIONSHIP, HELD IN SAN FRANCISCO'S DOWNTOWN BOWL. Irving Crane was there, as was three-time world champion Jimmy Caras, who was playing for the first time in four years. But the most intimidating player of all was Willie Mosconi, perhaps America's finest-ever tournament player.

As Fats lost himself in craps and cards in Norfolk, the dignified and haughty Mosconi spread balls in chandeliered banquet halls. As Wimpy conquered hustlers, Mosconi conquered champions. And when Wimpy screwed together his cue and combed back his hair and emerged for the first time on the world stage—when he first declared himself a competitor for a world title—Mosconi already had thirteen under his belt.

Some writers have distinguished between these parallel worlds of pool: between gambling and tournaments, between the so-called lions and the supposed lambs. Many top tournament players would wither beneath the pressure of high-stakes gambling—or so the argument went. Likewise, many gamblers (Minnesota Fats is the perfect example) appeared incapable of winning *without* such pressure.

Such arguments, of course, downplay the considerable pressure of world championship play, of stepping up against those of unspeakable talent, before spectators, journalists, sometimes TV cameras. Mosconi, despite his protestations to the contrary, had gambled early in life. By the 1940s he was playing exclusively in tournaments. He generally won at both endeavors.

In some ways, Mosconi, the man Lassiter met in San Francisco's Downtown Bowl, seemed to not even like pool. His father, a Philadelphia room owner, had encouraged Willie to play early in life. Pushed is probably a better word. Joseph William Mosconi took young Willie to the neighborhood rooms, where he set up exhibitions, pitted his son against local sharps, even set up a challenge match with the great Ralph Greenleaf. By his tenth birthday Willie was already sick of it. He could find no kids worth challenging, and he was nowhere near ready for the top pros. Besides, he had always preferred stickball and baseball. And so the juvenile champion of pocket billiards, with knee pants and a yo-yo, retired from the sport. "It was like having a weight lifted from my shoulders," recalled Mosconi in his autobiography.

For all he cared, he'd never go back. The years passed. Mosconi went to school, attended movies, eventually took a job in an upholstery factory. But in 1931, two years after the nation had plunged into economic depression, Mosconi suddenly found himself without work. And so, with his family suffering, Mosconi returned to pool, not out of love, but out of necessity. Out of hunger. Willie played local tournaments and gambled and went from room to room, picking up milk money and rent. He considered it a dog's life.

Some men work assembly lines. Some put on dark suits and balance columns of numbers. Mosconi's job was to win. He learned early how to steel himself against his opponents, even how to hate them, how to block out all distractions. At age seven, Mosconi had been able to run forty balls in a row. At age eighteen, when he returned to the pool hall, he doubtless could run fifties and sixties. He did so mechanically, blindly; he took pride in the effort, but perhaps not pleasure. Times were tough. His family needed the dough.

Loving the sport was totally beside the point.

"For Willie, the prospect of losing unleashed the demons of his deepest dread," Stanley Cohen, his biographer, wrote in 1993. "To Willie, the score never mattered. He played with a quickened intensity that was just the other side of despair. Any opponent, at any stage of a game, was deemed a threat he could not abide. He often said that he had learned to hate any man he was playing, but it was not the man he hated, it was the specter of defeat that the man embodied, the haunting recollection of his youth that bread might yet be snatched from his table."

This is who Lassiter confronted in March 1953, during the San Francisco tournament, held in the Downtown Bowl. Mosconi was a grim ball-running machine. *Bam!* Sixty balls. *Bam!* Sixty balls. Mosconi seemed incapable of running any fewer. And he was merciless. But Lassiter, too, had found that he could beat most men. And if Mosconi was a killer, then Lassiter was a stoic. Lassiter remained always calm, confident, sedate. When it came to pocket billiards, Luther Lassiter feared no man.

Not even Willie Mosconi

The format: a nine-man round-robin, meaning each player must challenge every other player. It then became a simple matter of math. Whoever won the most matches (there would be thirty-six over eleven days) would become champion. Although more intricate and unwieldy than single-elimination, such tournaments better test a man's skill. And Willie Mosconi, his hair already deeply gray, unleashed a great torrent of balls every time he stood to shoot. As expected, he began methodically beating every player that stood against him.

Crane went down early. Mosconi always had a special disdain for Irving, the Cadillac salesman from upstate New York. Crane had already won several world championships, and would win several more, and seemed perpetually a thorn in Willie's side. Beating Irving was fun. And then came Caras, also from Philly, who had come out of retirement to play in San Francisco. And others fell too, easily, one after the other.

Wimpy, however, had successes of his own. He had never played a world championship before, never competed at this level, but he suddenly found that he *could* win. These were the finest players in the world, yes, the best anyone had seen. Yet Wimpy stood there against them, pocketing ball after ball, winning game after game. This southerner, this player of nine-ball, this gambler, blocked out the spectators, the bright lights, the journalists. He saw only the pockets and the fifty square feet of green felt and the cascading balls. Wimpy doubled down low, and his eyes flickered from cue tip, to ball, to pocket. From cue tip, to ball, to pocket, ten times before the easiest shots, sometimes fifteen. And with all the strength of Norfolk and his years on the road, Wimpy would shoot, and the balls evaporated before him, one after another, and he began to win.

But something was not quite right. He felt a new burning down in his stomach, and a nausea. Perhaps the pressure made him sick. Perhaps the bright lights and the attention. But there it was, down in his gut, a horrible pain. And as he played, day after day, it became worse. He popped antacid pills and Broma Seltzer, but nothing seemed to work.

Jesus, it hurt. *Sweet Jesus!* He would sometimes hold his stomach, and it would make horrible, dreadful sounds. And yet he would keep playing. And sometimes, when he'd go take a shit, he'd find blood. But he kept playing. He was playing a world championship now. He was playing Caras and Jimmy Moore and Willie Mosconi. This was where he was meant to be.

Sweet Jesus!

And finally, as the tournament approached its end, and as he endured the pain and the sweats and the cramps, Lassiter found himself pitted against Mosconi himself. One more day to go. Mosconi remained unbeaten, confident, unstoppable. But with some luck, Lassiter could maybe catch him. Could maybe rob him of that prize, of the championship. And he meant to do so.

And so Lassiter broke the balls, sending whitey into the stack and then softly back again, two rails, leaving it tucked nicely in the jaws of the upper left pocket. Two balls emerged from the stack and then returned again, leaving Willie not much to shoot at. A little peeked out, but not much. Willie Mosconi quietly rose, and he chalked his cue, and surveyed the table. He ignored

Lassiter as one might ignore a wooden chair. The room was silent except for the squeaking of chalk against cue tip, of leather heel against tile floor, of a restrained cough from one spectator among hundreds.

And then Mosconi bent down, bent down low, and shot. And the heavens opened up. The cue ball slammed into its target, and that ball unerringly fell into the pocket. Of course. And the cue ball broke open the rack. Of course. And then the balls began falling one after another, rack after rack. He pocketed balls endlessly. He seemed incapable of doing anything else. Fourteen went down. *Rack.* And then 28. *Rack.* Forty-two. *Rack.* Sixty-four. *Rack.*

For thirty minutes Mosconi had pulled the cue ball around the table as if on a string. As if he had placed it there with his hand. Every shot seemed simple; he made no bank shots. His cue ball seemed to roll forever and miraculously close to his object ball. Never more than two feet away, ever. Just one easy shot after another.

But somewhere into his fifth rack, the cue ball went slightly astray. He found that he had a tight cluster, unbroken, that would cause problems. And with Lassiter seated at a small table to one side, and with spectators watching, and journalists scrawling notes, Mosconi played a safety. The cue ball drifted downtable, alighting softly on the end rail. And downtable he left one shot, a foolhardy shot, challenging Wimpy to take it. A miss, of course, would bring swift defeat. A miss would mean an open table, and one cannot leave the table open when playing Willie Mosconi.

Wimpy stood uncertainly. It was as if he were back in the Coast Guard again. A horrible, dull ache took hold of his stomach; he felt uneasy, as if he might stumble, and bile in his throat. Mosconi was looking at him. He'd ignored Wimpy before, but now icy hatred darted from his eyes. His sneer seemed to challenge the southerner.

Shoot it. Go ahead.

Wimpy took a deep breath and surveyed the table. Best to play safe. Mosconi had left a tough shot indeed. But Lassiter had seen worse. And whereas Mosconi was a straight-pool player, accustomed to easy shots, one after another, shots that depended on total cue ball control—Lassiter played *nine-ball*. And nine-ball encouraged risk. Encouraged the tough shot. And while Lassiter could not match Mosconi's cue ball control, would never match it, he certainly could match his shot-making ability.

Yes, sir, a mighty tough shot indeed.

Bam!

And sweet Lord Almighty, that cue ball raced from the far deep corner and struck the object ball with a calamitous snap, and the object ball dropped into the pocket. And he was on the table. Score: Mosconi 79. Lassiter 1.

But he had left himself nothing wonderful. And so Lassiter made another tough shot. And another. And then he broke up that troublesome cluster. And then he completed the rack.

Mosconi 79. Lassiter 14.

Wimpy continued shooting, and the shots began to come more easily. One after another the balls dropped for him. He seemed unerring, precise. He could feel the burning in his stomach, but he pushed it down. He drove it from his soul. He quietly went from ball to ball, from pocket to pocket. Twenty-five. Twenty-six. Twenty-seven. Twenty-eight.

Rack!

And the stack split apart, and the balls scattered like nighttime fireworks, and Lassiter kept shooting. Oh, glory be, they were coming fast now. Twenty-nine. Thirty. Thirty-one. Thirty-two.

He reeled off thirty-three straight. Thirty-three.

And then Wimpy took a deep breath. He paused. And for a second, he lost focus of the table. He lost focus of the game. Again he felt the burning in his gut. He touched his belly uncertainly with two fingers as he stole a glance at Mosconi. The great champion only seemed to glower.

Thirty-three. Straight. And now came the break shot, and Lassiter had left himself bad. The angle was not quite right. The shot was awkward. It would require a hand bridge—a device for which the nine-ball hustler had little use, and relatively little experience. The referee reracked the balls and called the score: "Seventy-nine for Mr. Mosconi. Thirty-three for Mr. Lassiter."

Wimpy could play a safety here. He could send the object ball uptable and tuck whitey up behind the stack. He could let Mosconi shoot his way out.

Or he could attack.

He stole another glance at Mosconi, and then quietly stooped for the hand bridge. He lowered the bothersome device to the green felt. *Attack or defend?* He sighted down his cue and drew a bead. *Attack or defend?* He began to stroke, his eyes rising from cue to ball to pocket, from cue to ball to pocket.

Attack!

And so the cue ball smashed into the object ball, and then the cue ball caromed inward, inward with all the power and glory of a rocket in flight, and the cue ball smashed into the tight rack, and balls scattered across the table. And the object ball, that awkward little ball far down the table, took off for the corner pocket. Wimpy watched it from the prone position: not rising, not moving. And he felt that burning tightness in his gut.

And then that awkward bastard ball struck the jaws. It did not go cleanly in—no comforting *pock!* It struck the damn jaws, and then it rattled for a second, like the hammer of an alarm clock, and then the rattling stopped. And the ball did not fall. Wimpy Lassiter had missed.

"The ball wobbled there and hung," recalled Mosconi, "and I ran seventy-one and out in a matter of minutes."

On March 12, 1953, Willie Mosconi defeated Luther Clement Lassiter at Downtown's Hollywood Bowl. And before Lassiter, Mosconi had beaten Crane and Caras. And he would beat Cowboy Jimmy Moore afterward. Mosconi pitched a shutout. But Lassiter, his insides burning, nonetheless acquitted himself admirably. The great maestro, who had dismissed Lassiter as a southerner accustomed only to small tables, acknowledged afterward that Wimpy could "shoot a respectable game of straight pool." Sometime afterward, Luther Clement Lassiter checked himself into a VA hospital. The pain in his gut had become unbearable. "The first tournament I played out in San Francisco in 1953, I had bleeding ulcers," Lassiter would later recall. "I was too dumb to know it until my doctor told me I was bleeding to death."

Luther Clement Lassiter, at the dawn of his professional tournament career, underwent major surgery. The doctor would eventually pull out his guts, cut half of them away, and then stitch him back together again. And Luther never felt quite right afterward. He suffered from gout. He suffered from a bad gallbladder. He complained loudly of sinus pain, of headaches, of a scratchy throat.

But even amid such tortures, Wimpy Luther Lassiter could focus on the tip of his cue, the ball, the pocket. He thought not of hands, nor feet, nor churning stomach. All of it evaporated into blue chalk and cigar smoke. No horizon now. No pitching sea. Just Lassiter, big balls, and hot lights. Rack after rack violently unfolded.

Wimpy the dog. Wimpy the dog sick.

Sweet Lord Almighty!

Rack!

6

THE DEATH OF POOL

"Pool was stone-cold dead, I mean cold enough to call the
embalmers."

— Minnesota Fats, from his autobiography.

 IMPY LASSITER BEGAN HIS PROFESSIONAL
TOURNAMENT CAREER FOR ONE REASON
AND ONE REASON ONLY: HE COULD NO
LONGER MAKE IT AS A HUSTLER. He would
never have gone to San Francisco, never played the Downtown Bowl, never
taken on Willie Mosconi—if only the gambling had held out. On this point,
there is broad agreement. Brother Clarence, for instance, recalled that "the
tournaments were nothing to him. The reason for him going pro was there
had come slack times for hustling." And Wimpy himself declared: "Times
were pretty bad for playing pool then. You couldn't make any money hustling,
so I started playing in tournaments."

By then, Norfolk was dead. The big money suddenly gone, the suckers
hiding. America's greatest hustling town had vanished like a dream. And so
Wimpy returned to the road. He went from town to town with the magnificent
Don Willis,[7] the so-called Cincinnati Kid, and they eked out a living. But even
that became intolerable. Action was dying everywhere—not just in Norfolk,
but in Chicago, Philly, and San Francisco too. For reasons Lassiter never fully
understood, poolrooms themselves were dying.

----

[7] See Appendix II

Sometime after World War II it began, this horrible black plague infecting pool, and it seemed to worsen with each passing year. The industry registered an 80 percent drop in the number of pool tables after the war, as compared to their numbers just a quarter century earlier. During the 1930s, Willie Mosconi's Chicago exhibitions outdrew the Bears. During the 1950s, few poolrooms remained in which to even conduct an exhibition. Mosconi held them in bowling alleys instead.

Fats and other hustlers blamed an overzealous politician—Senator Estes Kefauver, a Tennessee Democrat—who had declared war on the mob, racketeers, and gamblers of all sorts. "He kept pushing and pushing," said Fats, "and before long, the oldest established permanent crap and card and pool game Norfolk, Virginia ever knew was shut tighter than a drum." The collapse sent Fats back to Little Egypt, and into semiretirement with Evelyn, her mother Orbie, and twenty cats and dogs. He let a half dozen Cadillacs rust in the front yard.

Mosconi and the billiards establishment blamed gambling itself. "It appeared to be on a slow track headed for oblivion," Mosconi said of pool. The collapse sent Mosconi, then a pitchman for Brunswick Billiards, on a crusade: in billiard parlor and bowling alley, the champ railed against the professional gambler as if railing against the devil himself. "He hated gambling and always discouraged it," said Bill Mosconi, Willie's son.

It was a somewhat hypocritical stance for Willie,[8] who grew up wagering just to feed his family. But it was also understandable, given the history of the game.

---

[8] Mosconi once was asked by his son why he never taught the boy to play pool. "I want you to get an education and associate with a better class of people," came the response. Likewise, he told the boy, "I don't want you hanging around pool halls and betting the games." Quoted in Mosconi's autobiography, Willie's son said: "I think he even convinced himself that when he was young and supported his family by playing for money he was not really gambling."

In America, no other participatory sport has been so maligned by its association with gambling as pool. Recognizing this, Mosconi and the table manufacturers went to war with hustlers like Fats, Lassiter, and Red. The late-night wagers, the drunken arguments—that whole sorry *element*—made pool unfit for good, hardworking, decent folk. Mosconi fought them endlessly for the soul of his sport. He became the ragged prophet of a forgotten religion.

But neither Mosconi nor the hustlers were right about what went wrong with pool. Vice does not necessarily harm business. Prohibition had proven that. Just as Prohibition proved that the vice of men cannot be shouted down by angry moralists and politicians—no matter the shrillness of their tone. No, neither American vice nor American morality brought pool low.

The true culprit was the American dream.

SOCIOLOGIST NED POLSKY EXPLAINS WHAT *REALLY* HAPPENED IN HIS BOOK *HUSTLERS, BEATS AND OTHERS*—AND WHY NOTHING WAS TO BE GAINED BY CLEANING UP POOL'S IMAGE. Like a tribal anthropologist, Polsky spent years with Jersey Red and scores of other New York hustlers during the vicious 1950s. He noted their lifestyles, their personal honor codes, their career aspirations. He then took those observations and created a three-dimensional model of poolroom life, viewing it both in the wide context of mainstream culture and in the deep context of the subculture's history. Polsky concluded that neither gambling, nor its rejection by the middle-class moralists, undermined pool. Instead, Polsky blamed a fundamental change in American society.

Consider this: poolrooms have always been associated with gambling; moralists have always opposed them. Since the sport's very beginnings in

America, Polsky noted, poolrooms "were always associated with gambling and various forms of low life, ministers were always denouncing them, police were always finding wanted criminals in them, and parents were always warning their children to stay out of them."

As billiards historian Mike Shamos noted, this association extended to the sport's very name. During the nineteenth century, "poolrooms" were not billiard parlors, but rather places gamblers gathered to "pool" off-track bets. As gamblers waited for results—via telegraph—they often entertained themselves on billiard tables then typical in such rooms. Shamos reported that one of the popular games then was known as "pool." It was therefore a linguistic misunderstanding over off-track gambling that gave us the word "poolrooms" to describe billiard parlors.

Perhaps that's why New York lawmakers forbade the use of the word "pool" in connection with billiard rooms—as if a name change by itself could bring respectability. In 1919 Texas lawmakers outlawed poolrooms altogether. According to one newspaper account: "The 1919 law was mostly the work of women—pool halls having questionable reputations, wives and mothers wanted menfolk spared temptation."

So the preachers and the hustlers had been at war for a hundred years, during both pool's good times and its bad times. And yet not until the late 1940s and 1950s—with the collapse of Norfolk and America's other top action cities—did the American poolroom face the possibility of actual extinction. Polsky concluded that the blame lay not with the hustlers nor their adversaries, but rather with a change in society itself.

The events recounted in *The Hustler*, a film that eventually sparked the great renaissance of American pool, presumably unfolded during this dark time. But Polsky noted that the film more accurately described the pre-1930s poolroom, where there existed in America a different type of man. He called this man the *permanent bachelor*, and said he wandered without commitment through much of American history. Polsky argued that when the permanent bachelor disappeared from the American scene, so did the American poolroom.

Like Wimpy Lassiter, the permanent bachelor could go a lifetime without marrying. Like Jersey Red, he typically came from the working class. And like Fats's father, many were new immigrants. Through bits of lowbrow literature, common interests, and shared values, permanent bachelors formed their own self-identity and their own culture. They also had their own gathering places—and this point is key in understanding what really happened to pool after World War II.

As a gathering place, the upper-crust bachelors had the stuffy gentlemen's club often depicted in 1920s movies. The poor had the pool hall. There were other gathering places, to be sure: the barbershop, the neighborhood tavern. But the poolroom, with its clogged toilets and cigar smoke, became the refuge of choice for the working-class bachelor. "The poolroom was not just one of these places," wrote Polsky, "It was *the* one, the keystone." There, he said, men could escape the feminization of greater society. Among dust-covered tables, men could gamble, spit, and cuss freely. They loafed away their days without fear of nagging.

But unbeknownst to Willie Mosconi or Fats, unnoticed by the billiards industry *and* the hustlers, this crucial subculture had begun to disappear from the American scene. And when bachelors disappear, poolrooms close.

Polsky cited a 1959 study on marriage and divorce by Paul Jacobson that showed that permanent bachelorhood had reached its zenith during the late 1890s. The proportion of single males, age fifteen or older, then stood at 42 percent. By the 1950s, as poolrooms found themselves starving for customers, that proportion had dropped to just 25 percent. Likewise, the average annual marriage rate among single men rose from sixty-four per thousand in the 1900s to sixty-nine per thousand in the 1920s, dropped again during the Depression, and then soared upward in the 1940s to ninety-two per thousand.

The popularity of pool among Americans, as suggested by journalistic evidence, roughly paralleled this trend. In 1850, for instance, billiards star Michael Phelan wrote that "within the writer's memory, the number of rooms in New York did not exceed seven or eight, and perhaps not more than sixteen tables in all; now there are from fifty to sixty rooms." Nine years later Phelan played the nation's first billiards championship match for an astronomical prize of $15,000—large even by twentieth-century standards. Even at five dollars per ticket, the match, held in Detroit, sold out. Later, in 1913, A.C. McClung & Company published *Daly's Billiard Book*. It achieved a larger sale in its first ten years than any other book devoted to a physical sport or game.

While the proportion of permanent bachelors declined after the late nine-teenth century, Polsky argued that bachelors continued in sufficient numbers to maintain American poolrooms throughout the first three decades of the twentieth. There existed between forty thousand and forty-five thousand poolrooms in America during the 1920s, when Fats claimed the whole world was making whoopee; and poolrooms continued doing brisk business during the Depression, when the sour economy made marriage unaffordable.

Pool also thrived during the war years, when Wimpy Lassiter made a name for himself in Norfolk. Then, the installation of tables at military bases drove pool's popularity. The uber-bachelors—those new soldiers weighed down by the prospect of death overseas and signing bonuses in their pockets—made Norfolk heaven on earth for Lassiter and his ilk.

Polsky further noted that "the ideology of this bachelor subculture spilled over to married life itself; that is, married men spent more nights 'out with the boys' than they do today, which of course further helped poolroom attendance." Based on newspaper accounts and the number of billiards licenses issued and tables sold, billiards endured as the male sport of choice from the 1850s to the 1930s.

By the end of World War II, however, this trend had dramatically reversed itself. Fighting men returned home to a nation awash in money. Longing to leave behind the solitude of war and with a renewed optimism for the future, great numbers abandoned bachelorhood, built homes, created families. Suburbia came to America, and the suburban life—if it truly can be characterized as such—always stands at odds with the poolroom life.

Polsky wrote: "The once-great attraction of pool and billiards, both for spectators and players, was in large part factitious; it had not so much to do with the games themselves as with the poolroom's latent function as the greatest and most determinedly all-male institution in American social life. The poolroom got so thoroughly bound up with this function that it could not readily adapt itself to changed conditions; when the subculture died, the poolroom nearly died with it."

The end of the Depression, the end of World War II, *prosperity*—all of it conspired against the American hustler. Suburbia waged war with the poolroom; thousands closed. After the war, America's poolroom soldiers abandoned America's poolrooms. The poolroom bums, the old-timers, Minnesota Fats *and* Willie Mosconi: all spoke of the horrible diaspora. "Poor Willie," wrote James H. Winchester of *Bowlers Journal*, "the world's greatest pool player, 15 times champion, only he's got nobody and no place to play. He's a king without a country. Poolrooms are dead."

America's great hustlers came to a gloomy crossroads; desperation and hunger led many to diverging paths of straight jobs or outright thievery, into suburban homes or the county lockup. With fewer poolrooms, fewer suckers, less action—what else could they do? Norfolk was dust. The whoopie days were over. Men had to survive, even at the cost of their freedom.

A few, however, could not pay that bankrupting toll. Red, just starting out, survived the best he could. Fats went into semiretirement. He played during those years, and traveled, but mostly he lived off Eva-line and her mother Orbie. Luther Lassiter, the southern gentleman, went legit. He replaced the spittoon life of the hustling nine-baller with the tuxedoed life of straight-pool tournaments.

A year after his first major appearance in San Francisco's Palace Billiards, when he lost to Mosconi and then lost half his stomach to ulcers, Wimpy mounted his second major assault on a national championship. The year: 1954. The venue: Philadelphia's famous Allinger Billiard Academy. But this time, instead of executing hundred-ball ball runs before newspaper photographers and a packed house, Lassiter found himself playing before vacant seats.

And despite its billing as a world championship, opening-day coverage amounted to just two paragraphs buried backhoe deep on page twenty-one of the *Philadelphia Inquirer's* sports section. Here's that March 15, 1954, article, reproduced in its entirety:

Seven top pocket billiard stars will vie in a championship tourney at the Allinger Billiard Academy, 1307 Market Street, starting at 2 p.m. today. A pair of games will be played this afternoon and two games will be played this evening, at 7:30.

Top contenders are former world champions Irving Crane, Livonia, N.Y.; and Erwin Rudolf, Sayre, Pa.; Joe Canton, Watervliet, N.Y.; and Jimmy Moore, of Albuquerque, N.M.

Nowhere does the article mention that the Billiards Congress of America refused to sanction the event. Nor does it name Lassiter, then relatively unknown even among the cognoscenti. The southerner had won some fame as a road player, and had had that one prominent tournament appearance in San Francisco the year before, but otherwise had done nothing noteworthy. Mosconi sat out the Philly event even though it was held in his own backyard. He would have nothing to do with an unsanctioned tournament. And the hot-headed Jersey Red, then a nineteen-year-old poolroom bum, quite predictably never got an invitation.

The tourney ran two weeks. It featured four games daily—two in the afternoon, two in the evening—with the winner selected by double round-robin elimination. Each game went 150 points. Wimpy Lassiter won most of his early matches (including a 150-52 decision against Morris "Snooks" Perlstein of Atlantic City), and by the final day found himself with a single game lead over Irving Crane and Jimmy Moore, two of the finest straight-pool players in the world. To win the overall title, Lassiter would have to beat both of them. A single loss would throw the southern hustler into a tie; two losses would cost him everything.

Burr-headed, Stetson-wearing, slip-stroking Cowboy Jimmy Moore came first. Balls began dropping for Wimpy—uptable, downtable, cross cuts, narrow straight-ins. One rack, two racks, three.

Six ball, corner. Seven ball, side.

By whispering their names, Lassiter breathed momentary life into each. He brought them into soft focus; they danced alive; they pirouetted before him. *Eight ball, side. Nine ball, cross-corner.* For a half hour at least, Wimpy drove balls neatly to pockets, always leaving whitey precisely in position, like a soldier at a guard post. Only after nearly five flawless racks did Lassiter let whitey get away from him. And then the southern gentleman stepped back and scratched his head, and surveyed the table, and then called safe. He had sunk seventy balls.

Thus began a frigid war of defense, with both Wimpy and the Cowboy stranding whitey against the pack, or sometimes taking intentional scratches— anything to avoid an open shot. And the great burr-headed Moore, the cigar-chomping New Mexican Cowboy, managed runs of thirty-eight, twenty-six, and forty-seven. But Moore would not risk foolhardy shots. With a national title up for grabs, Lassiter and Moore, seasoned gamblers both, seemed unwilling to gamble much.

The game continued, safety upon safety, like an endless run-on sentence, punctuated only by the racking of balls and the applause of spectators. And then, after a record fifty innings, after two hours and thirty-five minutes, the game came to a sudden end. Moore had run twenty-six in a row, bringing his total to ninety-five. He appeared poised to overtake Lassiter, who had scored 138. But with victory perhaps too close, Moore rushed a relatively easy shot—and missed by inches. And pool, even more than football, is a game of inches. Lassiter, his face revealing nothing, ran twelve and out.

IRVING CRANE, THE MAN THEY CALLED THE DEACON, WAS TALL AND LEAN AND MORE DOUR THAN A MORTICIAN. Like Lassiter, he had gone prematurely gray. His face was a somber mask, his game play dispiritingly slow. So devoted to defense was Irving Crane that he would spend hours practicing safeties against *himself*. His offense could terrify the weak of heart. In 1939, for instance, Crane completed a mind-numbing run of 309—a straight-pool record that stood for a dozen years.

Only this man, the Deacon, now stood between Lassiter and his first national championship. And the Deacon was not a man to be trifled with.

Lassiter, blind to fear and unfettered by doubt, began with a quick Pearl Harbor sneak attack. He ran twenty-nine balls in the very first inning. It was a quick offensive flurry, with Lassiter going through one rack, then nearly finishing a second. He sent balls sliding down long rails or into side pockets, and then, when the shape went a bit awry, he buried whitey against the stack. A deft safety. He figured to beat Crane through a war of attrition.

But such a war, Crane would eagerly join. Against an impatient nine-baller like Lassiter, Crane felt he held the advantage. So Crane followed Lassiter's safety with one of his own. The two went back and forth like that for a while, both dropping whitey against the stack, or stranding whitey far uptable. Sometimes Lassiter would sink a single ball and then stop. Sometimes Crane would do the same. Anything to guard the table, to guard against the high run, to guard against disaster.

During the sixth inning, Lassiter left an open shot. It was tough and risky, and Lassiter must have figured that his conservative opponent would never even consider it. If Crane missed—if he *missed*—then Lassiter could begin his real game, his nine-balling, high-shooting game. Lassiter, having less cue ball control than Crane but superior shot-making abilities, could then put together a long run. He could prove his mettle.

And so Lassiter left a tough, open shot for the New York Cadillac salesman. Crane's expression belied nothing. Behind his eyes, few spectators could detect either fear, or annoyance, or eagerness—only the brow-furled intensity of a chess master. He sized up the table, perhaps noted that some pawns seemed spread a bit too thin; he spied a shot here, a shot there. Before him was opportunity. Or a trap.

And then the conservative Crane did something completely unexpected: he bent down low, and he sighted down his cue, and—he took the bait. His did not shoot gingerly soft as was his wont. He did not take the expected defensive shot. Instead, Crane, the former world champion, pulled back his piston arm and shot fairly hard—not a lightning bolt, but hard enough to knock the object ball into its pocket, hard enough to send whitey smashing into a cluster, hard enough to shave off a few balls while loosening the rest.

Colored balls scattered from the triangle; the cue ball stopped among them. For Irving Crane it was a beautiful thing, like a flower unfolded. The table was his. Shots everywhere. Easy shots. And so the Deacon went to work, plowing through one rack, then two, then three, then four.

And Lassiter could only sit, and wait, and listen miserably to the soft thudding of balls falling away. Hot lights burned his forehead, burned his eyes. He shaded himself with a thick palm; he closed his eyelids—closed them so tight that he could see the ghastly red beneath them. The horrible heat still beat down upon him, and the horrible thud-thud of dropping balls came from everywhere, like the dooming drumbeat in a suffocating jungle.

Two ball, side.

Three ball, corner.

Eight ball, corner.

Seven ball, side.

It was a dry, mathlike recitation of dropped balls and cleared racks. It was a solemn, hypnotic dirge marking time before Lassiter's seeming demise. *Two ball. Seven ball. Twelve and thirteen. Rack!* It was painful, disheartening, devouring.

It was endless.

And then suddenly, unexpectedly, it came to a halt.

Foul!

And with that single word, uttered not by Crane, but by the referee, Lassiter sat up, opened his eyes, and began to hope.

Foul!

Crane had run ninety balls, six racks in all—and then the master tactician had hooked himself, and so took an intentional foul. He failed to pocket a ball, or push one to the rail, and sacrificed a point. Anything to guard whitey, to guard the table against Lassiter.

The southerner returned to the table, pocketed three balls, and then played safe. Crane took another intentional scratch and Lassiter followed with two more balls.

On and on it went, Lassiter pocketing a ball here, Crane pocketing one there. Sometimes Lassiter took the intentional scratch; sometimes Crane took it. Lassiter was drawn into Crane's game: safety after safety after safety. In the eighteenth inning, Lassiter ran eighteen—giving him a total of 103 points—but then missed his nineteenth shot. Crane then stood at 110—only forty balls from victory—and in that inning pocketed ten more. But the eleventh ball went awry.

Lassiter, standing forty-seven balls from his first national championship, fired away. *Bam!* He sank one rack, then two. Somewhere in the distance he could hear the whispering of spectators, like the murmuring of a far-off storm. But he hardly noticed it, just as he hardly noticed the hot lights or the awful scowl of Irving Crane stuck on the sidelines. Lassiter quickly flew past Crane's 120 mark and he kept flying: ten balls, fifteen balls, twenty. Dropping soup cans into a grocery sack couldn't have been easier....

And then suddenly the southerner found himself stepping away from the table, blinking his eyes, looking with curious wonder at the green felt. It looked different now. It *was* different. And then he looked at his own thick hands, new powerful hands. He clutched his lucky cue stick. There was a silver dollar embedded in the shaft.

And finally Wimpy turned his attention to the sparse crowd all around him.

And that's when he realized people were clapping.

Luther Lassiter was thirty-five years old when he won his first national championship. The final reckoning: Lassiter 150. Crane 120. A thirty-ball margin separated the two, a thirty-ball margin created almost entirely during Lassiter's sneak attack during the first inning.

At the tournament's end Lassiter held twelve wins, two losses—both to Mike Eufemia of New York. Moore and Crane took home second place with ten wins and four losses, including two apiece to Lassiter. But Lassiter's first important victory earned him little. It came during pool's most difficult period: Mosconi refused to show up; the BCA refused to sanction it; the money somehow evaporated.

"In Philadelphia, I was to get twenty-five percent of the gate after expenses," recalled Lassiter, years later. "But the tournament didn't make expenses. I got twenty-five percent of nothing."

Two years later, in 1956, the Billiards Congress of America stopped sponsoring tournaments altogether. Pool's principal sanctioning body would no longer sanction an event. There just wasn't enough interest. There wasn't enough money.

Mosconi kept working, kept promoting pool for Brunswick Billiards, but to no avail. Even the great Mosconi himself could not revive the sport.

It seemed that suburbia, finally, had won.

RED'S LAST REFUGE

"I am the best one-pocket player that ever lived. I say that without qualification."

—*Jersey Red at the 7-11*

 ICYCLE CHARLIE LEFT HIS BIKE DOWNSTAIRS. Three-Fingered Gus just got beat up, bad, by Eyebrows Kelley. And Jersey Red—well, Red was hot on the five ball, looking for his pocket, and running, man, running. *Leave 'em broke and leave 'em happy.* He's down on the five, down hard, ready to go. *Man, watch this shot, watch it, here it goes, here it goes—fantastic.*

Before him were the twenty-one tables of New York's 7-11, the biggest poolroom of big-time pool. On either side sat a dozen smoking railbirds grooving to the poetry Red laid down on the green felt. And below were the sixteen balls, marching to the orders, going left, going right one-two-three, they just kept falling, one after another. And Red, he kept going too, working hard, putting the latest pigeon into a coma, into a body bag. *Where do you want this guy's body sent?* The old railbirds, the piss-stained men in loafers and work pants, watched from hard-backed wooden chairs. They cursed and they spat beneath horn-rimmed glasses.

As an unexpected consequence of pool's retreat everywhere else, its greatness became concentrated in a single geographic spot. America's last great hustlers—those not forced into straight jobs or outright thievery—came together in New York City. They motored in from dying Detroit and dead Philly. They came from no-action Norfolk. Some, like Fats and Hubert "Daddy Warbucks" Cokes, even came up from southern Illinois. Hustlers, hustlers everywhere. For only in the city that never sleeps did the action never stop.

At Manhattan's 7-11 poolroom, Red faced not just good players, not just excellent ones. Red faced past and future world champions. A desperate sort of competitiveness grew within him. Stomach-aching hunger whipped him on. Pool's darkest period thrust greatness upon him. Like a weed sprouting from frozen ground, Red would flourish.

Here's how it went, back in New York City, where Red became king. He was definitely a high-school dropout, maybe a reform school graduate, they said he once shot a man, and he just about lived at the 7-11. He slept on the tables, or at a nearby movie theater. He made outrageous spots; that is, he'd handicap himself in order to get a game. Sometimes he agreed not to chalk his cue. And sometimes, playing one-pocket, that game where each player has only a single pocket to shoot at, he'd sink ten to his opponent's five. Plus, Red gave away the break.

Eddie Robin, a former U.S. three-cushion champion, remembers how it went, remembers how Red ran him over like a Mack truck, smashed him flat. It was one of those embarrassing, hope-your-friends-don't-see, pants-down sort of humiliations; a drubbing so sound and final that it actually put future national champion Robin off pool for several years. "I was eighteen or nineteen years old and I was playing damn good and I kept hearing about this guy, Jersey Red, who spots any stranger that comes into the room an arm and a leg. So I walk in and I say, 'I hear you're willing to spot any stranger nine to five and the break,' and Red says, 'Get to the table.'"

"He gave me nine to five and the break, and it didn't make any difference. He kept running out. I sort of went into shock. I couldn't believe that anyone could give that kind of spot. I kept playing him and he beat me to death. I don't think I ever won a game. The guy put me into a coma. I had never seen anything like this."

From about 1949 until the early 1960s, a player could find no fiercer competition than that at New York's 7-11. Marriage had taken the suckers; suburbia had destroyed the roadman economy. America's last great hustlers came to the 7-11 like sharks drawn to blood. They schooled together, hoping, hunting, searching for money and glory in darkening waters.

They had no choice. There was nowhere else.

"The standards there were so high as to make the game barely recognizable," billiards writer George Fels recalled of the 7-11. "In that three-ring circus gone berserk, all those bona fide players, all that frenzied action, [Jersey Red] was just about unanimously considered the best of the best. Use your imagination as to how good that must have made him."

IN 1949, THE SAME YEAR THAT JERSEY RED DISCOVERED NEW YORK'S POOL HALLS, THE BASEBALL SCOUTS DISCOVERED JERSEY RED. He was then fifteen years old—still a kid—but big for his age. Like Lassiter, Red possessed a natural athleticism. Playing first base for several Newark sandlot leagues, Red terrorized opponents with his .400 or better batting average, his powerful left-handed longball. Brother Marty was then three years out of the infantry, working at the family diner. Dad flipped burgers; Mom waited tables.

A scout for the New York Yankees—Red remembered his name as George Weiss—invited him out to St. Petersburg for spring training. Weiss recognized

Red's talent, figured he could contribute to the farm team. "The Yankees were going to pick up the whole tab. It was all set." Red was supposed to show up in February.

"The week before I'm supposed to fly to Florida, I win seventy dollars shooting nine-ball," said Red. "The next day I win a few more bucks, and by the end of the week I'm making so much money shooting pool, I figured if I went to Florida with the Yankees, I might blow a fortune."

By then, home life at 75 Walnut Street had become intolerable. Red had abandoned school, refused to work at the family diner, wouldn't even wake up in the mornings. He fought with his father, just as his father fought with the bottle. The only person with whom Red remained close was his sister Ella, who, at age twenty-six, seemed more like a mom than a sibling. But even she couldn't stop him from leaving home for two or three days at a time. "He would go to the poolrooms and I would be the person that would work," recalled brother Marty.

Even by the standards of adolescence, Red was awful.

Red spent most weekdays at Steel's or The Chinese, near his Newark home. But on the weekends the fifteen-year-old took the PATH train to the city, trudged past the Honeymoon Lane Dance Hall on 47th, bounded up a long flight of stairs. The first time he witnessed the sordid splendor inside, his eyes must have grown wide like saucers and his heart must have pounded loudly in his ears. At the great 7-11, swirling all around like some surreal circus, men argued and spat and threw money across green felt. They dropped cigarette butts and leaned against walls laid bare except for cue racks and scoring slates. They argued with Blackie at the lunch counter while they drank their coffee and ate their PB&Js. A white-noise cacophony of cussing men and thunderous break shots and leather heels on hardwood floors enveloped the whole smoky, chalk-filled, magical scene where twenty-one steel bell-shaped lamps drooped over twenty-one unforgiving tables.

The 7-11 (also known as Paddy's after a previous, long-dead owner) remained open twenty-four hours a day, seven days a week. It became a midnight refuge for the forlorn and the unwary. They were all there: Three-Fingered Gus, Wagon Head (he never stopped waggin' his head), New York Blackie, Joey with Glasses. They stumbled by the prostitutes, over the stairwell-sleeping bums beneath newspaper blankets. The smoke and the crack of break shots drew them. The promise of easy money and cheap fame enslaved them. The stink of it clung to them like old sweat.

Brooklyn Johnny[9] remembers how it went, how he and Red became best friends—more like brothers, really. Red was just fifteen, Johnny thirteen. "He was living in New Jersey and I was livin' in Brooklyn," recalled Brooklyn Johnny, aka Johnny Ervolino, who in 1998 was still scuffling around pool halls, making games. "We'd play pool all night long—ya know, Paddy's was open twenty-four hours—and we also played at McGirr's and Ames.[10] We'd like make a circuit, 'cause they were all in an eight-block area. There wasn't much money in it—but you could always find a sucker."

And then, after fifteen hours or maybe twenty of this bloodletting, after the sun had gone down and then come up and their backs ached like a longshoreman's and they smelled of old sweat and smoke and chalk, Red and Johnny went to the air-conditioned Times Square movie houses. There they'd find a cool spot along the back row and they'd go to sleep. But even homeless in that midmorning darkness, Red and Johnny could not escape

---

[9] See Appendix II
[10] Two other famous New York poolhalls. Both have since closed.

the 7-11: always in their dreams the white ivory drifted silent as ghosts down long rails.

In 1971 Ervolino won the one-pocket title at the Stardust National in Las Vegas, then the richest tournament in pool. But in 1949 he was living that glorious bum's life—just like Red.

"Guys like me and Red—we would turn around and never make a ball. We'd let these guys more or less turn macho and just beat the pants off of us, and then let them pick the game they wanted to lose money on. We used to have it down so good, you know, so the games were close. We could make a shot and scratch intentionally—and not let the other guy know it. It used to be an art. The whole idea was to make it look like you were a hard-luck case."

Another legendary graduate of the 7-11 was five-foot, two-inch Larry "Boston Shorty" Johnson, the winner of several Johnston City events during the 1960s. Shorty possessed a somewhat unorthodox playing style. At the beginning of long gambling sessions, Shorty typically missed relatively easy shots or got bad position on good ones. He often found himself chasing his own money. But Shorty had phenomenal stamina—despite his fondness for cigars and beer—and so could stand for hours without losing his touch. In hustling, stamina can win more games than a powerful break or a wicked jump shot. Those who remember Shorty at the 7-11 remember a man who would play for days; the longer the session, the better his chances.

"I remember one time I saw Boston Shorty and Red playing Friday night through Sunday night—I didn't think they'd ever stop," recalled one of the old railbirds. "I don't remember who won it, but I remember they played and played, all day and all night. Shorty was a good player, and he'd wear you down. He'd never give up. He was like a pit bull and it would always end up like a war."

James Evans, somewhat older than the others, mentored Red. Many who knew him—Fats and Red included—considered Evans one of the finest players of that era. But because he was black, pool's sanctioning bodies barred Evans from world competition. Evans had his own four-table room (with poker action on the side) up in Harlem, at Lennox Avenue and 129th Street. Open all night, the room attracted the area's top hustlers.

It was against Evans, at the 7-11, that Red first unleashed what would become his signature shot—a stunning kiss-kick combination that to the untrained eye appears to defy the laws of physics. Red and Evans were playing one-pocket on a tight five-by-ten, located near the 7-11's front desk and surrounded by sweators.[11] Red fired his cue ball hard at the object ball, which then rested against the short rail a few inches from Evans' pocket. But instead of bouncing uptable, the object ball rocketed backward along the short rail—it somehow went in reverse—and right into Red's pocket!

Score one.

The secret of the shot, now known as the "Jersey Red shot" (and still performed on cable TV by trick-shot artists), is to get a double kiss off the object ball. After initial contact, the cue ball caromed to the long rail near Evans' pocket, then returned, kissing the just barely rebounded object ball into Red's pocket. Like a magician's sleight-of-hand trick, all this occurs faster than the eye can see. "It almost always brought the house down," wrote billiards author Eddie Robin.

Evans eventually went nearly blind—he got cataracts in both eyes before he died—and spent his last years living off a World War I pension in a Times Square hotel.

----

[11] "Sweator," a poolroom term for spectator, is spelled with an "or" to distinguish it from the article of clothing. See glossary.

Fats, during his visits home, also hustled at the 7-11. And it would have been there, during the 1950s, that Red first glimpsed the older player's machine gun style, his run-out game, his gambling strategy. Fats would then have been thirty-six or thirty-seven years old—two decades Red's senior. (Fats referred to Red as his "adopted son.") From Fats, Red learned a bit of showmanship: he laughed at the Fatman's stories, marveled at the attention Fats could draw, and then adapted the salty patter for his own use.

Eventually, Red's wisecracking skills, his flair for the dramatic, would nearly equal those of Fats. Few players could make such a boast. On the table, of course, Red quickly surpassed the Fatman. "He gave Fats nine to seven in one-pocket when Fats was at his peak and called New York Fats," recalled 7-11 regular Al Bonife, aka New York Blackie. "And Red beat him on the five-by-ten. Nobody did that to Fats then…There were a tremendous amount of good players there, but I think Red played better than anybody I ever saw on a five-by-ten."

FAMILY AND FRIENDS LATER DID NOT REMEMBER—OR WOULD NOT SAY—WHAT GOT JACK IN TROUBLE. The authorities do not release information related to the arrests of minors. But Red himself, through the years, vaguely acknowledged a criminal record. To one friend, he confirmed an actual shooting. An intruder—perhaps a would-be thief—appeared at the window of some flophouse, probably in New York. The intruder attempted to clamor inside. Too bad for him. *Bam!* Red fired a gun. Red never said what happened next.

Another time, after getting into a heated argument at a New York pool hall, Red hit a man so hard that the man's pants fell down. "You know, Red, I loved him, but he could be a hard loser," recalled Ervolino. "If you beat on him, he'd get pretty nasty. He could have this threatening style."

With animals, men, and hustlers, fear can prompt strikingly similar reactions: flee or fight. The hair stands up on the back of the neck, the pulse quickens, eyes widen. It was deadly fear that Minnesota Fats sometimes spoke about; it was deadly fear that Red—confronting both the prospect of homelessness and the skill of the nation's top players—lived with every day. To take the cash from those monsters, to go against Boston Shorty or Fats or James Evans, one must control one's nerves, control one's muscles.

In craps, say, or poker, it doesn't matter. Fear may prompt a bad bet on bad cards, or folding on good cards, but fear doesn't *change the cards*. In pool, fear changes everything. It invites disaster and self-loathing. Any micro-inch deviation in aim, any micro-foot-pound deviation in force, and a shot goes horribly, embarrassingly awry. And once that begins, the fear really takes hold, which then prompts the anger, and it makes of a man, as Minnesota Fats would say, a human cash register.

At the 7-11 Red came to accept fear, realized that one could not deny its influence, and so learned to use it to his advantage. He developed different strategies—some bullying, some avuncular—to mitigate its defeating power. For example, Red's famous cock-and-bull made him appear fearless, invulnerable, unbeatable. It could rob lesser players of any hope.

In a piece for *Saga* magazine, writer Dale Shaw described this ability. Red may have unconsciously picked it up from Fats, whose nonstop jabbering became his weapon of choice against the suckers.

Red leaned nonchalantly over the green-covered table, his 6-2, 180 pounds neatly balanced on one foot, and tapped in a two-ball combination shot for the winning money. He laughed uproariously...

"You know you are so good, sooo good!" came a cooing taunt from the ranks of drowsy watchers and backers surrounding the only table still lighted in the long pool hall.

"I do know it," grinned the hustler, pocketing two tens without exposing his roll. "I know it forever. There is no one, no one pockets the balls the way I do, evah! No-where! I pocket impossible shots, nevah-heard-of shots, I run balls forever. I start running balls now, if I want, I don't stop next year or the year aftah. I just don't stop."

The loser had been tired looking, morose. Now he clutched his sides, laughing, "Oh, Jersey, cut it out. Cut it out, Red!"

"Leave 'em broke, leave 'em happy," Jersey Red grinned, running practice balls joyously. "I leave 'em the brokest and the happiest ever heard of coast to coast and shore to shore. Seein' me run balls the way I do makes 'em appreciate livin'."

When confronting a player not so easily disarmed—a player, say, like Shorty—Red made every effort to equalize the impoverishing power of fear and doubt. If Red had to bet his own money, for instance, then he made damn well sure the other player also played his own money. No stakehorses. No moneyed backers. Imagine the difference: a hustler playing backer's money can afford to lose. If he does, he's out exactly nothing. But missing with one's own money cleans out one's own bank account.

When matched against a top player, it's always better to find a stakehorse. Or at least make sure the other guy doesn't have one.

Of course, a player can simply establish a direct psychological edge, and this can be as important as keen eyes and a smooth stroke. At the 7-11 Red sometimes simply intimidated his opponents. He was a big man, hotheaded, and those relentlessly tough years beat down upon him. Sleeping on the tables beat down upon him. As the decade wore on and he grew in experience, Red convinced himself of his absolute greatness. He lived with little dignity, sure, but he was still number one.

Red became the walking, talking, hustling cliché. He angrily cursed other players, fought with them and threw punches. Losing an edge in a tight money game could bring a dose of foul-mouthed abuse. The abuse made the opponent fearful. The fear brought the edge back to Red. "He was a different person during those hustler days," said Dottie Breit, the woman Red would eventually marry. "I heard him talk, heard him say how they did it up at the 7-11. But he was different then."

Yes, different. In some ways, perhaps, even diminished. But Wimpy's Norfolk glory days were over. Fats's Broodway whoopie days were done. A top hustler no longer booked the thousand-dollar bet, nor even the hundred, generally. Not even at the 7-11. Those glory days had turned to dust. And so Red did what it took: he slept in the flophouses or on top of the tables, and through cruelty or the quick hustle he survived.

DESPITE HIS FAILINGS—DESPITE THE FAILING THRUST UPON HIM BY AN AGE—RED NONETHELESS POSSESSED MORE HONESTY THAN MOST HUSTLERS. On this there is wide agreement. "Red was pretty much on the up-and-up," remembered one old-timer. "He used to bet his own money and he had plenty of backers because he wasn't treacherous."

Treachery, of course, has a special meaning when it comes to hustling, which, by its very nature, involves some element of deceit. Red and Brooklyn Johnny tricked suckers all the time. They performed their famous hard-luck show, playing on the lemon, dogging shots, losing games they easily, effort-lessly, could have won. That's dumping, sure—but that's *honest* dumping. That's dumping to gin up the wager. That's *hustling*.

Red, however, didn't engage in the other sort of dumping—the dumping of stakehorses, the sort of dumping that ran rampant during those tough New York years.

"Ames was a pretty good action joint in the afternoon, but 7-11 got the action at night," said one old railbird. "On the weekends, you know, on Friday and Saturday nights, we'd close up McGirr's, on Eighth Avenue, and it would be about two in the morning, and it would be hard to get in the door at the 7-11 at that time. In the middle of the night, there'd just be hundreds of guys there, and a small crowd around a few of the tables...

"And any stranger who struck his nose in a game usually got the worst of it because there was a lot of business games going on, and a lot of players cutting up the money in the bathroom afterwards. That was pretty much a given for anybody that hung around there, and so before you started betting, you had to find out what was going on."

That's how the railbirds remembered it, how the dumps went down at the 7-11, or at Ames or McGirr's or any of a hundred other action rooms. A stake-horse would back a player, agreeing to front hundreds of dollars with which to gamble. In exchange, 50 percent of more of the winnings would go back to the stakehorse. The stakehorse, however, swallowed 100 percent of the losses. So a disreputable, stakehorsed player—and there were plenty—could secretly throw the match. The stakehorse would pay the winner, and then both winner and loser would retire to the bathroom and split the jackpot.

Another typical dump involved side bets. A sweator would post a side bet, perhaps hundreds of dollars, with another spectator. One of the side-betting gamblers would then convince a player to intentionally lose in exchange for a percentage of the winnings. Some of the nation's finest players—players that figure in this very book—engaged in this and other deceptions.

But apparently not Jersey Red. Perhaps he had too much respect for the game. Perhaps, during those early 7-11 years, camping out at movie theaters and in flophouses, sleeping on the pool tables, at war with an alcoholic father—perhaps pool was the only thing Red respected.

In 1951, at age seventeen, Red left home for good. For a time he helped Abe Rosen run the 7-11, but mostly he just hustled pool. And hustling, then, was tough. Red went on the road, even though he had no car. He mustered up money games, even though he had little money.

Jersey Red became America's number one hustler during hustling's cruelest decade. Those relentlessly bullying years defined him, defined his playing style, defined his personality. This was Red's time: he grew to adulthood, found his greatness, received acclaim from his peers.

And he slept dead broke on top of the tables.

Red, more than Fats and Wimpy, came to embody pool's bankrupt years. Hustling, then, inadvertently prepared him for the renaissance to come. "I am the best one-pocket player that ever lived," Red boasted.

And most everyone agreed.

8

CROSSROADS

"It would take a miracle or a patron saint to bring billiards back. But we have to keep faith, those of us who love the game."

—Faye Procita, wife of pool legend Joe Procita

THE SCENE: A ROADHOUSE ALONG A HIGHWAY JUST OUTSIDE JOHNSTON CITY, ILLINOIS, POPULATION 3,900. The year: 1961. Earl Shriver, the pool hustler from Washington, D.C., craves action. And so does Marshall Carpenter, the Tuscaloosa Squirrel, an old protégé of Fats. Both have come to Johnston City in search of pigeons. Instead they find Georgie Jansco, fast talking and stout. The trio sit nearly motionless in his dark and dank, fabulously smoky and run-down J&J Ranch—Georgie's bar. They could play Georgie some gin, or maybe knock rummy, but both are broke. They could return to the road, but lethargy holds them firm. So they sit there, nearly motionless, and say nothing.

Goddamn, they're bored.

The Little Egypt of 1961 was not the Little Egypt of 1941. No longer was it the Las Vegas of Middle America. The action in Johnston City and nearby Dowell and Du Quoin had turned to dust and scattered in the wind, just as it had all across America. A decade-long drought, dry enough to choke a horse, had murdered tournaments, actions, and pigeons. And in that dark patch of the American soul—in that fertile place where pool and gambling and the vice of men should take root—one found only a yawning chasm, an empty hole.

And so bar owner Georgie Jansco absently pulled labels off beer bottles, and the Tuscaloosa Squirrel tapped his foot, and Earl Shriver looked dispiritedly into space.

And that's when it came to them—*bang!*—like a mortar shot from hell.

Hold a tournament.

THE IDEA FIRST CAME FIRST TO SHRIVER, LIKE AN EPIPHANY, ALTHOUGH IT TOOK GEORGE JANSCO TO MAKE THE IDEA REALITY.

"We were drinking beer and I remember Earl telling him [George] that he would call a few people and there would be a lot of action," recalled Squirrel. It was a great goddamned fabulous idea, everyone agreed. With the pigeons flown and the easy money gone, it now fell upon America's hustlers to create their own fun. And wherever hustlers gather, action always follows. So forget the stuffed shirts, forget the regular pros like Mosconi and Crane. And forget the BCA. The sport's sanctioning body had stopped holding tournaments altogether, the *fuckers*—not that they had ever invited Shriver or the Squirrel to play one.

Besides, the BCA understood only straight pool, a game for stiffs. So screw 'em. The nation's hustlers would hold a tournament, said Shriver, and it wouldn't be any of that straight-pool shit, the most mind-numbingly boring game yet invented. It would be one-pocket. The hustler's game.[12] Have a goddamned one-pocket tournament, for crissakes. There had never, ever, been a national-class one-pocket tournament in the history of the world—at least not as far as Squirrel and Shriver and Georgie could figure. This was an

---

[12] Mosconi once called one-pocket a hustlers' "gimmick" game.

injustice that they could remedy, right then, right there, down in Johnston City, Illinois. Earl loved the idea and Squirrel loved the idea and Georgie loved it too. And so did New York Fats, down in Du Quoin, just sixty miles away. They called his fat ass straightaway.

The J&J Ranch, Georgie's fall-down roadhouse on the outskirts of Johnston City, had no pool table, nor a place to put one. And neither did the nearby Showbar, the dance hall owned by his brother Paulie. "There was only one poolroom in town," recalled Fats, "and it was such a trap, it wasn't even good enough for a jamboree." But Georgie, like all visionaries, was driven, relentless, filled with the passion of his own imagination. And that imagination said: *beer shed.* Back behind the J&J ranch, Georgie had a damned beer shed! It had cement floors, cinder block walls, no windows...*perfect!*

Jansco knew a stocky, brown-haired carpenter—Fats remembered his name as Moore—who regularly drank on credit at the J&J. "Georgie told Moore that he would call the [bar] bill square if Moore would enlarge the garage," recalled Fats. "And so Moore is ripping out the walls and Georgie is feeding him the juice, and the more juice Moore consumed, the harder he worked. In a couple of days, he had the place looking pretty good. Then Georgie gets a secondhand table somewhere and the jamboree was ready to be launched."

Fats and Shriver got on the horn and called hustlers north and south *Come down, ya bum, and bring yer cash.* Jansco was putting on a jamboree—there'd be action, money, wipe yer ass, pull up yer shorts, get in the car, *drive!* Squirrel called too. And Jansco. And like drunken pirates they came: Johnnie Irish, Daddy Warbucks, Cowboy Jimmy Moore, the Knoxville Bear. He was a natural goddamned marketing man, Fats; and

Jansco knew a world of gamblers, and Squirrel and Shriver had been road players for-*ever*. Daddy Warbucks wouldn't come at first: "Why should I drive all the way down to Johnston City to play a bunch of brokes?" But the idea kind of grew on him, and the Indiana millionaire finally relented after Fats assured him that the Knoxville Bear would come too. And the Bear came down when he was told Squirrel would be there. And then Johnny Vevis had to come too, of course, and Handsome Dan. These men were hustlers—grit teethed, white knuckled. Each could win the tournament, but none would come to do so. Instead, they would come to gamble, to steal each other's cash, to drink a few beers, to maybe get laid, to have fun. The competition would be fearsome, the talent colossal, the smoke thick, the cheating a thing of grandeur.

AT ROUGHLY THE SAME TIME THAT GOERGIE, SHRIVER, AND THE SQUIRREL BEGAN WORK ON WHAT WOULD BECOME AMERICA'S MOST COLORFUL POOL TOURNAMENTS, TWENTIETH CENTURY FOX BEGAN WORK ON *THE HUSTLER*. The film was shot almost entirely in New York, with most sequences staged over six weeks in McGirr's or Ames, two old pool halls that have since closed. Director Robert Rossen hired Willie Mosconi as technical adviser, although most Americans then would not have had the foggiest knowledge of his world champion status. Paul Newman, for instance, said he never heard of Mosconi before production began.

Released in the fall of 1961, *The Hustler* describes a fictional rivalry between two of the nation's top hustlers: Fast Eddie Felson, portrayed by Newman, and Minnesota Fats, the elegant, refined, and then-undisputed king of pool. Obsessed with besting Fats, no matter the cost, the hard-drinking and mercurial Eddie abandons his former road partner and miserably mistreats his girlfriend. He eventually beats Fats, but at a horrible cost.

Besides Newman, *The Hustler* starred Jackie Gleason as Fats, Piper Laurie as Felson's luckless girlfriend Sara, and George C. Scott as Felson's amoral business manager. Each received Oscar nominations (although the lion's share that year went to *West Side Story*), and the film made the top-ten lists of both *Time Magazine* and the *New York Times*.

"*The Hustler*," wrote film historian David Thomson, "[is] a poolroom story about winners and losers, crammed with atmosphere and cleverly cast. It is a gripping movie; [its] pool scenes have a unique place in the filming of sports and games." Critic David Shipman called *The Hustler* a movie about "the small-time Charlies whose aspirations rise and die in the shadowy world of pool rooms…It was a subject that films had ignored, at least in the U.S., and Rossen's portrait of the seedy night city stands alone."

There is strong evidence that Georgie, Earl, and the Squirrel knew nothing of *The Hustler* when their mortar shell idea for a pool tournament struck them. The bartender and his pool-shooting buddies conducted the competition after the film's release, but Squirrel, George Jansco's daughter, and others later recalled that planning began *before* the movie. If true, then this was happy coincidence indeed. *The Hustler*, after all, led to an explosion of new media attention, new table sales, new poolroom construction, new players. Almost single-handedly, the film brought pool back from the grave. It's impact on that first Johnston City tournament was subtle yet extremely important. It made circuses of later ones.

The Hustler also delivered fame to Mosconi—fame dwarfing anything earned through his innumerable tournament victories, through his thirty

years of hard work, through his green-felt genius. The sport's doldrums—
which Mosconi always blamed on gambling—had robbed the champion of
real recognition, the sort of recognition reserved for giants of other sports. But
after hooking up with Rossen to film one of Hollywood's great homages to
gambling (Mosconi actually appears in the film briefly), fame came knocking.

In a conversation with author John Grissim, Mosconi noted the irony.

"I almost lost my job because of that movie. I was working for Brunswick
at the time and I didn't want to take on the assignment unless they were willing to let me do it. See, billiards at that point was at such a low ebb that I
figured anything that would get the game before the public, even a movie
about a hustler, couldn't hurt. Brunswick agreed, and I went ahead with the
project.

"Well, after they saw it they were very perturbed. You have no idea how
many calls I got from people all over the country accusing me of ruining the
game. My friend, Roy Gandy, a table manufacturer from Georgia who I've
known for forty years, calls me to say, 'Well, Willie, you've really gone and
done it this time.' But then a month later he calls me back and he's over-
joyed. He calls me all kinds of names and says, 'I can't believe it, Willie.
People can't get into the theaters down here fast enough to see the picture.
My sales are skyrocketing.' So after that I was a hero."

Twentieth Century Fox released the film on September 25, 1961. Like
summer lighting igniting a forest fire, the film put into motion a complex
sequence of events, which triggered other events, and—*bam!*—pool in
America exploded. Pool halls, pool playing, pool players—all of it, very suddenly, very unexpectedly—became hip. The movie transformed American
culture in an instant, transformed American pool for a decade, and it
changed one hustler in particular for a lifetime.

HE CIRCLED THE TABLE LIKE A STURDY LITTLE BULLDOG—NO NECK, ALL SMILE. A dancing tree stump. His words came in quick staccato bursts: *Rat-a-tat-tat HEEEY der FATTY rat-a-tat-tat FATTEEE!* He drank his beer from tiny Budweiser bottles, laughed often, seemed fond of dirty jokes. In his right-hand pocket, always, the bulldog kept a few hundred dollars cash money. Before him were the spread-out balls of a one-pocket game. Most were on his side, near his pocket. The cue ball was nestled up against the rail. He looked at Rudolf Wanderone square in the face, searching for acknowledgment. *What choo think, Fatty...rat-a-tat-tat...'bout dat?* The dancing tree stump seemed pleased with himself, with his break, with the game.

But Wanderone made like he hadn't even noticed. He'd seen plenty of top-notch pool playing in his day. He'd played plenty of champions. And his little friend Georgie Jansco, breaking balls out in the J&J Ranch, Johnston City, Illinois, could not be counted among them. Wanderone sneered at Jansco and then surveyed the table, stooped a bit—but not too much—and then spread his pudgy fingers down along the rail. He shot flawlessly into the cluster. A colored ball bounced off a rail and fell crisply into Fatty's pocket. *I could play better pool with my dick! With my DICK!* And then Wanderone began his run. One. Two. Three. Four.

The friends went back and forth like that for a while, playing and laughing and throwing down fives and tens. Cash exchanged hands with every game, automatically, but the contests never became too heated. Never unfriendly. Mostly Fats and Georgie played because they enjoyed each other's company. It was as if they had been playing the same game for fifteen years. Fats told the jokes; Georgie laughed. Fats won a few. Georgie won a few. The J&J—so named in reference to Georgie Jansco and his brother Paulie

Jansco, the co-owners of the bar—seemed insufficiently lit. It smelled deeply of smoke and stale beer. The jukebox, often played overly loud, remained silent. There were a few people there that night: Wanderone; Georgie's pretty daughter, twenty-one-year-old JoAnn; and JoAnn's boyfriend, David McNeal. It was the summer of 1961. John F. Kennedy was president. *The Hustler* had opened at the drive-in, but no one had yet seen it.

"We were sitting in the J&J, and Fats was playing pool with my dad," recalled JoAnn. "David asked where the movie was playing, and my dad said it was at the drive-in, the Egyptian, out in Heron, Illinois. And then my dad told Fats—and I'll never forget this—my dad said, 'You ought to go over there and set up a stand and claim to be Minnesota Fats.'"

The man who would become Minnesota Fats thought about this, but said nothing. Georgie was insistent. He said a fella could make some money with such a claim. He told Rudy Wanderone that he really did seem an awful lot like that Jackie Gleason fella. "He just kept telling him and kept telling him," said JoAnn. Wanderone, by then, had resided in Little Egypt for nearly two decades. He was semiretired, well past his prime, had very little money. In fact, he was broke just as often as not. He'd spent his life as a pool hustler but had very little to show for it. "Go out there," hissed Jansco. "Just go out there. *Do it.*"

AT ABOUT THIS TIME, SOMETHING ELSE VERY CURIOUS BEFELL THE VERY FAT RUDY WANDERONE, THEN KNOWN AS NEW YORK FATS. Willie Mosconi, speaking to a West Coast journalist then writing one of the innumerable features about *The Hustler*, made an offhand remark about

Gleason's character. It "was patterned after a real live pool hustler known as New York Fats," he told a reporter for the *Long Beach Independent-Press-Telegram*. The journalist asked if he knew this New York Fats. Mosconi replied, "Know him? He hustled me once." Mosconi said he broke Fats that day.[13]

At the time, Wanderone would have been completely unknown to most Americans. Many within the country's loosely bound community of hustlers may have met Wanderone—and likely held him in minimal regard—but to John Q. Public, Fats would have been as invisible as a ghost. When Mosconi made this remark, just an aside, really, he unwittingly gave Wanderone what Fats could never muster on his own: *legitimacy*. Mosconi's words were repeated over and over in newspaper accounts and magazine articles. Fats himself frequently alluded to them.

Mosconi may have served as technical adviser, but it was those comments to the *Long Beach Independent-Press-Telegram* that really brought *The Hustler* to life. No matter that author Walter Tevis denied, went to his death denying, any connection between the fictional Minnesota Fats and the real-life Rudolf Wanderone. ("I made up Minnesota Fats—name and all—as surely as Disney made up Donald Duck," wrote Tevis in a later edition of his novel.) Mosconi's words were like a charge of lightning to the Frankenstein monster. Mosconi had invited the fictional Minnesota Fats to jump off the screen and into real-life America.

----

[13] Fats also recalled the match-up—the game was one-pocket, his specialty—and Fats said it occured at a poolroom at Seventh and Morris streets in south Philly. He said Willie was managing the place. He put the year at around 1948. Fats said he "whacked Willie out." Such highly dubious claims—that he could and often did beat Mosconi—enflamed Mosconi's hostility as much as anything. Mosconi would even sue Fats over the claims—but not to much effect.

GRAVEL GRINDS BENEATH CAR TIRES LIKE A THOUSAND BB PELLETS, LIKE AN UPSIDE-DOWN HAILSTORM. It billows up in thick clouds of dust, white and gray, that swirl about in suffocating eddies. It becomes a giant fog bank—rising up quickly and then settling down just as fast—and it blankets any man who stands long beneath it. Just outside the Egyptian Drive-In, October 1961, there stood such a man. Before him was something like a lemonade stand—except with no lemonade—and he waved wildly at motorists lining up for the evening feature. The man was very fat, poorly dressed, with a pronounced facial tic. He would have been about forty-eight years of age and was covered from head to toe in the cake-flour dust. Behind him on the drive-in's backlit marquee, written in crooked fall-down crazy letters, was THE HUSTLER.

This was the Fatman: Rudolf Wanderone Jr., aka New York Fats, aka Chicago Fats, aka Triple-Smart Fats. But the sign taped to the front of the card table, a sign most likely comprised of poster board and sloppy tempera, identified him differently. Here, it said, was THE REAL AND TRUE MINNESOTA FATS. Twentieth Century Fox had perjured him, goddamnit! The drive-in movie had stolen his life. *Hey, lady, lookee here.* With gravel dust and exhaust fumes filling his nostrils and throat, the Fatman sputtered at passersby between violent bouts of coughing and sneezing. *You're looking at the real deal, right here, Minnesota Fats hisself.* The man was obviously deranged. *Hey, lady! I'm talking to YOU!*

Jackie Gleason, the famous TV star, portrayed in the Hollywood film a fat pool hustler from Chicago by the name of Minnesota Fats. He was dignified, elegant, soft-spoken. Rudolf Wanderone was none of these things—and probably had never, ever set foot in Minnesota—But Wanderone had lived in Chicago for a while. Everybody knew that. Walter Tevis, the author of the novel on which *The Hustler* was based, surely must have seen Wanderone there—and then fashioned Fats's character after him. But the similarities did not stop there. The novel, as Wanderone later noted, described Minnesota Fats as a man with a facial twitch. Well, Wanderone possessed such a twitch. Look—his face was twitching at that precise moment; it was completely contorting his face as he mounted a one-man protest at the Egyptian Drive-In, all shouts and arm waving. *Minnesota Fats— in the flesh! That's me, I tell ya! And I'll sue! I'll sue, I tell ya!*

The motorists would warily observe the Fatman as one observes the street corner antics of the harmlessly mentally ill. Likely there was amusement, caution before the unpredictable, bewilderment. Teenagers may have shouted obscenities. None of this, of course, would deter Wanderone, a man who at that very instant was transforming his life in much the same way as he had always lived it: with little dignity, much bombast. Down in Little Egypt, the heart of nowhere, holding a placard in the dust, a very small Fatman stood on the precipice of becoming a very big Fatman The world's greatest hustler had begun the world's greatest hustle.

ONE MONTH LATER, NEWSPAPERMAN TOM FOX, A MAN WHO WOULD UNWITTINGLY JOIN FATS IN THAT GREAT HUSTLE, TOOK A PHONE CALL FROM A LATE-NIGHT TIPSTER. "Make the drive to Johnston City," came the voice on the other end of the phone line, "check out the world's one-pocket tournament, watch for Hubert Cokes." The larger-than-life Cokes, the local millionaire known as Daddy Warbucks, would be making gargantuan back-room wagers, the tipster advised. And there'd be other gamblers too. A surefire instant feature story. Worth your time. Make the drive.

Tom Fox, about five feet, eleven inches, portly and red-haired, worked nights at the *Courier and Press* in Evansville, Indiana, about ninety miles from

Johnston City. He wrote sports mostly, had an eye for color, loved characters. He'd grown up in New Orleans—the south side—and spent some of his early years working at the horse track. And so Fox, then about thirty-five, took the call seriously, got the go-ahead from an assigning editor, packed into a beat-up sedan, and began his quest for a hustler's holiday.

"He grew up a block from the river in New Orleans, Algiers, just on the west bank," recalled Tom's widow, Karen, speaking in the summer of 2000. "He had a Mississippi understanding of characters and he knew how to get along with gamblers. Tom had been around, you know, and knew about back-room gambling. So he went over and he couldn't believe what he saw. We had just seen *The Hustler* a couple of weeks before and he could not believe that in the middle of nowhere, in southern Illinois, were all these incredible pool players. They played in the tournament—but when the tournament was over, that's when all this heavy-duty gambling was going on. Tom *knew* it was a national story."

Before taking the job at the *Courier and Press*, Fox had spent years covering sports for the *New Orleans Item*, long considered a writer's paper. Among the national-class journalists to graduate from the *Item* (eventually the paper went belly-up) was Jack Olson, author of several books, staffer for *Sports Illustrated*, and one of Fox's longtime friends. And so, flush with back-room excitement, aware that he had stumbled upon magic, real and true, and cognizant of the *Hustler*-inspired pool craze, Fox gave his old friend Olson a call.

"Sounds like a great story," came Olson's reply.

The *Sports Illustrated* editors, "went nuts," recalled Karen. "They loved it. He telegraphed the story to them and they sent over a sketch artist, because the hustlers wouldn't let in a photographer at first…And we just got to see it all firsthand. And oh my God, it was awesome. If not for Tom, nobody would have ever known about Johnston City."

HANDSOME DAN, COWBOY JIMMY MOORE, THE KNOXVILLE BEAR, THE TUSCALOOSA SQUIRREL: THESE TITANS MARCHED ON JOHNSTON CITY.
Moore, with his burr haircut, his white Stetson, his startling slip stroke (he actually let go the butt end of his cue for a split second), shot straights with a sniper's precision, his every move both effortless and wondrous. Eddie "Knoxville Bear" Taylor, the drawling southerner, was the world's best bank pooler. He banked from anywhere, from any angle, at any time. Rail-first eight and out, eight and out, over and over again, like a dream. And Squirrel had learned from the Fatman himself—but then transcended his teacher with nearly flawless one-pocket.

Titans, yes, but titans from a secret realm. As Fox would note, pool hustlers live in shadows. By disposition, by desire, for the sake of survival, for the sake of larceny—they don masks. The avuncular car mechanic. The traveling salesman. The stumble-drunk braggart. The Okie pig farmer. Possessed by a sort of anti-fame, these men hide from the public. And so the public did not come in great droves to that first Johnston City tournament in 1961. The so-called world's one-pocket championship was a solitary affair played for two weeks in a cinder block prison for almost no money. These men were strange, unknown, possibly dangerous. Their sport was little understood. As the sign said: MEMBERS ONLY.

"The public couldn't even go in," said billiards historian Mike Shamos in a 1997 interview. "They [the Johnston City tournaments] were held because the BCA wasn't doing anything at the time and Brunswick had become an international company, but wasn't sponsoring pool. Also, pool lost a big draw when Mosconi retired. The idea wasn't to make money off the audience, but to make money off the gambling and bar that the players would bring in."

But Fox's seminal piece, *Hustlers Holiday in the Lion's Den*, nonetheless brought it to the attention of the world. If the public did not come to the first tournament, Fox's article ensured they would come to later ones. And so too came the TV cameras, and eventually the national TV networks: ABC Sports, CBS Sports Spectacular. Fox understood gamblers, enjoyed their company, and eventually convinced them to allow photographers into their inner sanctum. He gained entrance for all of America; he threw open the doors of the Cue Club, the secret world of hustlers, *members only*. Fox, like the Johnston City tournaments, like Georgie Jansco and Rudolf Wanderone and *The Hustler* itself, helped fuel the renaissance.

And speaking to Fox, Wanderone insisted that Hollywood had stolen his life.

To be sure, other hustlers tried to mimic that success.[14] But only Wanderone—with his ridiculous shtick, his outlandish gumption—possessed personality enough to make the claim stick. And the world seemed a more magical place for it.

Tom Fox, in that seminal *Sports Illustrated* article, captured Fats as he was: hilarious, larger-than-life, ridiculous. Here's an excerpt:

----

[14] The most famous, perhaps, was one-pocket specialist Ronnie Allen, who was said to be the model for *The Hustler's* Fast Eddy character. Others included Louisiana's Ed Taylor, Missouri's Ed Parker, and California's Eddie Pelkey—each of whom also assumed the Fast Eddy persona. Reporters would repeat the contradictory and baseless claims—generally with no attribution whatsoever.

The spokesman for the Loyal Fraternal Order of Pool Sharks was a roly-poly 250-pounder called New York Fats (Rudolf Wanderone) who thrives on high stakes and egotism but lives not in shadows nor speaks in whispers. Fat Man is short (5 feet 8), with a shock of brown hair, a 52-inch waist and a philosophy to fit all occasions. He announced that the Johnston City promotion drew 14 of the "best one-pocket players in the world," and added modestly that he was once the best of the best.

"I was automatic champion one-pocket player of the world," Fat Man proclaimed. "They never had any tournaments. I always had to give great odds, most of the time two balls. The great champions would never play me. They dodged me at all times."

The hustlers listened when the Fat Man talked. They laughed and poked fun at him. But when an outsider asked questions about the hustlers, they let the Fat Man do the talking. He's the sharks' public relations man.

NOW BOSTON SHORTY (LARRY JOHNSON, 32, BOSTON) IS PLAYING.

Shorty is a short 5 feet 2 who gets sore when a hustler says he's "shorter than the cue stick." Says Johnson: "That's a lie, the cue stick is 58, 59 inches. I'm 62 inches."

A photographer is shooting pictures of the match. Boston Shorty stops the game and says he doesn't want his picture taken. The photographer wants to know how come. Shorty's backer climbs down from the gallery.

"Shorty ain't played the West Coast yet," the backer says with a forced grin. "You understand, he's still got some live territory to cover. He don't want them to know who he is or what he looks like. You understand don't you man?"

...NOW FATMAN IS MATCHED WITH TUSCALOOSA SQUIRRELLY, AND HE IS GETTING THE SHOTS. "Well, if I'm a has-been, I'm certainly glad I'm not one of these is-beens," Fatman says as he wins the match three games to none. (Squirrel got a total of three shots, two of them breaks.)...

"Look at Fatty," whispers Johnnie Irish (Johnnie Lineen, 47, Miami and Brooklyn). "He wouldn't hurt a miller moth but he'll leave you without a shirt playing pool. I know Fats all my life. I've seen him come into [a] town that looked like a desert, nobody at the pool hall. In two days, Fats had the place packed. He starts playing for $2 a game and pretty soon he's got the butcher and the baker playing $100 a game and they never saw a pool table before. If there's 100 people in town, Fatty had all 100 at the pool hall. Then he leaves and it's a desert town again.

Fats is a hustler's hustler.

DANNY JONES WANTS TO PLAY THE FATMAN. *Has* to play the Fatman. But Danny's got no money. And so he goes to the stakehorse, Daddy Warbucks—bow tie, bald, mean, and rich—the high-rolling oilman from Evansville, Illinois. Danny's shot against Fats before, back in Chicago a couple of years back, and lost thousands. *Thousands.* But Jones, twenty-nine years old, tells Warbucks his game is better now. Much better. No comparison. Before, he was driving a bus, he explains, just shooting part time back home at West Point, Georgia. Now he hustles full time. His chest expands with pride. He's up to Fats's speed, he explains, he *knows* he can take him. Shit, Danny reminds Cokes that he won the national snooker championship just last March. No way Fatty can stand up to him now.

"Mr. Cokes, let me play him four out of seven for five hundred dollars" Jones pleads, insistent like a child begging for candy. Fox witnesses the entire exchange.

Hubert "Daddy Warbucks" Cokes, cigar planted firmly in jowl, frowns. "No, Danny." The Fatman smirks. "Get your backers to put up some money, sonny boy," Fats taunts. "You guys all gotta have stakehorses. I only got one partner and that's Eva-Line."

Somehow, Jones rustles up $200—a consortium of backers believes Dirty Dan can put the screws to Fats—and Cokes hands out the rest: three crisp one-hundred-dollar bills. The Knoxville Bear holds the bet. "I got a stakehorse, Fatman. Four out of seven. Five hundred dollars." Jones seems gleeful.

The Fatman, unimpressed, washes his face, powders his cue stick. He gives the Bear his $500 and turns to Jones, ready to play, confident, eager. "Daniel," he says, "you're in the lion's den."

And so they start: Danny Jones, the snooker champion, Handsome Dan or Dirty Dan, twenty-nine years old, the handsomest of the hustlers. And Rudolf Wanderone, the man who would be Fats, 220 pounds, round, fat fingers, skinny tie. The first game goes to Fats, easily, but Jones takes the next two. He seems able to lock Fats against the rail over and over again, leaving only tough shots, and Fats, maybe, begins to feel the heat. "I'm not getting the breaks," he moans. "I shoot seven hundred balls and I don't get a break." Fats misses the six. "Look at that, will ya? I put a million dollars' worth of spin on that ball and only a nickel's worth took hold."

Jones eyes Fats suspiciously. Something seems wrong. "You're dogging it, Fatman." Jones wins the first match and the two play again, this time five out of nine. The stake grows: $1,000. Eddie Taylor tucks down the money.

"They'll break you, Fatty," whispers one of the hustlers. "You're all washed up, Fatman," says another. "If you were intelligent, you'd quit."

But Fatty shakes it off.

"I'm the most intelligent man I know. The more I hang around with you imbeciles, the more I realize I am the most intelligent man I know. I could spot Einstein the ten ball. I know everything that everybody knows, and *nobody* knows what I know." But Fatty, somehow, impossibly, still cannot get position. Jones keeps him locked up, shot after shot, leaving whitey on the long rail, or deep in Fatty's own pocket, or hard in the center of the short rail, between both pockets, leaving Fats a ridiculous length of green, sell-out long shots. "Unbelievable, positively unbelievable," says Fatty, surveying the predicament. "In all my life, I've never seen anything like it."

And so it continues. Fatty leaves the table for a moment to wash his face and hands—again. He becomes momentarily enraged because Jansco provides no towels. "For three nights I've asked them to get something so I can dry my hands." Fats's voice has gotten away from him. He's yelling now. "No napkins, no toilet tissues. You can't dry your hands. It's ridiculous, ridiculous beyond compare." Fats returns to the table, but perhaps it would have been better if he had stayed away—because he loses the second match just like the first. And now, suddenly, Double-Smart, Triple-Smart, New York, Chicago, *and* Minnesota Fats finds himself down $1,500. In a twinkling, fifteen big ones. But he plays Danny again. This time it's $2000. And the Fatman, playing with wet hands now, perturbed, enduring the taunts of the gallery, still can't get a damn shot.

"Looka that, you think he ain't scared," mutters Jones to nobody in particular. Jones has left the cue ball frozen against the rail again. "How do you like it on the rail, Fatman?" And so the snooker champion wins again and Fats goes down $3,500. But Fats won't quit. Seems eager, in fact, to keep going. The wager increases to $4,000.

And then suddenly, miraculously, with the wager astronomical, Fatty's game somehow gets better. And Danny's game, somehow, gets worse. Danny loses a bit of touch, can't seem to lock up the Fatman like he did before. Instead, it's Fatty who leaves Danny up against the rail, or down in his own hole. And Danny, sweat gathering on his upper lip, falls silent. His taunting ceases. The whole gallery gets quiet: just the clicking of balls, scooting chairs, chalk squeaks against a leather cue tip. And through the tense light, the thick smoke, the genius of the Fatman finally emerges. First come the banks, one after another—always a thing of beauty in one-pocket. And then come the quick run-outs, one after another. And suddenly, the $4,000—as much money as went to all Johnston City prize winners that year—goes to Fatty. For Handsome Dan, it's an $8,000 turnaround, a stunning turnaround, and he sees now that Fatty remains eager to play. No quitting now. But Jones, and Daddy Warbucks, and the stunned gallery of would-be backers, seem to have lost their appetite. Four-thousand-dollar one-pocket is Fats's game. High stakes. High pressure. A fortune won or lost very quickly. And so Jones quits him.

The match, which lasts most of the night, ends just about even for the two players. Fats pockets the stake—including Danny's $500—and drives home.

GEORGIE JANSCO, MINNESOTA FATS, TOM FOX, AND *THE HUSTLER* HAD FINALLY SUCCEEDED WHERE THE BILLIARDS INDUSTRY AND WILLIE MOSCONI COULD NOT. And it all came together in a roadhouse along a highway just outside Johnston City, Illinois. Here a small-time con man would become the greatest hustler the world has ever known. Here a small-time bookmaker would organize the greatest pool tournaments of all time.

The truth had finally revealed itself—and it was not as Mosconi and the billiards industry would have us believe. In Johnston City, it became clear that pool's romance had little to do with pocketing balls and polite applause. It was not about tuxedos and crystal chandeliers.

Rather, the romance of pool is about cussing men and spitting and petty larceny.

The romance of pool is about hustling.

The romance of pool is about *freedom*.

A liar and a cheat, certainly, but in this one regard Fats possessed more honesty than the great Mosconi, a champion who forever denied the true nature of his sport. And the proof would come with Fats's fame, which grew and grew—first through interviews with magazine reporters, then through an autobiography, and eventually through TV appearances with Johnny Carson and Howard Cosell. Ultimately, the fame of Minnesota Fats would eclipse that of Willie Mosconi himself.

And it all began, said Fats, with *The Hustler*, Tom Fox, and that first Johnston City tournament.

"The [first] jamboree out in Georgie's beer shed was by no means a staggering success. As jamborees go, this one lacked the most essential asset—a flow of liquid cash. But it was the start of something real big, because a year later every pool player in the country was talking about Johnston City, Illinois."

9
WORLD'S GREATEST
ROADHOUSE

"There ain't a fine, worthwhile hustler in the world who ain't here."

—*World-famous golf hustler Titanic Thompson, commenting on the*
gathered talent at the 1963 Johnston City hustler's jamboree

N 1962, GEORGE DECIDED THAT HIS "WORLD" TOUR-
NAMENT HAD GROWN TOO LARGE FOR A BEER SHED.
So he and his brother Paulie, who had become a full partner,
moved their Wild West show to the Showbar, out along the
Herrin–Johnston City road, just west of Johnston City. Owned by Paulie (whom
they sometimes called Joey), the Showbar looked like a giant flat shoebox
with a farmhouse roof. The parking lot was unpaved. Surrounding the giant
shoebox were meaningless houses—all in vague states of disrepair—and
weeds. The whole area had a look of impermanence, as if something big was
coming, or something big had just left. It was hard, driving into the gravel
parking lot, to imagine that this was *it:* the world's greatest roadhouse, the
world's greatest pool tournament.

JoAnn McNeal, Georgie's daughter, described the Cue Club as a sort of
cinder box building, with three separate rooms and two floors. "They had
three tables in one room, where the bar was, and three tables in the front
part, where you came in," she recalled. "It was all concrete, but there was
linoleum too. There was an upstairs, where you walked in, and they would
put bleachers in. It was a pretty good-sized room. It could probably hold, I'd

say, two hundred people. Maybe three hundred. But there were no windows. It was just a concrete building."

Eventually, George and Paulie ordered the excavation of a three-foot-deep pit into the floor of the adjacent Showbar. Into this, they lowered twin Gandy tables. Tall bleachers surrounded the pit on three sides. This become the crater at ground zero, a dogfight arena for the world's greatest: Wimpy, Shorty, Cowboy Jimmy Moore, Weenie Beenie, the Knoxville Bear, Irving Crane, the Squirrel. The roadmen nestled their cars along patches of weeds and unkempt grass, pulled cue cases and brown-bagged whiskey out from behind back seats, went to work.

A gaudy painted plywood sign outside Johnston City advertised the 1962 event. WORLD'S POCKET BILLIARD TOURNAMENT, OCT. 26 TO NOV. 18 it read, right above a red-painted arrow. Daily admission was $1.75. About sixty competitors were on hand—Lassiter and Fats among them—up from about a dozen in 1961. Red (who rarely left the 7-11 and who couldn't drive a car) stayed in New York. Crowds remained sparse.

Unlike the year before, the 1962 tournament featured one-pocket, nine-ball, and straight pool. George Jansco dubbed it the "all-around" championship and put up $10,000 in prize money. The BCA refused to recognize the event. "The true world champion of pocket billiards should be the champion of all three games," Jansco explained to Mort Luby, publisher of *Billiards Digest*. "Willie Mosconi, for instance, is world champion of straight pool. But how well does he play the other games? What we are trying to establish here is the overall champion. Like the decathlon champion in the Olympics."

Fats bombed out quick—in the very first round—after entering only the one-pocket division. Handsome Dan, whom Fats had beaten the year before during a high-dollar action session, simply dismantled him. The loss did nothing to diminish Fats's growing fame. Neither did it keep Fats from going after Detroit Whitey.[15] The two conferred briefly, set the game and stakes (one-pocket, best of seven, $150), and then settled in for a long session. Fats carefully draped his olive suede jacket over a chair, washed his hands, then dusted them up with talcum. Whitey began by taking a shot of Alka-Seltzer.

"One more night and it's going to be like Ghengis Khan going through the big wall of China," said Fats. He ran four balls straight, missed, then Whitey took over. The two went back and forth for two and half hours before Whitey declared uncle. "I offer to play anybody living," says Fats. "I always have. If a guy's afraid to play me, I say, 'It wouldn't hurt you for me to beat you because I beat everybody that ever was.'"

Lassiter, by contrast, grandly proclaimed that he did not hustle pool. And then, just to prove his point, he got himself beaten by a much younger, much less experienced player. He gazed upward in mock prayer. *"Oh Lord, thou hast forsaken me. I have been thwarted by a mere amoeba of our species!"* Lassiter followed that stunning loss by taking one hustler for $3,700, running 125 balls against another. "He shot out the lights," yelped Fats.

Johnston City continued for three long weeks. Lassiter won first place in nine-ball, and then first place in straight pool. He took away $1,200 and $1,000 for the victories, respectively. Not a bad payday considering the sorry state of pool just a few years earlier. Lassiter then won another $1,000 for his

----

[15] Detroit Whitey, whose real name was Eddie Beuchene, said he once hustled a Miami department store owner out of $72,000. It took days of losing to the department store owner, who gave Whitey increasingly more generous spots. When the spot got to four balls to the department store owner's eight—and the per-game wager to $5,000—Whitey lowered the boom.

play-off victory against Marshall Carpenter, the winner of the tournament's one-pocket division.

Lassiter faced the nation's gathered hustlers and beat every one. In 1962 he became their all-around champion.

The BCA be damned.

PERHAPS THE SEXUAL REVOLUTION AND THE CULTURAL REVOLUTION HAD CREATED A SPACE IN AMERICA'S UPTIGHT PURITAN HEART FOR A HUSTLER REVOLUTION. Perhaps Americans had finally tired of their prissy, nine-to-five suburban lives. But whatever the cause, the result was clear. As *Playboy's* Craig Vetter observed: "The second Golden Age of Pool had begun...That movie *[The Hustler]*, along with the Jansco brothers and Rudolf Wanderone—Minnesota Fats—put it all back together." By 1963—a full three years after the release of the film—everybody still dreamed of hustling like Jackie Gleason, still dreamed of back-room challenges. Pool halls were popping up in every fucking place—in the new shopping malls, in the strip centers, in towns small and large. Even women started playing.

Women, for crissakes.

Jersey Red could not have helped but notice the new pigeons, the new money, the growing public interest. A magazine writer actually came to interview Red in 1962, proclaimed him King of New York, made him famous for a day. Sociologist Ned Polsky spent hours observing Red's playing style, watching his 7-11 gambling methods.

From the sidelines, Red enviously followed the World's Invitation 14.1 tournament, held in the spring of 1963 at New York's Commodore Hotel. Ignoring Red's repeated victories in important regional tournaments, ignoring his growing legend, the Billiard Room Proprietor Association of America refused to let him participate. The tournament promoters correctly pegged him as a hustler.

Lassiter won the BRPAA event, but Red figured he could have taken the southerner—given half a chance.

George Jansco held a disdainfully low opinion of the event. "This so-called world tournament in New York was a dried-up, old social affair—like a tea party," Jansco told *Bowlers Journal*. "I wouldn't care if they gave a hundred thousand dollars in prizes—it would still be dead, dull, and flat." Much to the chagrin of BRPAA promoters, Jansco rented five rooms at the Commodore Hotel and blew $380 on food and booze "just so people wouldn't think they were at a wake." Many of the players got fall-down drunk. There, at this wild after-hours party, Red would have learned of the goings-on at Johnston City.

Hustlers, said Jansco, could make some money there. "The greatest in the world" would come, Jansco promised. And it wouldn't be like an uptight BCA event, or this uptight BRPAA straight-pool tournament where, Jansco sneered, "I never saw a dollar bet." This would be a hustler's event. "A straight-pool tournament is absolutely the dullest thing known to man," he said. And so Red, drinking a beer and chatting up George Jansco, figured he'd mosey on down to Johnston City, see what all the fuss was about.

He also figured he'd see if he could beat this Wimpy Lassiter. Red was pretty sure he could, given half a chance.

JANSCO SOLD FIVE THOUSAND TICKETS FOR THE THREE-WEEK TOUR-NAMENT, INCLUDING 180 FOR THE STANDING-ROOM-ONLY FINALS. Running from late October through early November, the 1963 event drew players from thirty-four states. Again the Chicago-based BCA refused to bestow their blessing. ("What's wrong with the people in Chicago?" Georgie griped.) But CBS came to town that year. Technicians knocked out the north wall of the building—and the roof—to make room for six cameras. And they positioned one directly above the principal tournament table. Two TV trucks, one from St. Louis and the other from New York, housed electronic equipment, about two dozen technicians, and producer Bill Creasy. Jansco, sensitive to the image being broadcast across America, admonished the more brutish in attendance against "unruly remarks." CBS put the total cost of filming the event at $37,000.

Red started strong, beating future hall-of-famer Cicero Murphy 125-76 in straight pool. Two days later Red beat another future hall-of-famer, Cowboy Jimmy Moore, 125-124, again at straight pool. Against Moore, on several occasions, it looked as if Red would never shoot again. But Red would come from nowhere, winning that game and others that by rights he should have lost. As the event wound into its final days, it became clear that Red could finish no worse than fifth.

But Lassiter won too. The southerner amassed a string of victories in both the straight-pool and nine-ball divisions, beating Cornbread Red, Jimmy Moore, Marshall Carpenter, and Weenie Beenie.[16] The hustlers fell to the hacking gentleman from North Carolina with alarming regularity. Eventually, even Jersey Red fell to Wimpy Lassiter. The northerner did well in each

----

[16] Weenie Beenie, also known as Bill Staton, owner of a chain of hot dog stands in Washington, D.C., was robbed at gunpoint during the rough-and-tumble 1963 event. Bandits forced Weenie Beenie and a friend into a car and made them drive into the country. The bandits took more than $1,000 from Weenie Beenie and about $475 from his friend. They left both men, unharmed, on an isolated road miles from Johnston City. The pool hustlers flagged a passing truck to get back to town.

division, beating players at one-pocket, nine-ball, and straight pool. But somehow he could not match Wimpy Lassiter. Red took home second place in the nine-ball division.

Wimpy, by contrast, took first place in nine-ball and then won the straight-pool division. For the overall title, Lassiter faced Eddie Taylor, the so-called Knoxville Bear,[16] and the winner of the 1963 one-pocket event. The play-off featured all three games—nine-ball, straight pool, and one-pocket. Lassiter began by beating Taylor at one-pocket, 3-1, and then beat Taylor again at straight pool, 150-116. The southerner took home $3,150 in prize money, more than that in back-room wagers—and the 1963 Johnston City all-around title.

RED BOARDED A NORTHBOUND BUS TO CHICAGO THE VERY NEXT DAY. With him was his pool cue in a case, a tiny suitcase containing a couple of shirts, and a wad of cash, wrapped in a rubber band and stuffed in his pants pocket. He had his second-place trophy in the suitcase. When Red wasn't dozing, he was fiddling with a pack of playing cards, or chatting amicably about the Jets, or sometimes just staring vacantly at the hypnotic blur of fence posts and telephone posts whizzing past the window.

Somebody with a portable transistor radio first heard the news. Other passengers then frantically reached for their own radios, retrieving them from duffel bags and purses, while those without radios—even politically apathetic passengers like Red—did their best to crowd around, clutching the backs of

---

[17] Hall-of-famer Eddie Taylor was perhaps the world's best-ever bankshot artist. He often deflated other players by running 8-and-out playing bank pool, that game in which every pocketed ball must hit a rail first.

seats, lurching into the aisles at every bump and curve. The reactions of the men and women on that northbound bus were much like the reactions of men and women all across America: first came the chaotic jabbering, then the weeping, and then, finally, as the hours wore on, a stunned and sullen silence. The president of the United States was dead.

November 22, 1963, the day after that year's Johnston City finals, was a day of change for both the nation and for Jack "Jersey Red" Breitkopf. Commentators often note that the assassination of John F. Kennedy marked an end of innocence for the nation. The same, perhaps, could be said about Jersey Red: for waiting at his eventual, final stop was a new home, a wife, responsibilities, and…one day…his deathbed. Red spent a week or so in Chicago (he made an appearance at Bensinger's) but it would be Houston, Texas, where he would eventually settle. There he found all the accoutrements of the grown-up life. And while he would forever remain a poolroom hustler, it was perhaps in 1963 that he left behind the life of a poolroom bum.

IT WAS FREDDY SESSIONS, AN OLD FRIEND WHO HAD SPENT TIME IN BOTH TEXAS AND LOUISIANA, WHO DIRECTED RED TO HOUSTON. Red had become too well known in the Northeast—too feared—so the action remained fast, but no longer easy. Red could still make games, sure, but the spots became too big. Either that, or he'd make games with Shorty or Steve Mizerak, Jr.—and with games like that, well, hustling becomes gambling. Better to play cards, which Red did for a while, but then that began robbing him of his stroke.

So Freddy Sessions told Red: Go south, where you're an unknown. Like buffalo hunters, pool hustlers ranged far in search of game and Freddy said he'd found plenty in Houston, especially down at the Central Cue, just outside downtown. Freddy gave rather specific instructions. Find a woman named Dottie Thorpe, he said, and tell her you want action. She ran the Central Cue, knew all the players, knew their speed. All this, and Dottie couldn't play a lick.

A little after 9 p.m. on Friday, December 6, 1963—not long after JFK was shot, just a week or so after the Johnston City event—Jack "Jersey Red" Breitkopf walked into the Central Cue. Dottie was perched on a barstool, her gaze upward at a prizefight telecast flashing on the TV above the bar. Henry Hank, out of Detroit, was favored over former light heavyweight champion Harold Johnson. The fight was at Philly's Blue Horizon Arena but televised locally on channel 13, the ABC affiliate. Dottie knew just enough about boxing to place a small wager on Johnson, the underdog. Red liked boxing, too, liked Johnson, and liked that this slender blond was in on the action. It was a long shot, but Red agreed with Dottie's bet: Johnson should win.

"He was very quiet when I first met him," Dottie recalled of her first encounter with Jersey Red. "When he didn't know people, he could make friends real quick—but he wasn't a loudmouth or anything. A lot of people would come in, just spouting off, but Jack didn't do any of that. He was very quiet.

"And when he walked in, I was betting on that boxing match on television. I think I caught his eye at that time, because he loved boxing and there I was, betting on that match. And all I remember of that day was 'Hey, here's this guy, and he's watching us while we're watching the boxers.'"

The two fighters went around for a while, waiting each other out, throwing jabs here and there, but not to much effect. The TV was in the back of the poolroom, behind a counter where they served beers and gave out the balls and marked playing time. There was a big snooker table near the counter.

Neither Jack nor Dottie had much use for beer, although a lot of other guys there were tossing them back. Dottie, a slim woman with a high stack of Texas hair, puffed on a long filtered cigarette and gabbed with one of the guys. For a woman, she had a big voice, and when she laughed, people knew it. She honked and twanged and smoked and watched Hank and Johnson beat each other up.

Johnson, of Philadelphia, was declared the winner by unanimous decision. The fight lasted ten rounds. And it was then that Jack "Jersey Red" Breitkopf, who had not opened his mouth for the entire fight, finally turned to Dottie and said, "I'm looking to play some pool. I like to gamble."

Dottie scanned him up and down—she had already noticed him, but now she had an excuse to really look. She saw a man who was tall, but not awkward. His eyes were gimlet green. His shirt was wrinkled; his smile wide— like the Cheshire Cat, like a man without fear. But could he play? Dottie knew a lot of players who thought they could, thought they could beat just about everyone-—but she also knew that most were self-deluding chumps.

But Red just flat-out told her, "I play good."

And when she asked how good, Red's expression didn't change, his gaze didn't waver. His grin remained chiseled to his face, as if he would smile forever. And his response had an uncharacteristic taint of modesty, of under-statement—but there was arrogance there too. It was a response born of both hunger and strength. "I play good enough."

This divorced mother of two who managed two pool halls had stood wit-ness to plenty of bullshit in her twenty-nine years. Some of it had come from her ex-husband, some of it from the guys down at the Central Cue, and some of it from strangers who carried break-down cues and said they played *good enough*.

"I wasn't too sure," recalled Dottie. "A lot of these guys think they play real good, but they can't play worth a damn. So I sent him to play all the weaker players, who played for money, and then I just steered him up the ladder, until he got to the better players, and then he kept going up the ladder, until he got to the top. It didn't take me long to tell how good he was."

DOTTIE THORPE—THE LAST NAME WAS THAT OF HER FORMER HUS-BAND—WAS BORN IN HAYNESVILLE, LOUISIANA, ON APRIL 7, 1927. At the time, she was called Dorothy Brazeltown, after the daddy she never really knew. Dottie said her parents got divorced when she was real young—maybe two years old, maybe three—and that she never had much to do with her biological father. As far as Dottie was concerned, her real dad was her stepfather, Walter Barnett. She also had two siblings, both older—although her brother, Willard, died when she was quite young.

Dottie did okay in school, although she didn't make it to college. Rather, she went to work at J. Ray McDermott, an oil industry company, after graduating from Reagan High School in 1944. A year later she married her high-school sweetheart and bore him two children. That marriage lasted thirteen years, ended poorly, and the kids went off to live with their father in Corpus Christi.

At South Houston's OST Bowling Lanes, where Dottie worked after leaving the oil company, she got to know Houston's players. There was a single table there that for some reason attracted all the city's best. (Dottie also became an adept bowler—she had a 175 average, which she said was "pretty good for a girl"). After a couple of years, the owner of the Central Cue asked Dottie to come work for him, figuring—quite correctly—that if the very cute Dottie Thorpe came to the Central Cue, many of Houston's pool players would follow.

She had been working there about a year when Jersey Red blew into her life. And after that first meeting they hardly left each other's sight. Even after midnight, when the Central Cue closed, Jack and Dottie remained together: she'd give the pool hustler a ride to TJ Parker's, an all-night room that was a drive but good for the action.

Red, still without a driver's license, eventually invited Dottie to go see Count Basie, who had a concert scheduled down on South Main. Pool hall proprietor T. J. Parker ended up driving them. Jack gussied himself up nice in dress slacks and may have even put on a tie. It became their first real date. And so the love affair began: born from pool, nurtured by Jack's inability to drive a car, and sealed by Jack's quest to gamble.

Here's how Dottie remembered it:

"I was just carrying him around to the different places [to shoot pool]. Sometimes I'd drive him out to TJs, and then, all of the sudden, it was like we were going together. It was then, as I was steering him around, that we became attracted to each other…

"You know, he hung out in the poolroom all day long, and he was just about *always* there when I was working. I was working in the evening. And we'd go out to TJ's, or if I was too tired he had a little apartment that wasn't too far from there.

"It's funny. We seemed to get along real good, and he just…grew on me. I didn't think much of anything about him at first, but then the fascination grew when I saw how he could really play pool. That really impressed me. He wasn't like the run-of-the-mill pool players, and I wouldn't never go out with any of them.

"Our love started like a deep friendship, and it just bloomed. I'm not even sure that I was all that deeply in love when we got married, but later on it just kept on growing. And sometimes, you know, I think that's the best way. To be friends first. I think everything works out better that way."

Jack and Dottie got married by a municipal court judge on June 1, 1964. Jack had a suit on, but no tie. Dottie bought a special dress for the occasion. Their courtship lasted just six months.

JOHN "DUKE" DOWELL, ONE OF RED'S BEST FRIENDS, HAD HEARD THE STORIES ABOUT RED AND THE 7-11—OF GOING BROKE AND SLEEPING IN THE MOVIE HOUSES, OF GETTING ARRESTED FOR SHOOTING A MAN, OF SPENDING TIME IN JUVIE HALL. But Duke said that in Houston Red became a very different person. Once married, Red got *responsibility*. It may be okay to play yourself just absolutely fucking broke if you're living on your own. But not here, not now. Red's bankroll—that great whopping bulge held tight in his left-hand pocket—now had a significance greater than poolroom status and money for the ponies. Now Red had someone to care for. He had a *wife*—just like the straight lawyers and architects he played for pigeons.

In the lock-up games, for instance, Red always tried to gamble his own money. It's just plain dumb, said Duke, to share that action with a backer. It's like giving money away. But in the tough games—the ones with California one-pocket specialist Ronnie Allen, say, or when Red was pushed into gargantuan spots against a good player—he would look for the insurance. Better to have a backer than lose grocery money. And while guys like Ronnie Allen and Weenie Beenie may have been happy to gamble thousands, Red generally kept his wagers to the hundreds. Red gambled, sure, but he also managed his money. He didn't want to book a loss that could put his lovely Texas bride on the street.

"After Red married Dottie, he became a very responsible-type person," said Duke. "He'd take their money, and when he'd bet, he had the nuts to win, because he didn't want to be missing no meals and he didn't want to be sleeping in the car. If it were just him, he wouldn't worry too much about it, but after he married Dottie, he became very responsible towards her, and she might get a job working in the poolroom while Red was doing something else—either shooting pool or playing dominoes in the back."

One night at the Le Cue, on Rusk and Fannin in downtown Houston, Red got himself into a fistfight. From outward appearances, Red seemed then to have reverted to the biggest, dumbest cliché of pool. But the thing was, Red wasn't drunk, and he wasn't fighting over a bad bet. Instead, the hotheaded Red was fighting against his past.

It started when this guy named Larry—an exceedingly loud pool shooter from Delaware—came to the Le Cue talking shit. Larry began ragging Red about how he was back in New York, back at the 7-11, when Red was sleeping in the poolrooms, scraping around for five-dollar games. Right in front of Dottie, Larry brought it all up. After Dottie left the poolroom, after she went back to their hotel to sleep, Red let the guy have it.

"Look man, when it's me and my wife, I don't want you to say anything about what I did in New York City," snapped Red. "So just keep your fuckin' mouth shut."

But Delaware Larry kept on him.

"Yeah, Red, I remember you used to sleep in the poolrooms out at the 7-11..."

"Look, man, I don't want you saying anything about that, especially around my wife. You know that's all in my past, and I don't want you fuckin' with me."

It was as if Red wanted the world to believe he'd never booked a loser, that he'd never lived the harsh life of a hustler, that somehow, impossibly, he had security. It was important that Dottie believe—that everyone believe—that Red was not a poolroom bum.

Duke Dowell was there that night and watched the whole sorry exchange unfold. Duke is mostly a quiet man, and not one prone to loud outbursts or wild hyperbole. He grew up just south of Houston, and it shows when he talks. His *o's* become *u's* and unexpected syllables grow onto four-letter words and pool players are really *good ol' boys* or sometimes *pieces of shit*—except when Duke says it, it's more like they're *pee-yesus uh shee-yut*.

And that's what he said about Delaware Larry.

"Red was pissed, I could tell," recalled Duke. "But Red kind of surprised me, because I didn't think he would do anything, and Larry just kept ragging on him a little bit and Red says, 'Yeah, you're going to bet this and bet that, but just don't bet I won't whup your fucking ass.' And Larry thought Red was on the rib, you know, and so Larry just says, 'I'll bet you fifty dollars you can't whup my fucking ass.'

"And so Larry pulled out a fifty-dollar bill and threw it out on the bar, like that, and Red was so fucking hot, that Red didn't even think about getting change. He just pulled his bankroll out—he only had hundred-dollar bills—and he pulled a hundred off and he says, 'I don't have any change, so I'll just lay you a hundred to fifty that I can whup your fucking ass.'"

And then the combinations began. *Wham, wham, wham.* "Red hits this son of a bitch with a left, and a right, and another left," said Duke. "This guy was an Indian, and he had this big jaw, and he was a big guy, and Red just teed off on him, and he just punched this son of a bitch...

"The guy just stood there, and then he reached out and grabbed Red, and said, 'Aw now, Red.' You know, Red hit him flush on the button, first punch. Red's left handed, and he hit him flush on the jaw, and the guy didn't even blink a fucking eye. You could hit this guy with an anvil and I don't think it would have hurt him. The guy never threw a punch, he just reached out and grabbed Red and they were struggling and Red was trying to get free and this guy just reached out and bear-hugged Red.

"And Red said, 'Man, don't fuck with me, and don't ever talk about my past, because I *will* do something to you.'"

WHILE RED WAS A MUCH BETTER POOL PLAYER THAN DELAWARE LARRY OR ANY OF THE OTHER PLAYERS WHO MADE IT DOWN TO LE CUE, HE OFTEN TRIED TO HIDE THAT ABILITY. It was called lemoning, or playing on the lemon, and Jack stayed on the lemon for two or three months after first arriving in Houston—just barely booking the win, just showing enough to go home with the money. He took advantage of a central principle of pool: unlike cards and board games, it's very tough to cheat. About the only way would be to secretly move the balls around with your hands. Which is, of course, madness. Get caught doing that—and what else would happen with such an obvious ploy?—and the hustler could very well get those hands broken.

So what does that leave? Lemoning. A hustler can't cheat, but he can play below speed. A fraction of a fraction of an inch off, and a ball ricochets from the pocket. Too much force, and it bounces into the side pocket—and then bounces out again. Too much follow, and the hustler pockets his ball, but whitey gets hooked downtable. And if pool hustlers have a credo, this is it: when possible, play on the lemon.

And so that's what Red did, day in and day out, at the Central Cue. Dottie said she watched him play, watched him go from one player to the next, quietly dispatching all—until the day his lemon got found out.

"It didn't really take me that long to begin to see that Red could win whenever he wanted to," said Dottie. "I could see the stroke and the position that he could get. That was three-fourths of it, you know, getting the position.

"But he wouldn't go all out—he wouldn't just run out to show that he could do it. He wasn't going to do anything like that. He would just keep it close enough to where they always thought they had a chance. He would win, but it would be closer than it needed to be. But watching him, you weren't too sure, because he'd be just good enough—*just good enough*—to beat everybody I ran him into.

"He wasn't a known player at all, you know, at that time. He hadn't played yet in [that many] tournaments—except in New York. But around the country, he wasn't known. I forgot who came in that recognized him and knew who he was. He got wind of a left-handed player that was playing real good. It was some guy that was there for a week or two, and he said [Jack] was known as Jersey Red, way back in New York."

After that came the spots, which were legendary, incredible, the stuff of wide-eyed stories decades later. And the secret, too, was to first give a small spot and then slowly ratchet it up. That is, a hustler like Red might give away one ball in one-pocket, win; give away two, win; give away three, win; and keep going on like that until the spot becomes truly outrageous. One of the most incredible was "six no-count"—a feat never before witnessed in Houston.

Bill Lee, who has spent years scuffing around Houston pool halls, said it made his jaw drop.

Red lines up a shot in Johnston City, Illinois. Although Red played all games well, his specialty was one-pocket. He was said to be absolutely unbeatable at one-pocket on the big 5' by 10' tables, then popular in some poolhalls. Here, he plays on a smaller 9' by 4 ½' tournament table. **photo © Billiards Digest**

Promoter George Jansco, left, congratulates Wimpy Lassiter after a first-place finish in Johnston City. Jansco's brother Paulie stands behind the trophies. Through their tournaments, the Janscos contributed to the sport's 1960s renaissance.

photo © Billiards Digest

◄ Jersey Red looks on with concern as Wimpy Lassiter surveys the table during the 1969 U.S. Open in Las Vegas. Red, the hot-headed northern one-pocket player, always had difficulty with Lassiter, the cool-witted southern nine-baller.

photo © Billiards Digest

▲
Unlike Red, Fats played from an upright position. He probably got into this habit because of his fat stomach. During his early years in Little Egypt, Fats' waist ballooned to 55 inches and he tipped the scales to nearly 300 pounds. **photo © Billiards Digest**

During tournament play, Wimpy Lassiter was a picture of suffering. He complained of gout, clogged sinuses, and headaches. Lassiter even played through bleeding ulcers during a world-championship clash with Willie Mosconi.

photo © Billiards Digest

◄ Boston Shorty, a.k.a. Larry Johnson, lines up a shot during a pressure-cooker match in Johnston City, Illinois. Shorty was known for his phenomenal stamina and his love of cigars and beer. At 5' 2'', Shorty stood taller than his pool stick—but just barely.

photo © Billiards Digest

Lassiter gets down low over a shot. The Elizabeth City, North Carolina native began hustling pool as a teenager during the Great Depression, and dominated the tournament circuit during the 1960s—when he was well into his 40s.

photo © **Billiards Digest**

The fame of Minnesota Fats ▶ would far outstrip that of Wimpy Lassiter, Jersey Red, or any other player before or since. Fats would host two TV shows, including this one that featured celebrity guests. That's Milton Berle leaning over a shot on a pocketless billiards table.

photo © **Billiards Digest**

Hubert Cokes was known as "Daddy Warbucks," after the similar-looking character in the Little Orphan Annie comic strip. Like the cartoon character, Cokes often walked around with several thousand dollars in his pocket. Unlike the cartoon character, Cokes also carried a loaded pistol.

photo © Billiards Digest

After coming to prominence with the 1961 release of *The Hustler*, Fats made a living playing exhibitions and promoting products for Rozel Industries. Sometimes he won; sometimes he lost. But Fats always entertained the crowd.

photo © Billiards Digest

▼

The left-handed Jersey Red typically got down low over the balls. The one-pocket specialist also drew plenty of sweaters, as can be seen here during one of the early hustler jamborees in Johnston City, Illinois. Red was considered the king of the New York pool hustlers.

photo © **Billiards Digest**

Wimpy uses an unusual ▶ bridging technique—note how he has placed his right hand knuckles directly on the felt for this shot— while on the hustlers circuit. Straight pool genius Irving Crane, a textbook player, appears to disapprove.

photo © **Billiards Digest**

▲
Rudolf Wanderone, Jr., had many nicknames in his life: Double-Smart Fats, Triple-Smart Fats, Chicago Fats and New York Fats. But he was best known as Minnesota Fats, after the Jackie Gleason character in *The Hustler*. Walter Tevis, author of *The Hustler*, always denied there was a connection between the fictional character and the real-life pool hustler. **photo © Billiards Digest**

Lassiter's precision ▶
shotmaking keeps Red
glued to his chair during
the 1969 U.S. Open,
televised on ABC's Wide
World of Sports. Willie
Mosconi served as
moderator for the event.

photo © Billiards Digest

Fats and Willie Mosconi lag ▶
for the break during one of
their famous televised
match-ups. Mosconi was
arguably the finest pool player
to ever hold a stick. He was
contemptuous of the
loud-mouthed Fats, even
though Fats brought more
attention to the sport.

photo © Billiards Digest

◀ The Valentine's Day battle between
Fats and Mosconi in 1978
became the highest rated
sports program that year, after
the Ali-Spink fight. It was telecast
from the posh Starlight Roof of the
Waldorf Astoria. Howard Cosell
served as moderator. A frustrated
Mosconi would admonish Fats
to shut up and shoot.

photo © Billiards Digest

"You know, that's where Red had to run six straight [at one pocket] before it even counted," said Lee. "He was playing that way, and the other guy had to sink eight any way he could get them. And Red just killed that guy, like four times in a row. The guy couldn't win. I couldn't believe it. It was fucking incredible, man."

Duke remembered how Red would spot opponents eight balls playing one-pocket. *Eight balls.*

"I saw this guy—used to love to play Red—and his name was Buddy Bealer. Buddy was playing Red one night, playing five-dollar one-pocket, and Red was giving him sixteen to eight. *Sixteen to eight!* And Red had the absolute mortal nuts, and he just beat this guy out of a hundred and fifty-five dollars in three hours playing one-pocket.

"Red was raining balls in from all angles, and he was loving it. You know, if you're playing a guy sixteen to eight—that's a total of twenty-four balls—and so you have to spot eight balls back up in order to make the score come out even. And so Red would run whatever he would run, and spot them up until he had eight balls spotted up and then he'd just go and finish out the game.

"But the strongest thing about that session was that Red ran sixteen and out three times. In one-pocket, that's *phenomenal.* He would just make a long-rail bank and then start running balls from behind the head spot. *Sixteen and out—three times!*"

IT WOULDN'T BE LONG BEFORE RED RETURNED TO THE ROAD, NOW WITH DOTTIE BEHIND THE WHEEL. But despite his best efforts, he almost drove them both broke in San Francisco. Dottie remembers crying in a motel bathroom, completely hysterical about the crazy marriage, seeing their bankroll shrunk to just seven dollars. But Red came roaring back, just as he always did, and before long they were living easy. It was also about then that Red changed his name: dropping the "kopf" from Breitkopf. Red said he liked the ring of the shorter "Jack Breit," which fit better on tournament and exhibition posters.

One of the first tournaments that Red attended with his new wife would have been the 1964 Johnston City Hustlers' Jamboree. The Billiard Room Proprietor's Association had barred Red from the previous year's world tournament—probably because of his hustler's reputation[18]—but George and Paulie Jansco loved the hustlers, loved the action, and so Red and the other gamblers came in great numbers.

It was also in 1964 that ABC signed a production contract with the Janscos. With the added network money, George and Paulie doubled the total purse to $20,000. TV crews strung lights and cables, reporters crowded into the stands, bona fide hustlers told bona fide lies. The 1965 jamboree was the biggest and most spectacular to date.

And the public went nuts.

"The beer and bourbon—standard playing equipment—had to be served in paper cups, and the lights were a little hot, but ego runs high around the hustlers," wrote Craig Vetter, of *Playboy* magazine. "The only things to do are drink and play pool. The two are far from mutually exclusive, and...Jansco has them both sewed up."

Red's performance was not particularly noteworthy in the 1964 Johnston City event, but Lassiter's was phenomenal. Wimpy won the nine-ball division, the straight-pool division, and the 1964 all-around. It was a blitzkrieg repeat

---

[18] Because of his race, the BRPAA in 1964 also barred Brooklyn's Cicero Murphy. The exclusion prompted pickets outside the hotel. Murphy was invited the following year.

of his phenomenal finishes in 1962 and 1963. It also came on the heels of Lassiter's victories at the controversial BRPAA events in 1963 and 1964.

By the mid-1960s, in fact, Lassiter had won every major nine-ball tournament ever held in America.[19] He had beaten every man there was to beat: hustlers, tournament players, champions, chumps. The soft-bellied and sickly southern gentleman rocketed through the ranks like a moon-bound Saturn V.

What makes this early trajectory even more startling is that he had accomplished almost nothing during the previous decade. His only significant tournament victory had been against Irving Crane, back in '54—and that's not even noted in most record books. So by the time *The Hustler* rolled around, most players did not consider Lassiter much of a threat.

He was too old, too sick, too frail. He was a has-been. Sure, he played good—for an old roadman.

And so what to make of Wimpy Lassiter? How to explain his down-and-up career? He exploded onto the pool scene. He came from nowhere. Based on his early dominance alone, Lassiter's contribution to pool was as significant as Ty Cobb's to baseball.

Why, then, did Luther Lassiter suddenly begin to fail?

---

[19] There had been a few other national nine-ball tournaments prior to 1964—U.J. Puckett had won one back in 1960, for instance—but never with the top-notch talent of Johnston City.

10

1965

"I'm looking forward to the day when I will hear the referee say 'playing for one' and the next sound will be that of the cue striking the ball just right. Then will come the sound of the ball being pocketed and then the roars of the crowd when they announce that I'm the champ. It may sound corny, but it's something that I continually think of—being the champ."

—*Jersey Red*, National Billiard News, *February 1967*

L ASSITER'S FIFTIETH BIRTHDAY APPROACHED— THE TREMENDOUSLY DEPRESSING FIVE-OH, AN AGE FOR GRAYBEARDS...EVEN IN THE GRAY-BEARD WORLD OF WORLD-CLASS POOL. And by 1965, after his earlier victories in Johnston City and New York, it appeared that those years had begun taking a toll.

Lassiter was lonely, sick, and burned out. So far he had sacrificed everything to this grasping whore of a sport: companionship, a home, a wife. Cancer had killed his mother in 1957; his father was already gone. His one-time road partner, Don Willis, had abandoned him.[20] Lassiter once said he'd walk 2,800 miles for the companionship of a single friend. "What could be better than having that far to walk if you had a good friend to walk with you?"

------

[20] The two road partners had had a falling out some years previously—no one seems to remember why. A dejected Wimpy went off to the tournaments; Don Willis kept hustling.

Sickness dogged his every step. Like a return to those unsettling Coast Guard days, it seemed that Wimpy might drown in his own gout and clogged sinuses and bile-filled rumbling stomach. His soul burned with the suffering—and Wimpy's intolerable suffering made those around him suffer. He complained endlessly.

Lassiter rattled as he walked—*tap, tap, tap*—literally rattled, as if some part of him had become unfastened. It was a little thing, just a gentle clicking in the right-hand pocket—but everyone noticed it. And those who knew, those that had spent years with Wimpy back in Elizabeth City, and those that played him on the road, understood what that tap tap tapping was: it was the insistent rattle of a tiny vial of sedatives. "C-O-M-P-O-Z," he explained. "It's supposed to calm you down." Wimpy was also said to have a fondness for Percodan.

And so maybe, by 1965, the round pills, the frayed nerves, the tight undershirts and the long, long years—perhaps all of it had finally undone Wimpy Lassiter. Three decades of road life, of late-night honky-tonks and big-hoorah whisky; three decades of Don Willis, of Beefy Laden, and car wrecks; *three decades of gambling!*—these things come not free. Lassiter had gone too far, played too much, become too experienced. He was wearing himself out.

"I've been so infected, it's sapped all my strength," he would say, smacking the side of his head.

RED, MEANWHILE, WAS MAKING GAMES ALL ALONG AMERICA'S OLD BLACK RIVER. He and Dottie rode her grinding brown Mercury up and down, east and west, searching, always searching, for the accidental score, the forgotten pool hall. Quick entry and quiet escape. In and out, two hours max—and always, *always*, with the shuffling joy of dead presidents flowing flush across his long, long face. *Made seventy-five, honey. Let's eat!*

Like Bonnie and Clyde, Red and Dottie in 1965 took flight. Out of Houston, out of Le Cue and JR's, searching for action. It came with thunderclap nine-ball games. It came in syrup-slow one-pocket, race to five, a flood of balls and a fat pay-off. Five dollars and ten dollars and twenty dollars and more. Small bills changing hands quickly—the quick action. Large sums changing hands more slowly—the big action. On that old black river, at 1,001 pool halls, Red found them both.

But that rarest action of all, and the sweetest, Red could not find. Nowhere in that everchanging, wanton river did Red find that day-in-and-day-out action that brings a hot plate and a real apartment and a fridge. Nowhere did Red find that island of security—that *steady* action—the action that meant Red could march off to the same poolroom every day, just like some square pigeon in a square suit, and come back every time with cash money in his pocket. Steady meant a rent-by-the-month apartment with his big-haired beautiful wife, and steady meant Dottie could get a job slinging hash or bartending, and steady meant that sometimes, in the evenings, Red could share a meal with Dottie—just like a real-life married couple. The black river could not surrender the steady action, because *steady* remained a thing foreign to the road. Jack hustled for a living: he could only play at real life.

And so the river washed over Jack and Dottie, taking them to accidental pool halls, sudden hotels, cursing fights. Hand in hand, they crossed a great divide of gravel and dirt and desert grime. The accidental and uncertain, for a very long time, defined who they were. *Made one-twenny-FIVE, baby!* he'd say. *Made two hun'red, baby! Jes look! Two hun'red!* Red could give Dottie his cash, but he wanted for her something more. He could give his love and loyalty, but love and loyalty were nickel-and-dime. He could show Dottie the whole wide world, beat chump after hapless chump, stay forever sober, curtail his famous foul mouth. But it made no difference. Jack was a bum, the son of a drunk, a high-school dropout. The action both quick and big could not erase who he was. It could not erase Jack "Jersey Red" Breit.

What Jack wanted, most of all, was to become a new man. His wife said it. His friends remember it. A review of his life leaves little doubt. Becoming a better man, achieving greatness, transcending his reputation as a poolroom bum: this was Jack's dream. This was his only salvation. Proving himself worthy meant becoming greater than the daily hustle. Proving himself worthy—of both Dottie's gamble in marrying him, and the gamble of his own life—meant becoming a winner. A thousand fat paydays against no-talent hacks meant nothing. A fifty-ball run in some backwater back room against some bent-dick sucker meant nothing. Red knew—he must have known—that hustling, by itself, could not save him.

His accidental life could only end with *pool*.

And so by 1965—the first full year of his marriage, the fourth of the *Hustler*-inspired billiards renaissance—the urge to end his accidental life must have burned Red beastly hot.

ON MARCH 25, 1965, JERSEY RED CONFRONTED LIMPY LASSITER.

The venue: the world's straight-pool tournament in New York City. Lassiter came to the table with a tournament-leading 7-0 record. Despite a loss to Babe Cranfield at a world championship challenge match three months earlier, despite his deteriorating state, most old-timers still considered Lassiter the man to beat.

Red, by contrast, possessed a 0-4 career record against Lassiter, and a 4-4 record at the tournament. Yet Red remained in contention, and the New York old-timers—the ones who had seen him work his magic down at the 7-11—understood his potential. With Dottie at his side, Red had both his reputation and his pride at stake.

So down in the cellar of New York's Commodore Hotel, in the chandeliered Windsor Ballroom, wearing tuxedos in the Hades of world competition, Red and Wimpy unscrewed their cues, lagged for the break, went to work. And the young northerner, coming on like the first promise of the rising sun, opened up long runs, maintained tight control of whitey, broke up ball clusters with unerring speed control. He demolished rack after rack—one, two, *three, four*. He kept firing, kept sinking balls.

Red led first, then Wimpy, then Red again. Finally the game stood at 121-118, Red's favor, with Red controlling the table. And here Red came to a crossroad. He could see the great Lassiter could be beaten. The lay did not look too treacherous. Lassiter was stuck in his high stool, away from the table. Here the young northerner saw a chance.

A long shot confronted him. Easily makable, but long nonetheless. Red would have to stretch his tall frame to address the cue ball. He could grab that bridge, he could take the rake, and set the shot up—*but why?* Red felt so close now, very close. The murmuring crowd recognized imminent victory, the scribbling newspapermen could see it in the eagerness of Red's eyes, and the still air seemed thick with its promise. Red felt the exhilaration, the excitement.

He bent down low; he locked his eyes on the object ball. A long shot, sure, and a stretch—but quite, *quite* makable. Easy really. He could use a bridge...but that would slow down the run, and he couldn't slow down.

Not now. Not yet. Not with victory so tantalizingly close. Red braced himself. His time had come.

"And then," the *National Billiard News* reported, "something happened—something that oldtimers were still talking about days after the tourney wound up."

As Red stretched for the shot, stretched to bring his final judgment against Luther Lassiter, his tuxedo jacket opened a bit, just a bit, and the edge of it came down, soft as a feather...and it touched a ball.

FOUL!

121-118, playing to 150.

FOUL!

Luther Lassiter stepping to the table.

FOUL!

JESUS Christ! Jesus CHRIST Lord ALMIGHTY!

FOUL!

The air left Red's lungs; the blood rushed from his head. The groans of the audience filled his ears; the sour bile of self-recrimination filled his gut. Red must have known, then, the horrible sickness of self-doubt. And of fear. The groans engulfed him, and yet as loud as they were, they could not drown out the frantic dialogue within his own soul: *Stupid. So STUPID. Fucking STUPID imbecile.*

Red watched with panic as Luther Lassiter, the calm and sedate and unerring Luther Lassiter, took his practice strokes. Red felt victory slipping from his fingers, saw his defeat written in the pattern of the balls, in the sureness of Lassiter's steady gaze. He felt his stomach sink as Lassiter surveyed the table.

Lassiter fired; the scorekeeper marked another point: 121-119. Playing to 150.

Lassiter resurveyed the table, eyed a shot, thought better of it, found another more to his liking, bent down low, sighted.

And then—Luther Lassiter did something he very seldom did.

He missed.

And Jack "Jersey Red" Breit, the two-bit hustler from the 7-11, ran out the table.

A stunning upset—that's what the *New York Times* called it. In beating Lassiter, Red managed to do what no other player so far had accomplished in that tournament. The victory also cemented Red's reputation as a first-rate tournament player. The old-timers grasped Red's hand, shook it vigorously, told him victory had been a long time coming. Dottie gave her big man a big kiss. "I never wanted to win a game so badly since I started playing fifteen years ago," said Red.

Although neither he nor Lassiter came out on top during the 1965 World's tournament,[21] the 1965 event was something of a turning point for both.

For Red, the New York event marked the beginning of an obsession. He knew, then, that he could beat any man living. The 150-121 straight-pool score stood testament to that. Red convinced himself that he would conquer all of pool, and that the *New York Times* would write of that conquest, and the TV crews would come, and the magazine writers too. And he'd finally prove to Dottie that she had married more than a two-bit hustler, more than a poolroom bum.

The future seemed bright, beautiful, and wonderful.

----

[21] That year's title went to Pennsylvania's Joe Balsis.

But for Lassiter, the event marked the beginning of a free fall. The southerner had lost his world crown to Cranfield just a few months earlier and now lost it again. Just as America's pool renaissance reached a crescendo—and just as Jersey Red finally began knocking on the door of his own greatness—Lassiter peaked. His rocket paused at high pinnacle; it shuddered in midair; it plummeted back earthward. In 1965, Lassiter's grasp on pool began to fail him. The old railbirds, the players, the press—they nodded and clucked knowingly. They whispered among themselves, noting his bad shape, his missed balls—how he lost whitey like a dog through a broken fence. "The pressure's got to Wimpy," they'd say: "Look what it did to Mosconi."

FATS DID NOT ATTEND THE NEW YORK TOURNAMENT BUT RATHER ATTENDED TO HIMSELF, WHICH, BY 1965, HAD BECOME SOMETHING OF A GROWTH INDUSTRY. Magazine articles. Appearances on *The Tonight Show. A job!* By virtue of his new position as executive vice president for Rozel Industries, Fats even got himself a Social Security number. The government assigned 322-42-2372 to one Mr. Minnesota Fats—not Rudolf Wanderone, but "Minnesota Fats"…*got the card right here*—and so the big lie became legit.

The endorsement deal brought big money, big exposure, a fat expense account. "Overnight I became the biggest attraction the billiards industry ever knew," said Fats. But there was a downside too: as executive VP, there'd be no more sleeping till 2 p.m., no more searching the countryside for wheat fields and watermelon. Fats, suddenly, had places to go, people to see.

"Getting up early in the morning isn't so bad, but fighting the sunshine is brutal beyond compare," he complained. "I always avoided sunshine at all costs on account of sunshine is one of the most dreadful things on the entire earth.

"[But] sometimes the grief is a lot worse than just standing out in the sun, because more and more I'm getting robbed of sleep, which was always one of my favorite hobbies. Zee [Rozel boss Mr. Phil Zelkowitz] won't let me get the proper rest because he had me running all over the country making more personal appearances than a Miss America. Sometimes I feel like a tourist."

From D.C. to Detroit to Delaware, Fats spread his bullshit like fertilizer. He mixed the truth and lies for a thousand reporters in a thousand pool halls, telling stories and jokes and signing autographs. The lies rolled off his tongue like spittle: colossal, ridiculous, utterly entertaining lies. *I played at the North Pole twice last year,* he'd say. Or, *I've played for every king and queen, every maharajah that ever lived. You can't name a place, Zanzibar to Timbuktu— I've been to every place but the moon.*

Fats appeared in lengthy profiles for both *Esquire* and *Life* magazines (even donning an odious tuxedo for one photo shoot) and appeared on the Tonight Show, where he hustled Johnny Carson out of a buck.[22] On the Irv Kupcinet Show, Fats went toe-to-toe with Cassius Clay in what amounted to a thirty-minute no-holds-barred debate. "At the end, the viewer can judge for himself just which gentleman is 'The Greatest,'" the Chicago TV host told his viewers.

Fats told a nationally syndicated newspaper writer that he never miscued more than six times in a single year—*and I used to make these shots with concrete balls, ya understand.* The lies inflated Fats, made him bigger than his already elephantine proportions. And so he ballooned during the mid-1960s,

[22] At that time, the Tonight Show paid all guests $320—whether they were Frank Sinatra or Tiny Tim, Fats wrote in his autobiography. "But when Johnny Carson added the dollar to my talent fee, making it exactly three hundred and twenty-one, I became the highest-paid guest in the history of the Tonight Show."

becoming bigger than old Cowboy Weston who led the parade in a white Stetson and six-shooters, bigger even than jazz-age sensation Ralph Greenleaf shooting wing shots beneath the hot lights of vaudeville, bigger than Red and Lassiter going head-to-head for a world title.

Minnesota Fats was becoming bigger than all of pool.

THIS, FROM A FULL-PAGE ADVERTISEMENT IN A 1965 EDITION OF *BOWLERS JOURNAL:*

Enter the 1st Annual

Stardust Open

All-Around

Pocket Billiard Tournament

3 tournaments in 1: Straight Pool—Nine Ball—One Pocket

June 2—June 16, Stardust Hotel Las Vegas, Nevada

The ad notes that the first annual event received the official endorsement of the Professional Pool Players of America and sanctioning from the Billiards Congress of America. The tournament promoters promise $30,000 in prize money—supposedly the most in pool history—plus trophies. At the very bottom appear these very tiny, very curious words: "Tournament consultants: Jansco Brothers, Johnston City, Ill."

And so finally, this was it: the country circus of quick-talking, quick-thinking hustler promoter Georgie Jansco had made it to the big city. Georgie possessed oversized ideas—ideas that never quite fit into the tiny confines of Little Egypt. And Las Vegas was his Xanadu. His Mecca.

The notion first came to him, like a bullet, during a family vacation. The Janscos—Georgie, wife Sadie, daughter JoAnn—had taken a room at the Flamingo Hotel, on the Vegas strip. The year was 1965. "He was really fascinated by Vegas," recalled JoAnn. "He was a gambler, you know, and he liked the action. That's when the idea popped into his head."

A tournament, a desert tournament, thought Georgie—and one like his famous Johnston City events, featuring pool's three major disciplines: nine-ball, one-pocket, and straight pool. Jansco would invite the game's greatest players. The casino, he figured, could front the prize money. In exchange, it would get free publicity and scores of the hardest-drinking, hardest-gambling men in America. That would be the pitch.

And so, with an open phone book on an unmade bed, Georgie made phone calls. Down the list he went, marking off one casino after another, looking to cut the best deal. The family's Flamingo Hotel vacation room became Georgie's makeshift office, HQ for America's pool renaissance. The game was exploding everywhere, he explained, and a tournament—a world-class tournament—would attract the networks and the newspapers.

With Milt Jaffey, vice-president of operations at the Stardust, Georgie finally agreed upon the right combination of salary and perks. Four to six weeks every year, the Janscos would stay at the hotel. The family would swim and gamble and play golf. Georgie would work the phones, set up the bleachers, rent tables. Players would receive fat hotel discounts.

Her father scheduled the tournaments for each summer, in contrast to the Johnston City events every winter, said JoAnn. "And I just went out and had fun. It was wonderful. Those were the good years." Her father had finally bridged his patch of nothing with a bejeweled oasis in the desert. This was it. Snake-eyed dice. Suicide jacks. Pool, pool, and more pool!

The inaugural event lasted fifteen days, and drew 102 entrants from twenty-four states. It also attracted an astounding five thousand paying fans, who filled bleachers at the casino's second-floor International Room. JoAnn remembers table after table in neat lines and hundreds of spectators. A reporter for *Bowlers Journal* described the Stardust event as a near-perfect reproduction of Johnston City, albeit on a much grander scale. "Janscoian touches included George's special lighting system (a battery of blazing lights surrounded by a skirt of black bunting), seating capacity for 400 spectators and a torrent of publicity."

Georgie and his brother Paulie partnered at the event, and both received salaries. The cost of admission, the TV contracts, and presumably the player's entry all went to the casino. But Georgie and Paulie had another source of income—perhaps their *principal* source of income—and its promise brought them back year after year.

"My father was good at one-pocket," JoAnn said. "I remember he was in Vegas one time, him and his brother, and the pool tournament had gotten over with, and Uncle Joe [Paulie] went to bed. After that, my dad got a pool game with a guy named Sarge. He played with the guy from twelve at night until seven the next morning, and my dad came out twenty-five thousand dollars ahead."

JoAnn said it again, for effect: "Twenty-five thousand dollars. Playing pool."

Shortly afterward, JoAnn's dad went down to the Stardust restaurant for breakfast. And that's when Uncle Joe showed up, said JoAnn, and her uncle seemed none too pleased that Georgie had won so much money. "He comes in and asks, 'I'm half of that, aren't I? And he [my dad] says, 'No, you went to bed. That's my action.'

"You know, Uncle Joe was arguing that they were in the pool tournament together, and so they should be together with this money that my dad got. But my dad made the game. My uncle thought that because they were in the tournament together, that any profits that were made, they had to split."

JoAnn shook her head, recalling the absurdity. Her words seemed imbued with both pity and disdain—sentiments that often arrived hand in hand when discussing Paulie "Joe" Jansco. Georgie Jansco, her bigger-than-life father, had helped create the pool renaissance. Uncle Joe, years later, would help destroy it. Gambling would fuel both its resurrection and its destruction—just as gambling fueled that midmorning dispute between the Romulus and Remus brothers of America's great hustler days. "Uncle Joe cried and cried and so he [my dad] finally gave him half the money," said JoAnn. "That's the relationship between two brothers. That was the relationship with the family. My dad took care of him."

JIMMY "THE GREEK" SNYDER, IN A JUNE 3 EDITION OF THE *LAS VEGAS SUN*, RANKED RED NEAR THE TOP FOR THE FIELD FOR THE INAUGURAL STARDUST INVITATIONAL. Fifteen-to-one odds—that's what the Greek put on Red. The Greek ranked Boston Shorty a twenty-five-to-one winner and gave twenty to one to Cicero Murphy, the top-rated black player. The Greek put Lassiter way up above almost everyone—judged him a five-to-one winner, even though Wimpy did not excel at all three games featured in Vegas and had been on a long losing streak.

It appeared at first that the famous Vegas oddsmaker had called a winner. Lassiter beat Red at straight pool on June 11 by a score of 125-41. A day earlier, Lassiter had beaten Eddie Taylor 125-0 at the same game. He also topped Irving Crane 11-4 at nine-ball. "Luther Lassiter of Elizabeth City, N.C. continues to lead all divisions in the Stardust Open National Billiard Tournament going into the final three days of competition," read a June 13 edition of the *Sun*. "Trailing Lassiter, but rated strong contenders are Harold Worst, Irving Crane, Joe Balsis and Jack Breit."

A strong contender indeed, Breit took down Handsome Danny Jones, 4-3, at one-pocket on June 7 and then toppled Eddie McGehean of St. Louis, 11-6, at nine-ball. He also beat Hugh Pearson, of Las Vegas, four games to two at one-pocket, and Dallas West, 125-40, at straight pool. "Breit finished very strong in Burbank's World's tournament, made a big showing in Johnston City World's Tournament, and [is] "confident and aggressive," wrote the Greek in a June 11 column. "[Red is] capable of beating any player at any time."

On June 14, Red leaped into the one-pocket finals with a 4-3 victory over the very wiry Harry Petros. Only three-cushion champ Harold Worst now stood between Red and the one-pocket title and a chance for victory in the richest pool tournament in American history.

Lassiter, by contrast, had resumed his downward spiral. Already bounced from the one-pocket and nine-ball divisions, Lassiter now faced former world champion Irving Crane at straight pool. And there Lassiter fell for good. With the adroit precision of a Harvard-trained mathematician, the New York tournament player dismantled the gentleman hustler. Crane scored nearly two balls for each of Lassiter's. Final score: 125-66.

Lassiter, then, was out. He fared no better at the Stardust Invitational than he had just a few months earlier at the world championship in New York. Lassiter watched from the cheap seats as Irving Crane took the straight-pool division title, beating Cowboy Jimmy Moore, and he watched from those seats as Baltimore's Eddy Kelly took the nine-ball division. And it was from the bleachers that Wimpy watched the last-division finals—one-pocket—pitting the spectacular Harold Worst against the sensational Jersey Red. It went on all night.

As always, Red came on like fire. He sent balls to pockets just like in his old 7-11 days. He showed the old magic, winning one game, then two, then three. But Worst played strong too—terribly strong, and with confidence. Worst understood the tables, had an instinct for the two- and three-railers. His prowess at three-cushion billiards—he was, after all, a world champion at that pocketless variety of pool—served him well.

Game to Worst.

Game to Worst.

Game to Worst.

And then, late into the night of June 15, 1965, it came down finally to one final game, eight balls. Red and Worst were tied at three apiece, but Red held the table. And Red could see the shape, the run-out. He could see it all, just like at the 7-11, against Wagon Head and Joey with Glasses, playing on the big five-by-tens. But this time Red played not for bums, but for newspaper reporters. This time he played not for cigarette money, but to conquer the richest tour-nament in American pool history. Red, finally, was playing for true respect

There he stood, at the very precipice of glory, with one game between him-self and salvation. And maybe it was precisely then, just as that intoxicating promise swam within him, that Jersey Red began to drown. The crowd went silent like a mountain lake, and through that suffocating silence Red's own awful doubts emerged. He relived past mistakes, tragic errors, his wrong choices.

Concentrate. Focus.

But what about that fucked-up foul against Lassiter—the one back at the world championship just a few months earlier? Such urgent thoughts would always cloud Red's mind at exactly the wrong moments—he frequently said he would often look back when life demanded that he look forward. This was the tragic pattern of Jersey Red's existence.

Concentrate.

Red held the table, needed just a few balls. Tied three games apiece. He bent down then, down low for the tight shot. He played it in his head. Imagined it. Judged ball speed. Calculated distance.

Focus.

He cocked his left arm, took a few ghost strokes...*fire!*

Red did not stand up. He did not disrupt the follow-through. Instead he watched from that low, prone position as the object ball fell crisply into the pocket, just like he had envisioned. —*Perfection.* Whitey continued on, striking one rail, two rails, three rails. He watched as whitey glided back like a ballet dancer...but coming too fast, coming too fast...*too fast, goddamnit!*

And he watched as bastard whitey glided straight into a side pocket.

Foul!

Jersey Red did not shoot another ball at the 1965 Stardust Invitational. Harold Worst pocketed $4,350 for first place; Red placed second in one-pocket, fourth overall. Red pocketed $2,050. The free-falling Lassiter failed to win a single division.

DOWN IN SOUTHERN ILLINOIS, MINNESOTA FATS WAS STROKING A TWENTY-OUNCE CUE, LOOKING AT THE BLUE TWO AND THE CORNER POCKET, FIGURING HOW WHITEY WOULD SAIL OVER THE VAST LAKE OF GREEN FELT AND HIT THAT TWO JUST RIGHT AND HOW IT WOULD DROP—*PLOP!***—INTO THE CORNER POCKET.** Beneath him were the hard concrete floors of Jansco's Cue Club, all around him the bleachers, and off to the side, serving drunks, was JoAnn McNeal, the pretty daughter of Mr. Georgie Jansco himself, the club's fast-talking owner. And the Fatman, Mr. 250-pound, all-around-town Fatman, looking at that blue two and the corner pocket, perhaps was thinking about the bankroll in his pocket, hoping it would stay there...or maybe even grow some. His fifty-five-inch stomach pressed against the table, suffocated the rail.

The Fatman fired. He could feel the stick's follow-through—not the recoil, but the follow-through—as it went right through whitey and died, as if to impale the sacrificial lamb. The Fatman *believed* his shot to be true; the Fatman believed he had charted a course that was smooth and straight and good. But still, somehow, in that fraction of a microsecond between follow-through and recoil, something felt wrong. And his game face contorted: it got that weird tic that always came when he focused, but also when he became rattled with all the money to be lost or won.

Goddamn it. Goddamn it all to hell.

To those who didn't know, to those who had never seen Fats play and believed the hype, the miss came as a surprise. After all, it was an easy shot, and Fats often boasted that he never, ever, lost for money, even though he'd been hustling around saloons since he was three or four years old. But that night in Johnston City any newspaperman or TV journalist still sitting in the bleachers could see the *other* Minnesota Fats.

THE 1965 HUSTLERS' JAMBOREE, HELD SOME FOUR MONTHS AFTER LAS VEGAS, SEVEN MONTHS AFTER THE NEW YORK WORLD'S STRAIGHT-POOL TOURNAMENT, WOULD BE AMONG THE LAST FOR FATS. Lassiter also was a no-show. But other top players made the October 20 through November 17 pilgrimage: Worst, Handsome Danny Jones, Boston Shorty, Jersey Red. Great numbers of the media came as well: newspapermen from Chicago and Philly, TV crews, magazine shooters. Tickets went for seven bucks each. George Jansco's country circus had begun.

"The action will be filmed by an ABC-TV crew busily engaged in setting up myriad lights and miles of wiring for the event," the *Marion Daily Republican* reported. "Stationary cameras are located directly overhead and at the south end of the table. A mobile camera above the pit at the north end of the table will give viewers a clear view of every shot made during the program."

Dottie Breit, Jersey Red's new bride, remembers watching that long action session between Cuban Joe and Minnesota Fats. It went down in the Cue Club, the private sanctuary out back, after the regular action concluded at the Showbar. The game was one-pocket, Fats's game, but he had given away too much weight—that is, a handicap—and Cuban Joe began running balls effortlessly. When Fats missed that blue two—an easy shot—a shot he should have made, a shot he *had* to make, Cuban Joe came to the table, lined up the shot, and fired. Fats had left the table wide open, unprotected, and Cuban Joe started raining down balls like it was judgment day.

Oh shit. Oh fucking shit!

Dottie and Red watched the humiliation from the stands. They watched as Fats got the worst of it, and they watched as his avuncular *how-ya-doin'* bullshit turned mean and profane. His curses spewed forth as if from a garden hose. *You mother-fucking, shit-licking goddamned ASSHOLE.* Red couldn't take it. At the 7-11, Red would have matched Fats word for word. But not now, not with Dottie there at his side. "Hey, man," he said, standing from the bleachers. "Just shut your filthy mouth. There are *ladies* present."

Red was hot. This was his princess, and he could not tolerate any disre-
spect "That's just how he was," said Dottie. And Red gingerly took his Texas
bride by the hand and together they walked from the room. The journalists
paid off their side bets. Cuban Joe cleaned up.

**ON OCTOBER 21, ON THE TOURNAMENT'S SECOND DAY, RED STRUNG
TOGETHER FOUR STRAIGHT NINE-BALL VICTORIES TO BEAT JOE
PROCITA 11-6.** The show dazzled everyone—the press, the sweating
railbirds, the competition. Dottie beamed from the bleachers as her talented
husband ran off rack after rack. "The left-hander gave added indication that he
could be the man to be beat for all the marbles," the *Marion Daily Republican*
reported after the match. Four days later Red beat Tom Cosmo twice: once
in the nine-ball division (11-6), and then again in straight pool (125-108).
The next day Red ran over Cornbread Red, the wild-man one-pocket
specialist from Detroit. On November 1 he took down Al Coslosky of Philly,
125-68, in straight pool.

In fact, Red continued undefeated in all three divisions for half the tournament. Not until November 3 did he drop a game, when he got upended by
Racine's Al Miller in one-pocket. The two players had been tied at three
games when suddenly Racine got hot. A quick succession of tough shots
from Miller drew applause from the gathered pros. Red went down 4-3.

Red beat Coslosky again four days later—again in straight pool—and then
played a nail-biter against Joe Procita on November 9. Procita won three straight
in the one-pocket match, putting Red down 3-0 in the race to four. But then Red
won the next four in a row. The unexpected victory eliminated Procita from that
division. With a victory a few days later, Red likewise eliminated Al Miller.

But somehow, in the end, it didn't quite come together. It was as if those early successes in all three divisions had begun working against him. While others would get eliminated from one division or the other, Red continued playing in all three. He played back-to-back matches in two or three divisions against well-rested opponents who were then competing in only one division. And as the tournament progressed, the days got longer for Red. The sessions went on for hours. It was exhausting.

Boston Shorty, Red's old 7-11 nemesis, eventually emerged victorious in the one-pocket division. In straight pool, Red defeated all challengers but one: Harold Worst. The winner of that year's Stardust Tournament also won the nine-ball division and the overall competition.

Red took second place in straight pool, fourth overall, a check for $1,000. And then suddenly, as if returning to a troubling, unfinished dream, he and Dottie were back on the road.

That old black river seemed to flow on forever.

11
THE WOLF

"The undershirt is the most foolish item in a man's wardrobe.
I shall never wear one again."

—Luther Lassiter, Johnston City, Illinois, November 1963

I
N LATE 1965, *BOWLERS JOURNAL* AND *BILLIARD REVUE* SUMMED UP PREVAILING THOUGHT THEN CIRCULATING ABOUT WIMPY LASSITER. His "domination of pooldom," the magazine reported, "has apparently ended." Such a conclusion was easy to make. In 1965 the drawling hypochondriac from Elizabeth City (as *Bowlers Journal* would call him) lost all the big tournaments. And then 1966 came along and Lassiter kept losing.

In February, for instance, Lassiter placed third behind Joe Balsis and Jersey Red at the U.S. Invitational Pocket Billiards event held in Long Beach. He had a chance at that title until running into Red, who sent him through the meat grinder during a tie breaker play-off.[23] He then went on to lose to Joe Balsis at both the U.S. Open in Chicago, and the Hustlers' Jamboree in Johnston City. He failed to take even a single division.

----

[23] With victories in Las Vegas and Johnston City, Harold Worst arguably would have been considered the tournament favorite. But Worst had received bad news three years earlier: doctors diagnosed him with lymphoma, a cancer of the lymph glands. He was literally dying on his feet during the 1965 competitions, and likely too ill to compete at Long Beach. Worst died that summer—on June 15, 1966—at Blodgett Memorial Hospital in Grand Rapids, Michigan. His death came just one year after his spectacular conquest of pocket billiards—and while he still held the U.S. three-cushion title. He was thirty-seven.

Lordy.

But even if the press, the fans, and the railbirds had lost faith in Wimpy Lassiter, Wimpy Lassiter had not lost faith in himself. Yes, he was tired, sad, and worn out. Yes, he was without children, parents, or friends. Yes, he was...*disappearing*. But it didn't matter. None of it mattered. For there still lived within that old heart, way down deep, a secret knowledge that warmed him a bit.

Luther Lassiter understood that he possessed one thing in life, and one thing alone. It was both his gift and his curse.

Luther Lassiter could still pocket balls like a son of a bitch.

The following year, in January 1967, just as the Long Beach Invitational Tournament of Champions got underway at the Lafayette Hotel, Luther Lassiter made a dramatic declaration.

The desire to play pool, he said, had utterly left him.

And then he demolished straight-pool ace Johnny Ervolino.

Held in Long Beach, California, the twenty-two-day tournament attracted the usual crew: Jimmy Moore, Las Vegas's Ed Kelly,[24] the great Cicero Murphy of New York, and Jersey Red. Like Johnston City, the Long Beach tournament featured straights, one-pocket, and nine-ball. A play-off would determine the overall winner.

Lassiter fared especially well in straight pool. After running 121 and out against Ervolino, he went on to bust Balsis, Kelly, and Cowboy Jimmy Moore. Only one player surpassed that performance during the early going: Jersey Red. Playing straights, the fast-talking northerner sailed past Kelly, Murphy, and Moore. At his specialty, one-pocket, Red took down one of few players

---

[24] Winner of the 1966 Johnston City nine-ball and one-pocket divisions.

considered his equal at that game: Burbank's Ronnie Allen. The California hustler fell three games to four.

With both Lassiter and Red in top form, a showdown seemed inevitable. It came, finally, during an evening match—straight pool, 150 points—near the tournament's end. Lassiter and Red possessed nearly identical division records and both needed this single victory to advance. Red, however, had control of the table and was running balls effortlessly. And everything seemed in order for the northerner: the shape unfolded like a flower; the balls found their targets; whitey remained the obedient, well-heeled dog.

All Lassiter could do was wait.

Red methodically clicked off points; an unsmiling referee kept score. *Seventy-five for Mr. Breit. One hundred one for Mr. Breit. One hundred twenty-two for Mr. Breit.* At ball 145 Red tangled himself up. He made the shot, but got lousy shape. Standing just five balls short of victory, Red confronted a difficult choice: go for a tough cut and gamble victory against a sell-out; go for the safety and let Lassiter back to the table.

With a forty-five-ball edge, with victory so tantalizingly close, Red chose offense. He would not willingly let Lassiter back to the table—not even with a difficult shot. The spectators watched in amazement as Red sighted down his cue; they watched as Red's ball cut neatly across the table; they gasped as the bill struck the pocket jaws and rattled dead.

The bastard ball would not go in. He returned to his seat.

Lassiter began almost wearily running racks. He put together combinations. He sank long treacherous banks and awkward cuts. He slid the object ball down the rail, or caromed it off the pocket's edge, cheating it, while sending whitey to break clusters. Red watched his forty-five-ball lead melt away. Lassiter would not stop.

And then, with but three balls remaining—three balls between himself and victory—Wimpy took a moment to survey the damage. He reviewed the table and then affixed his gaze upon his young opponent. It was as if Wimpy suddenly felt the weight of his years, and the loneliness, and understood what he had become.

The fire that burned within him—his passion for pool—had melted away more than Jersey Red's lead. Lassiter was more than halfway through his life and yet remained without children, friends, or love. The burning ember of his passion, the certainty of his greatness, the magic of his right arm: these things had distilled Lassiter down to his essential core. He was forty-eight years old. And he felt every damn second of it. That fire had left but one thing: *Victory.*

Wimpy held Jersey Red in his baleful gaze, and with neither malice nor disdain nor anger summed up the burden of his long years and evaporating life.

"Sometimes," he said, "Forty-eight seems like eighty."

Jersey Red could not smile, but neither could he turn away.

Wimpy beat Red that day, and then posted victories in the straight-pool semifinals, finals, and eventually the division play-offs. On January 28, the final day of the tournament, Lassiter played fourteen hours straight. He began with an early afternoon match, kept playing throughout the evening and into the night. Between innings, he sat "sprawled in his seat, straddle-legged, tie-loosened, looking wilted, exhausted, and an eyelash away from sleep."[25] But by 3:40 a.m. no other player remained standing.

Lassiter, the tired and old Luther Lassiter, was back.

---

[25] According to a tournament report in a March, 1967 issue of the *Bowlers Journal and Billiard Revue.*

"I DO BELIEVE I NEED AN OLD-FASHIONED." The southerner wore a rust-colored sports shirt, no tie, a dark brown suit jacket. He seemed his usual, ill-at-ease self, as if forever constrained by ill-fitting trousers. Frank McGown, a respectable straight-pooler from New York City, had just trounced Wimpy badly. It was Lassiter's first defeat during the 1967 World Championship, sponsored that March by the Billiard Room Proprietors of America and held in the Terrace Ballroom of the Hotel Statler-Hilton in New York City. It came two months after Lassiter's resurgent victory in California.

"Now, lawdie, I ask you, sir, wasn't that just awful?" Luther said as he sidled up to the hotel bar. "Why that danged rascal McGown played a real slowdown on me, he did indeed."

Lassiter now stood with a 10-1 record. Jersey Red and Joe Balsis nipped at his heels with 9-2s. Only a few days remained. With journalist Tom Fox at his elbow, Lassiter had passed into the Penn Bar, at the far corner of the lobby. With them was one Nubby Cheek, a husky, square-shouldered used-car salesman from North Carolina, close to Luther's age. Nubby was an old friend and so bought the first round. The date was March 30, 1967.

"A great drink for *unlaxing*," said Lassiter as he savored the sweetness of his Old Fashioned. "Oh, they tell me there's no such word as unlaxing, but they don't know. They watch a man shoot a game of pool and they don't know how he's burning inside. That's why I've got to unlax some with my old-fashioned here. Yes, sir, a mighty fine drink. A little whisky and a slice of orange. I do believe they might put a li'l sugar in it, too, 'cause it tastes mighty, mighty sweet. Yes, sir, mighty, mighty sweet."

Lassiter turned to Nubby: "You married again?" he asked.

"Oh, hell yes, Wimp," said Nubby. In fact, it was his new bride that had brought him to New York—he'd come to buy her a diamond ring, and that's when he saw Luther's picture in the newspapers. "She's my third wife and a beauty," said Nubby. "She's looking to give you a preaching about that article in the New York paper today.

"My wife read the article and she said, 'Nubby, I've got to meet your friend, Mr. Lassiter, and straighten him out on age and marriage.' See, Wimp, this one's twenty years younger than me, but she's a helluva woman. She's right over here. Wait, I'll go fetch her, Wimp. She sure wants to meet you, boy."

Tom Fox, in a May 1967 article for *The Bowlers Journal and Billiard Revue*, described Mrs. Cheek as a "lovely thing—a tall, dark-haired belle with a drawl as thick as cotton." She told Wimpy that he simply must visit, that he must come home soon, and that she'd get him dates with pretty young girls. "A man should never marry unless his wife's twenty years younger—at least twenty years," she said.

"That's right, Wimpy," said Nubby. "I'm a happy man married to this pretty chile."

Fox recalled how Lassiter blushed. The stories of Lassiter's *swolls*—that is, the painful swelling of his lips whenever he was confronted with the affection of a pretty girl, had become the stuff of legend. And yet Lassiter was tired of being on his own. Perhaps he was now ready for a new case of the *swolls*. "Well, now—if you can arrange something like that, Mrs. Cheek, I'll be mighty pleased to drop in on you folks one day real soon, ma'am."

Lassiter allowed that he'd have one more drink—another old-fashioned— but across the street at McAnn's Saloon. The Penn Bar was closing. And so Fox and Lassiter continued their conversation, and Lassiter drank more than one old-fashioned—*Why looka here, Mr. Bartender, I seem to have hit a dry hole down here*—while ruminating on a lonely life.

"Being forty-eight and a cantankerous old bachelor, I have no family. Not anymore. Oh, the old home place is still there on Pearl Street, in Elizabeth City, but nobody really lives there anymore. I'm always in Norfolk and my brother, Charles, he's still home, but he's mighty sick. The rest of the children are all married, so nobody's ever home. Nobody's there since Mama died...

"I never really appreciated home until Mama went away," he continued. The whisky had taken hold. It felt warm, comforing. "Oh, I always seemed to be off shooting a silly game of pool somewhere when Mama was alive and well. Then one day they called and said Mama was going to die. The cancer had Mama in an awful weak state...

"So I went home. I went home because I knew Mama was going to die. We were all there, all of Mama's children came to be with her...We spent all our time with Mama. We took her for long rides in the country, and we passed the afternoons and evenings with her. Every last one..."

Lassiter prattled on for a while, about Elizabeth City, and brother Charles, and his beloved home on Pearl Street. He spoke of solitude and love. And then he called for one last drink before shuffling back to his room on the tenth floor of the Statler-Hilton. Tomorrow would be a big day.

"Man is the strangest of all the Lord's creatures," he said, finally. "The trouble with man is he doesn't know how to live...I'm a pool player, so they ask me, 'Haven't you done anything with your life except shoot pool? Haven't you ever worked?' I always tell them, 'Well, no, sir, I can't say that I've ever worked.' That always gets those rascals, 'cause they always ask, "But how have you managed to live?' Oh, Lawdie, that's so silly.

"I tell them, 'Sir, I live like a tree—3 percent from the soil and 97 percent from the air.' You know, that's true."

THE VERY NEXT AFTERNOON, THE VERY HUNGOVER LUTHER LASSITER GOT BEAT. Joe Balsis, who was then tied with Jersey Red for second place, played repeated safeties on the southerner. Lassiter held an early lead—at one point, he was up forty to minus three—but he couldn't sustain it. Twice he violated the three-scratch rule (by scratching on three consecutive innings) and thereby sacrificed thirty crucial points. Final score: Balsis 150. Lassiter 75.

But that safety strategy would not work against Jersey Red, whom Balsis faced during the second featured match of the day. Balsis found himself reeling from Red's spectacular hundred-ball run in the first inning. Red then continued sinking balls, one after another, while the seemingly defenseless Balsis foundered like a stricken warship. After falling behind by 111 points, Joe finally managed a few good safeties to slow the hard-charging northerner. But too late. Balsis fell 150-71.

Red's victory catapulted him to one final match against Lassiter. At stake: the American straight-pool championship. The date: April 1, 1967. And so, before TV lights and newspapermen, Red and Wimpy bent down low, took a few practice strokes, lagged downtable. One final game. The show was on.

Dottie, a picture of southern beauty, sat near the front, smoking and fidgeting. She knew Lassiter had several titles to his name. She knew that Red, as he bent low to lag that ball downtable, dreamed of his first. She watched the balls sail to the end rail, drift back slowly over nine feet, and then settle up close to the rail. Lassiter won the lag and gave Red the opening break, a disadvantage in straight pool.

Red stood for a moment to envision the shot. He did not look to break open the rack, or even to pocket a ball. In straight pool, every ball must be called. And because calling a ball off the opening break is a very low percentage undertaking, Red would instead attempt to play safe. Just drift the cue ball downtable, hit the far edge of the triangle of balls, and then—if everything goes right—bring whitey back uptable, where it would nudge against the near rail, or maybe settle into the jaws of a corner pocket. If he could do it just right, he would leave Wimpy with no shot, or a very difficult one.

In a single, deft motion, Red set the cue ball back behind the head string—into that rectangular part of the table called the kitchen—and began pumping off left-arm practice strokes. His cigarette smoldered in an ashtray on a small, high-runged table set off to one corner of the playing area. He fired whitey downtable. It gently nudged the far end of the racked balls. Red watched as two of those balls separated from the rack, slowly, and then hit nearby rails.

But they did not scurry back. They did not come home.

Red had applied too little force—just a fraction of a foot-pound off—but there it was: an open shot. Two object balls remained free from the stack: unprotected, vulnerable.

Red had left a horrible open shot.

And so Luther Clement Lassiter, the rattling and snuffling and aching southerner, ambled to the table, surveyed the lay, and quietly began picking off balls. *Five in the side. Four in the corner. Three in the side.* He hit the opening shot, and he hit more. He moved from one side to the other. He went uptable and down. He made every shot easily, leaving whitey always just twelve or fifteen inches from the object ball. He played straight pool as it was meant to be played: quietly, methodically, with southern grace. The *New York Times* called Wimpy's opening run "brilliance."

And it would not end for four racks.

Finally, on ball sixty-four, Lassiter left the table. But unlike Red, he left no open shot, no vulnerable balls. The game, as reported by the *Times*, then "developed into a battle of strategic safeties and intentional scratches." The score went from 89-2, 113-8, 120-18, 144-31—each time, Lassiter's favor.

At 2:15 a.m., after sixteen innings of hiding and ducking and before two hundred stalwart fans, Wimpy Lassiter earned his third BRPAA national title. Jersey Red had managed late-game runs of twenty-nine and twenty-four, but it would not be enough to overcome Lassiter's early surge. The final tally: 150-73. Red had lost the national title with his opening break.

When it was all over, Lassiter gulped down three pills.

"Good for whatever ails you," he muttered, "and today I had myself a few ailments. I did, indeed. Lawdie, it sure was a horrible day."

BRPAA officials awarded Lassiter a trophy and a $3,000 check. Red received a second-place check, a picture taken with Lassiter, a big kiss from Dottie. "I'm proud of you," she said.

LASSITER WOULD THEN GO ON TO WIN THAT YEAR'S JOHNSTON CITY MEET, HELD AGAIN IN NOVEMBER, DESPITE STRONG COMPETITION FROM RED, IRVING CRANE, AND OTHERS. Fats, by contrast, never even showed up. He had competed in the first two Johnston City tournaments, bombed out in each, and then boycotted most of the rest. But probably not from spite or sour grapes. Rather, Fats simply had become too busy, too big for Johnston City.

Or at least, that's what's Georgie Jansco figured.

"Him and my dad got a little separated, because he wouldn't come down," said JoAnn Jansco, Georgie's daughter. "I remember my daddy making the statement that he had helped him [Fats] to where he was, and he was not coming back and helping my dad make his deal bigger. He [Fats] just wouldn't have no part of it. And so they weren't close anymore. Fats wouldn't come down. He was too much of a big shot. He just got too busy. He got too big."

So that's how it went: Fats helped create Georgie; Georgie helped create Fats. The Johnston City tournaments drew the media, just as Fats did—and the two became mixed together in the public's mind. Georgie even set aside a personal parking space for Fats's fat caddy.

But then Fats simply stopped coming.

Fats, by the late 1960s, had managed to land two TV deals: *Celebrity Billiards with Minnesota Fats* and *Minnesota Fats Hustles the Pros.* The first featured the likes of Milton Berle. The second featured Lassiter, Jersey Red, and Jimmy Moore. Fats usually got trounced. Not that it mattered.

Fats's old friend Tom Fox, the writer who made both Fats and Johnston City famous, also approached him with the idea for a book. Fox had managed to sell the notion to Roy Channells, senior vice-president of World Publishing Company, after meeting him outside a taxicab in New York City. He explained that Minnesota Fats was as crazy as a sprayed roach. It would be a surefire hit.

Getting Fats to cooperate was another matter. Although Fats loved the attention, getting him to sit still was nearly impossible. Fox did all the writing: all Fats had to do was be Fats. "But he would go into these rages," recalled Karen Fox, Tom's widow. "They were kind of funny. He would just have these ego attacks. And so Evelyn would have to fill in the blanks so Tom could get the book out." The result of this tense corroboration was *The Bank Shot and Other Great Robberies*, an autobiography published the next year. Karen Fox acknowledged that the book, written supposedly in Fats's voice, was largely based on Evelyn's recollections. "It was just too hard to get him to fill in the glue between all his little gems," said Karen.

And then the legend continued to grow. *Sports Illustrated, Rolling Stone,* and *Esquire* published profiles. He made more TV appearances. Fat checks rolled into his Du Quoin post office box. He hobnobbed with celebrities at the Illinois State Fair. "Hell, ABC was in town half the time," said Dowell mayor Luciano Lencini. "Him and Howard Cosell would come into the tavern laughing. He'd give them a song and dance, you know. Hell, he drew them here. He was just a wicked hustler."

"LISTEN, THE MATCH TONIGHT IS GOING TO BE ONE OF THE BEST OF THE TOURNAMENT." Paulie Jansco had brought *Playboy* writer Craig Vetter back into his office. And there, in a rapid-fire monologue, he listed both the games and the players of the 1969 Hustler Jamboree, held, as always, in Johnston City, Illinois. Lassiter had reached the one-pocket finals against one of one-pocket's best: LA's Ronnie Allen.

And Lassiter *hated* one-pocket.

"Luther's going to be way over his head against Allen in one-pocket," explained Paulie. "In nine-ball or straight pool, he'd eat Allen alive, but in one-pocket, it ought to be the other way around. It'll be a good match. Luther's a pro, he's been playing pool for thirty-eight years and when he goes down into that pit, he goes to shoot. No matter what, there'll be some no-forgiveness one-pocket pool in there tonight."

Paulie explained the particulars: "The trick is to keep your opponent from having a shot," he told Vetter. "You hide the cue ball: behind the pack, on the wrong rail, anywhere you can. Just so you leave the other guy nasty. That's called playing safe. It's maybe the toughest game in pocket billiards, because you have to know how to shoot straight, bank, play combinations, perfect position; and hardest of all, you have to know how to shoot a safety. It's a nervous game, gives everybody those sneak-up kind of heart attacks. It's beautiful."

In the pit, two new tables received a final brush-down. About three hundred fans settled down into the grandstand seats surrounding the tables. Others stood on chairs behind the grandstand, or found spots along the aisles. It was about 7:30 p.m.

Allen—head-to-toe in mod clothes: bell-bottoms, a shirt with loose long sleeves and a large pointed collar, vermilion corduroy cap—strolled in through the back. He was about thirty years old, cocky, laughing, smiling. He overheard a few spectators placing bets on the match. He turned to one, a man wagering on Lassiter.

"You want to bet? I'll take your bet. What do you want?"

"Seven to five on a hundred."

"*Seven to five?*" Vetter, the *Playboy* correspondent witnessing the exchange, wrote that the LA hustler was shouting. "Man, do you know who I'm playing? Lassiter—*Luther Lassiter*—and you want seven to five?"

The man remained unconvinced, insistent. Seven to five or nothing. Allen turned to a stakehorse, apparently one of several. "Take it," he told him.

Vetter wrote that Lassiter was wearing a white shirt, dark tie, gray sports coat. He quietly seated himself on a stool at the corner of the pit, one foot on the ground, one foot on the crossbar, his head slightly tilted to the left. He held in his hand a Balabushka cue.

"Ladies and gentlemen," said Paulie, who had now stepped into the center of the pit. "Welcome to the ninth annual World All-Around Pocket Billiards Championship…Tonight, we'll crown a one-pocket champ in either Ronnie 'Fast Eddie' Allen of Burbank, California, or Luther 'Wimpy' Lassiter, of Elizabeth City, North Carolina. The best four out of seven games will win."

The lights dimmed on all but one of the tables. "May I lag, Mr. Lassiter?" says Allen.

"Yes, sir, I hope it's your pleasure."

The two men sailed their balls downtable and back again. Lassiter's ball came closest to the near rail, and so he made Allen break. The LA hustler applied a bit of outside English on the cue ball, sending it into the rack. It glanced off two balls—the six and the three, according to Vetter—and then settled along the rail on Lassiter's side. A textbook, nearly perfect safety. Allen returned to the stool, where he took up his cigarette.

Lassiter took deep breaths, almost gasping, and blinked painfully. He shook his head back and forth, chalking his cue. "Boy, I wish you'd put me out of my misery," he muttered. But Lassiter still managed to play a safety, and a tough one at that.

"Very pretty," said Allen. But then, using a carom, he managed to send whitey uptable and back, and nestle it into the rack. The shot brought applause, much of it from those with money on the game. He had left Lassiter even worse than before.

Lassiter shook his head nervously as he returned to the table. He could see just one shot, and it was dangerous. He could attempt a tough kick combination. Failure would mean a sell-out—but with no possible safety, Allen had forced his hand. And so Lassiter bent to shoot, then straightened again to reexamine the table, bent again, fired. Whitey hit the rail, came back perfectly, smashed open the rack. The five ball scurried forward, disappearing into Lassiter's pocket. The yelping and clapping began even before it dropped.

The position looked good, and Lassiter had room to move. He knocked the two ball in with a thin cut; he knocked the three straight in; he banked the eleven; he sent the six downrail; he banked the four. "Mr. Lassiter shooting for two," said the referee. Lassiter easily knocked in the fifteen, but then saw that he had gotten stuck again and so played safe. "Mr. Lassiter needs one ball to win," said the referee.

Allen had one possible, wretched shot. He put his eye very close to his possible target—the seven, nestled at the rail. Very close, but not frozen. It sat about a foot from Allen's pocket. Whitey sat on the opposite side of the table, behind an insurmountable cluster of balls.

Allen took the shot, sending whitey downtable, off the side rail, and into the seven. Perfect. The seven slid a foot down the rail, fell into Allen's pocket. The crowd clapped wildly—some even spilled their drinks. "The blitz is on," said Allen. And without hesitation, he banked the eight, knocked the one straight in, sent the thirteen along the rail, sent the ten straight in, cut in the nine, knocked in the fourteen. In not much more than a minute or two, Allen had sunk seven balls. Both players needed just one to win: the twelve.

Allen bent to shoot. He knocked the twelve against the rail, and it came back unerringly. But then it hit the side of the pocket and jawed out. "Should have had a hamburger," cracked Allen, returning to his seat.

Lassiter, however, had nearly nothing. The twelve sat dangerously close to Allen's pocket. Only a cross-table bank was possible, and a miss meant a scratch—and almost certain defeat. "Don't miss," said Allen.

Lassiter knocked the twelve against the long rail on Allen's side of the table, and then it slowly, slowly went toward Lassiter's pocket. "Will it go?" Allen asked, stretching from his stool.

"It will, my boy, it will."

By the end of it, as usual, the old veteran seemed haggard and worn out. His entire body trembled. And yet with patience and defense, Lassiter had out-smarted the younger player. He would shoot a ball here, a ball there, and then play safe; Allen would knock in five or six balls in quick succession, but then get stuck. Lassiter became the old tortoise who defeated the mocking hare.

During the final game, a drunk in a tweed jacket who bet twenty-five dollars on Lassiter began to shriek: "Atta boy, *Wimpy!* Did ya see that, Chuck? He never misses that cut." The drunk stood from his chair. Allen smiled, weakly, shaking his head. "Nice and easy, nice and easy, *goddamn*, look at that!" The drunk clapped and yelped and whistled. "He's still the greatest, Chuck! Shit. Come on, *Wimpy!*"

12

THE HUSTLER KING

"First time I ever got busted for eating a bowl of soup."

—*Jersey Red, 1969*

LAS VEGAS, NEV., DEC. 5, 1969 (AP) *Luther Lassiter of Elizabeth City, N.C., won the fourth annual United States open-pocket billiard championship today with consecutive victories over Jack Breit of Houston.*

Lassiter, who had been defeated in a game earlier in the four-night event by Steve Mizerak of Carteret, N.J., downed Breit, 150-114, and 150-124, in the double elimination tournament.

Jersey Red played until his legs grew heavy like pea gravel, until his left shoulder—up above that smooth, smooth piston arm—grew hot like fire. He played day after day, dispatching Cicero Murphy and Boston Shorty and Weenie Beenie and all the giants, one by one, who sometimes grew scornful in defeat, leaving the table with an evil scowl or harrumph. He shot down Cowboy Jimmy Moore. And Irving Crane. And Handsome Danny Jones. And all the while, Jack kept smiling, kept pocketing balls, kept convincing himself he could beat anyone. Anyone.

Jack witnessed his own greatness in the eyes of the bleacher-sitting, cigar-champing sweators, who murmured and nodded as he tore off fifties and sixties. And he saw his greatness in the adoring but sometimes mournful gaze of Dottie, sitting there too, with her great big hair and long cigarettes.

And soon, very soon, Jack felt his greatness would be known to the whole wide world. For it seemed then, as he lined up shots in Las Vegas, Nevada, on network television during the 1969 U.S. Open of Straight Pool, that Jack "Jersey Red" Breit really would be king.

There is no one, no one, pockets the way I do. Evah! No-where! I pocket impossible shots, nevuh-heard-of-shots, I run balls forever. I just don't stop.

But then came the finals—the championship match—with the possum-grinning Wimpy Lassiter shuffling to the table, complaining about his sinuses, about his ulcers, always distracted, but somehow managing a smile. The two locked eyes—Wimpy's periwinkle blues on Jack's gimlet greens—and the two shook hands, reaching across four and a half feet of green felt, fifteen colored balls, TV lights, big time. And Wimpy, with small, deft hands, pieced together his two-piece cue with the lucky silver dollar embedded in the butt. And Jack put together his, too, and the two lagged for the break, drifting balls silent like fog over an algae pond, and the balls returned, landing on the near rail.—*Thud*. Wimpy wins the lag.

It was then that Jack began to hear the whispering doubt, like a question in the back of his mind, too faint to grasp, nagging at him from somewhere deep in his heart. He refused to embrace it. And under those big lights and big cameras, he managed runs of twenties, thirties, and more. The balls fell one-two-three, his left arm worked like a machine, he sighted down his cue.

And when he finally left the table, he stood far ahead in the ball count, and he left nothing to shoot. Red could have left whitey buried in the rack, awkward, but instead he decided to drop it along the near rail with no way to actually pocket a ball. None. Just to get safe, Wimpy needed to navigate a long, treacherous cut. It was, as anyone could see, a layout fraught with peril. Wimpy misses: Jack wins. The calculation was simple.

Lassiter understood this, but it didn't matter. It never seemed to matter. Without much hesitation, he got down over the balls and fired away, shooting safe right back. And then it began: guerrilla warfare. The two went back and forth, shooting and ducking, until Wimpy finally got a clear shot. He opened a big run on Jack, pocketing balls, one after another. And no matter how many balls dropped for Jack, Wimpy came back with more, always more, a great goddamned torrent of balls showering into every hole—on the left side, on the right, all the way downtable—colors exploding beneath TV lights and smoke whorls. And when Wimpy got bad at the end, when he lost the shape and there was no good shot, no good safety—that's when the banks began, and the impossible combinations and the long, evil cuts.

And Red could only sit and watch, and that whispered question became louder, more distinct. *Are you really the best?* The whispering turned to fear, and fear never arrives alone. Always in tow comes her bitch sister: defeat.

Jack placed second at the Las Vegas Open, losing twice to Lassiter, 150-114 and 150-124. He returned to Houston, as he had many times in the past, with the second-place check and not even half the glory.

"Lassiter, at age forty-nine, won about everything there was to win," recalled Jack's old friend John "Duke" Dowell. "Red played Lassiter numerous times—either in the tournament at Johnston City or Los Angeles—and he beat Lassiter about as many times as Lassiter beat him. But Red [during those years] hardly ever beat him in a tournament or a championship and he would be frustrated about that a little bit. A couple of times, he thought he should have won, that he had Wimpy locked up, and that Wimpy would just run out on him and Red wouldn't shoot again."

For Jack, those also-ran finishes had become a curse. He placed second at the 1966 World Straight Pool tournament, second at the 1967 World

Straight Pool tournament, second at the 1969 U.S. Open. Always there in front of him, blocking his path, stood Wimpy Lassiter.

IN SEPTEMBER 1969, A FEW MONTHS BEFORE WIMPY BEAT RED IN THE U.S. OPEN, HOUSTON POOLROOM OWNER DON S. SIEGEL SPONSORED A NATIONAL-CLASS POOL TOURNAMENT. Dubbed the Houston Invitational Nine-Ball Tournament of Champions, the event was conducted in double round-robin fashion—that is, each player matched up twice against every other player. The player with the most wins at the end of fourteen days would receive the first-place trophy, a write-up in the local newspaper, appropriate glory. The game was nine-ball—Wimpy's specialty—with matches played to eleven.

Siegel held the tournament at his downtown room, the Le Cue, and hired Dottie to assign the tables, organize players, book hotel rooms—all the innumerable and mind-numbing details that go into running such events. He also paid for transportation and accommodations for the out-of-towners, put up prize money ($2,500 for first), and contacted the newspapermen and television stations. But in an uncharacteristic move for a southerner, Siegel elected to begin the tournament on September 1—when the city remained in the heavy, sweaty, suffocating embrace of summer.

Although other Americans migrate south to celebrate the heat, most true southerners despise it. They complain constantly of how it sweat-drenches their work shirts; of the burning, blinding sun everywhere, blasting an entire city like a nuclear bomb; of the horror, the *true horror*, of a broken air conditioner. And the spring, although beloved elsewhere, only reminds Houstonians of the approaching nastiness. Everywhere in the Parking Lot

---

City, with its miles of eight-lane freeways and chains of smoke-belching oil refineries and shimmering pavement, are sweat and indolence. This is summer in Houston.

For pool players, the dog days also brought slow and treacherous tables. In the middle of the season—during the wretchedness of June and July—Siegel would turn the air conditioner up high, make it run hard. It was the only way to prevent a fleeing-customer exodus from the furnacelike second-story room. The air conditioner, in turn, created moisture, which, when combined with Houston's legendary humidity, both perceptibly slowed the balls' movement across the green felt and dulled play off the rails. Sauna nine-ball. Steam bath one-pocket. The Houston old-timers gleefully tell of Yankee hustlers sent packing, beaten in part by a strategic adjustment of the Le Cue thermostat.

An old hydraulic elevator squeaked up the side of the flat-roofed downtown building at Rusk and Fannin. Once up, the hustler found stucco walls, a lunch counter (serving soup, sandwiches, coffee, Coke, and draft beer), and high stools. Among the twenty or so tables were two for snooker, two giant five-by-tens (although only the half-brained would play Jersey Red on those monsters), and smaller four-and-a-half-by-nines. The walls were bare, as were the tile floors.

Like moths before summer lights, America's big-time hustlers came to Le Cue: drinking beer, popping pills, sweating games. Jersey Red, Handsome Danny Jones, Big Train Stevens—each victimized the unwary and the stupid. They climbed the tables, both feet dangling, neither foot on the floor, their bellies flat against green felt. Sprawling wino snipers hunting long balls, eyes intent.

Siegel tried to clean up the place for the 1969 tournament, tried to make it respectable, but to no avail. If anything, the action only increased. Duke said the tournament drew gambling men from throughout Texas—"the place was real crowded every night"—and that these men would get games or side-bet the games of others. "There were a lot of people there—people coming in from all over Texas, staying during the weekends, just showing up for the tournament," said Duke. "The big mistake was that Siegel hired two Harris County sheriff's department officers, and some of those idiots [pool players] were blatantly gambling in front of them. You know, the sheriff's department guys—one was working the front door, and the other was working the cash register—and they would occasionally walk through the crowd, and they probably saw people passing money."

Besides the cops, old newsmen like the mercurial Zarco Franks, a *Houston Chronicle* editor famous for his violent mood swings, and Tommy West, of the *Houston Post*, stood witness to the stakehorsing and side-betting. The TV guys arrived too—although less frequently—along with various other hangers-on, many of them back-slapping the players, buying drinks. Grady Mathews spent much of the event looking for one-pocket action. Mike Massey, the famous trick-shot artist, exchanged great wads of cash with local do-nothings.

Tens and twenties fell across green felt, accumulated in short stacks along the rail, fell into the wells of corner pockets. The stake money—the insurance premiums of gambling, the money set aside before action begins to ensure pay-off when it ends—that money got stashed, quite openly, in the Le Cue cash register. With a paper clip, Dottie affixed little slips of paper identifying the stakees: *Jack/Allen, Stevens/Allen, Duke/Massey.*

An explosive mixture of cops, hustlers, and newspapermen swirled together at Siegel's pool hall: the hustlers plied their trade, the newspapermen got drunk, the dick-faced cops marveled at the audacity of both. A tinderbox—that's what Don Siegel had created—a tinderbox of vice and arrogance. There was sure to be a reckoning.

RED STARTED THE TOURNAMENT STRONG, PLOWING THROUGH OPPONENTS WITHOUT PAUSE, WITHOUT MERCY. He quickly downed Jones, Big Train Stevens, and Richie Florence. Cicero Murphy and Cowboy Jimmie Moore also fell. Only Fort Worth's U. J. Puckett—that "sharking son of a bitch" from Fort Worth, as Duke called him—beat Red during the early going. By the midway point of the tournament, that loss to Puckett was Red's only loss.

But Lassiter at that midway point had also suffered but one loss. Red and Wimpy were like two Thoroughbreds running neck and neck—with the rest of the field, the Big Trains and the Handsome Dans, fading away. And it was here, during that last sickening stretch, with Red's stroke uncoiling and the tension mounting, that he always seemed to fail. Always, *always*, would Wimpy Lassiter pass him by. And this was not one-pocket. This was not straight pool. This was nine-ball: this was Wimpy's game. He was the undisputed king, the world champion, the greatest shotmaker living, the greatest shotmaker that ever lived. And at Houston's Invitational Nine-Ball Tournament of Champions, Luther "Wimpy" Lassiter was the favorite—the absolute, hands-down, watch-him-go favorite. He was the emperor in ragged clothes, and Red knew it.

At the midway point of the tournament, Jersey Red confronted his old nemesis. The rivals had already played one another twice that year, perhaps as many as twenty or thirty times over the course of their careers. As the two lagged for the break, Red was probably remembering how many times Wimpy had beaten him in the past. He got to thinking about how Wimpy had lost just that one match so far in Houston—just that one against Richie Florence. He had easily plowed through the opposition, just as Red had, just like a knife through warm butter. And even though Wimpy ambled about in tired old leather shoes, always suffering, always looking as if he might collapse, he seemed unstoppable.

And so Red felt a twinge of nervousness in his stomach, and he likely felt that tightness along the back of his neck, and maybe he perceived that whispered doubt way down in the well of his soul. The doubt, he later said, that he always felt at precisely the wrong moment, with victory so tantalizingly close. Red won the lag and began taking his practice strokes. The tall northerner pushed his left arm back and forth and tried to focus.

Bang. The nine-ball rack exploded, obliterated, followed by a quick succession of pocketed balls. Red found his target easily, and found the shape. He won one game after another. He did not miss. But neither did Lassiter miss. Nor did he foul. And so the North Carolinian won games also, won them beneath a barrage of thunderclap breaks. He scattered colors across the green sea, drove balls like scurrying rats into holes.

The games went fast now, no time for thinking, no time for doubts, just play, concentrate, move, race to eleven. And Wimpy and Red would duck and shoot, duck and shoot, each grimacing when the shape unfolded less than perfect. The old spitting railbirds up in the bleachers watched and marveled. They clapped as Red sank cross-table banks, as Wimpy unleashed miraculous long shots. Sometimes the shape went bad, sometimes nothing dropped after the break, but both seemed incapable of missing.

Bang. Bang. Bang.

And then, somehow, under the lights and the whirling smoke, and the wheezing, hard-running air conditioner, it was over.

And Jersey Red had won.

The final tally, as the old men stretched from hard-ass bleachers and ambled back to the bar for coffee and Cokes, stood 11-8. Red stood atop the pile, in first place, waiting to get knocked down. He'd suffered only one loss. And straggling just behind, like some old hacking dog, came Lassiter, whose losses to Red and Florence put him in second. Wimpy, however, remained the tournament favorite. And then came the rest of the field: Florence, third; Stevens and Murphy tied for fourth; Jones and Allen tied for fifth; Puckett holding up the rear.

But to win, Red would have to amass the best record after going through the field *twice*. To win, he again would have to go through Danny Jones, winner of the 1967 Las Vegas Stardust Nine-Ball Open; and through U. J. Puckett, winner of the 1960 U.S. Nine-Ball Championship, and through old friend Cicero Murphy, sometimes called "Rush Out," winner of the 1965 World Tournament in Burbank. And then, of course there was his old nemesis, Lassiter, who had won just about everything there was to win, a man who had beaten Red plenty.

Success became more difficult in the second round. Allen, with whom Red matched up frequently in Le Cue one-pocket action, beat the northerner. Cicero Murphy beat Red as well. And catching up quickly was Lassiter, who galloped past Allen and Jimmy Moore and Murphy. For every match Red would win, Wimpy would win one of his own. Neck and neck—*Red and Wimpy, Red and Wimpy*—rushing to the finish.

But then, somewhere along the way, came Big Train Stevens—the dark horse of the tournament and a maniacal, pill-popping, 210-pound, fleshy freak.[26] He was a man whom Jersey Red described as "one of the best nine-ball players in the world," a man who could bust anyone, anyone, when the speed hit him just right.

Big Train Stevens was to play Wimpy Lassiter. And "it was," recalled Duke, "one of the damnedest matches ever."

----

[26] See Appendix II.

The time: 4 p.m. Stevens arrived that day looking fresh, as if he'd gotten himself some sleep. This was not a typical look for Big Train, who often played for days beneath the relentless whip of trucker's speed. "That Lassiter was the most shot-making son of a gun you ever saw, but Greg [Big Train] won the lag for the break and won six racks, just to start off," said Duke. "And he never won [any of those racks] off the break, you understand. He'd just break and run out. Then broke, made a ball of the break, and run out again."

And then Stevens, who was rested, fresh, playing against perhaps the most wondrous nine-ball player to ever wield a cue, got hooked. Duke said he remembered how it went: Wimpy kept racking and Big Train kept running, one game after the another, without pause, moving fast, pushed by amphetamines, eyes wild. And then, on that seventh game, after running six racks straight without a single miss, Big Train got hooked off the break. And so Big Train played a roll-out; that is, he made use of the rule whereby a player rolls the cue ball to an awkward position and allows his opponent to decide whether to shoot or pass.

And Wimpy, who had lost the lag, and who had not taken a single shot in six games, did not like what he saw. The cue ball had settled uptable against a rail, and the low ball remained nestled at the bottom, leaving no good shot, no good safety. This was not the roll-out to accept, Wimpy thought. This was craziness. And Stevens' luck, after all, would eventually have to end. And so the usually aggressive Lassiter, a man known for his never-heard-of shots, for his cut shots that no longer get cut, quietly returned to his seat. And to Big Train, he said, "Shoot it."

Big Train returned to the table, his pupils perhaps beginning to dilate from unseen lights and red bennies, looked at the lay he'd given himself. And old Wimpy sat there, his pupils slightly dilated too—maybe from his own pills, maybe from the darkness behind closed eyelids. He was a picture of deep contemplation, his head cradled in his open palm. "Shoot it," he had told Big Train. *Go ahead. Take it.*

"It was a long, tough cut shot, and Lassiter thought Greg was about ready to miss a ball, you know," recalled Duke. "But Greg wouldn't miss, *ever*, if you caught him in his stroke. Any time you ran into him like that, you wouldn't get to shoot. He'd get hit by that speed, just right, and he'd run out and run out and run out. And so he made that shot, and a bunch more, and ran out the other five games. Lassiter never got to shoot the whole session. He was hit by a barrage. And Lassiter was one hot sucker because of it."

WHAT SURPRISED EVERYONE ABOUT BIG TRAIN, OF COURSE, WAS THAT HE COULD PLAY AT ALL. Big Train, like many of the others, would get to gambling after the evening matches, throwing money back and forth on the tables, getting action where he could get it. But unlike Wimpy and Red and anybody else who hoped to actually *win* the Le Cue Invitational, Big Train wouldn't stop. For days he'd stagger around the tables, never leaving, getting sloppy, money everywhere, liable to have mustard and hamburger grease slicked down his shirt. The hours pounded on him like a mean boxer. After a while he smelled of beer and sweat and bad aftershave and cough drops. He smelled like shit.

And Big Train would gamble with anyone who gave him a game—or better yet, *weight*.[27] And so would Duke and Red and Richie Florence and just about anybody at that tournament, tossing money back and forth, stashing stakes in the cash box up front with Dottie, or below the tables, or into the

---

[27] A handicap. See glossary.

corner pockets. The action began every night at about 11 p.m., after the conclusion of the evening matches, and went on at every table, in every quadrant of Le Cue, in front of the women, in front of the tourists, in front of the newspapermen. And it went on in front of the brown-and-whites, the Harris County sheriff's deputies hired by Siegel to protect the joint; and they would stand at the front door grim-faced beneath their cowboy hats, watching as the obviously hopped-up Big Train and the brash Jersey Red and the sharking Puckett plied their larceny.

There was to be a reckoning, there had to be, and it came on September 11, 1969. It came near midnight.

The pool hall had cleared out a bit, but not too much. A security guard who worked the graveyard shift at the Texaco Building, across the street, had just come in to get some dinner. He ordered soup, as he did most nights at that hour. Several women were in the room too, including Dottie, who sat with Red at the lunch counter, smoking cigarettes. Red ordered a bowl of soup, which was ladled from a deep pot.

Not far away, on one of the tournament tables set up behind the yellow curtains strung up along the back of the room, Handsome Dan and Big Train waged pitched battle for high stakes. Duke, across the room, also found action. He had set up a short nine-ball match with Mike Massey, the renowned trick-shot artist, for forty bucks. Duke and Massey had left their stake money in the cash box, binding the roll with a paper clip, and were playing even. Duke doubted, however, that he could beat Massey.

Not far away, a light-haired man sat at a small table, watching the action. He looked familiar—real familiar—like an old football player. A linebacker for the Houston Oilers, maybe. He just sat there, looking grim, no cue, no game, no friends, smoking cigarettes. An old bookmaking acquaintance of Duke's thought he recognized this man, and went to ask about an upcoming Oilers game. "The football preseason had started, and this old man, this old-timer bookmaker, saw that guy sitting there and so he went over to show him the football line sheet," Duke recalled. "And the guy says, 'I don't know anything about that,' and the bookmaker says, "Didn't you play for the Oilers?" and he said, 'Not me.' And it was at about that time that somebody said the police were there."

And so Duke, thinking he knew what was what, left his game with Mike Massey and approached this man, and asked respectfully, kindly, in his least-turdlike voice: "Sir, are you a member of the Houston Police Department?" Duke, of course, had heard the story that if you ask a cop up front to identify himself, he has to comply. Because that's the law. Plainclothes or not, cops couldn't just go around *lying*. But, of course, they could, and this one did, although it hardly mattered because at that very instant, suddenly, every-where, coming out of the walls, there were cops. They came streaming up from the stairwell like marines—the plainclothes guys and the harness bulls—arresting everybody, *everybody*, and the players scattered, but not before the TV cameras arrived, and then more newspapermen.

Duke, seeing Danny Jones getting jacked up by the cops, rushed to the cash box to retrieve the stake money ("cuz, sometimes, the cops will just *swaller* that"). But he had hardly taken two steps when he felt his arm pushed up behind his back, and a cop breathing into his ear, hot, but not too threatening. It was the stranger, former Oiler defensive back Bobby Jancik, now of the Houston Police Department vice squad. Plain clothes.

"And where do you think *you're* going?" growled Jancik, and Duke, feeling a bit helpless, a bit sick to his stomach, said, "Well, sir, I'm leaving I guess." But by then, no one was leaving. They hauled just about everybody to jail, loading them into paddy wagons outside—ten people a wagon—

arresting nearly a hundred people in all. It was, according to a Houston Police Department spokesman, the biggest gambling bust in Houston history.

Duke ended up getting stuck in a cell with Puckett, who spent the night cracking jokes. Dottie said they arrested Red too, even though he wasn't even holding a cue stick. He was just sitting there, Dottie recalled, eating his dinner at the bar—but the cops grabbed him, pushed his arms behind his back, took him to jail. The cops let the women go—no need for scandal— and Lassiter, complaining of his ulcers and sinuses and stomach, had gone back to the hotel to sleep, so he got away too. Records show that Lassiter, probably lying in bed at the Montague Hotel, was the only tournament competitor *not* arrested.

98 ARRESTED AT LE CUE
RAID RACKS UP POOL HUSTLERS

(HOUSTON CHRONICLE— Sept. 12, 1969) A police raid on the Le Cue Club, 1104 Rusk, after play at a Nine-Ball tournament, netted 98 persons, including a group of the nation's top pool hustlers.

The names on the police blotter today read like a Who's Who of pool players, including Handsome Danny Jones, 37; Greg (Big Train) Stevens, 37; Jack L. (Jersey Red) Breitkopf, who also uses the name Jack Breit, and Ronnie (Fast Eddie) Allen.

Don S. Siegel, owner of the Le Cue Club and host of the 14-day tournament that ends Saturday night, said the raid came after tournament play had ended.

"It's unfortunate that this happened," said Siegel today.

Six of the 98 were charged with gambling on a pool table, a misdemeanor. The other 92 were charged with remaining on the premises while gambling was going on, also a misdemeanor.

*The six charged with gambling—they included Handsome Danny and Big
Train Stevens—all were released on $25 bond.*

Eventually, of course, they all got out. Duke said the players posted a bond
equal to their fine and then never went to court, forfeiting the bond money.
Siegel also hired a lawyer to fight the convictions, and reimbursed any player
who could provide a court receipt for the bond.

Dottie recalled that she spent most of the night worried sick, weeping,
hysterical, pacing the floors at the downtown cop station. She had witnessed
the roughing up given to one old bird, with the marauding cops pushing him
struggling to the floor and brusquely ripping out his back pocket when he
didn't hand over his identification quickly enough. And while she knew that
everybody liked Red—even some of the working stiffs down at HPD—Dottie
still dreaded what might befall her husband, taken away against his will,
pushed headfirst into a van under the blinding television lights and the
babble and midnight confusion on Rusk Street. And so Dottie went to the
police station, was ushered back and forth, got stuck in a waiting room, and
then finally recognized a plainclothesman earlier befriended by Red. It was a
vice officer—Dottie couldn't remember his name—but he ended up pulling
some strings, talking to the desk clerk, doing whatever needed to get done,
and Red got released, along with some others.

"I drove up to the police station and sat there, trying to find out what was
going on, what I could do," recalled Dottie. "It was like five in the morning
until this guy walked in that I recognized. And he asked what I was doing
there, and I said that I'm waiting to get my husband. I told him that they had
arrested Jack with all of them, that I couldn't find anything out.

"He [the vice officer] was really hot that Jack was still in there, and he just
put a release on him and let him loose. You know, Jack had shot a bunch of

trick shots and stuff for him, when the vice guys would come up and look around [making rounds at Le Cue]. Jack could make friends with anyone."

The tournament resumed the next evening—and the gambling got going too, although with a bit more discretion. Jack returned with a flourish, announcing to anybody who would hear that it had been the first time ever that he had gotten arrested for eating a bowl of soup. And when Jack returned to play, he began winning, cutting through player after player, invigorated, his brow furled, bearing down with his mouth puckered into a tiny O, shooting, running balls. *Heh, heh, look at me go!* And when he would step away from the table, it was always with the satisfaction of whitey stranded against the rail, beached behind an obstructing ball, and it was there on the rail that his opponents would founder too. Defeated, dead.

Stevens returned too, having survived his own night in jail, and perhaps more rested for it, because he beat Richie Florence at about 5:15 p.m. the next day. At first it looked as if the Big Train would wreck, with the fresh-faced Richie methodically connecting the dots, quietly, quickly, going up early seven games to two. About twenty spectators sitting on back-wall bleachers shifted and fidgeted on the rickety, hard wood, whispering about the Big Train going down. But then Richie got stuck, and then sat, gasping for air, as Big Train ran out seven games in a row. "Damned!" cursed one spectator, seeing that Big Train's victory would cost a side bet. Richie banged his stick on the floor as Stevens slapped in the winning ball.

One table over, the recently sprung Handsome Danny had also fallen behind fast, early, three games to zero, to Cicero Murphy. Jones would never really recover. Although one rally brought Handsome Dan even (at four games apiece), he lost the next three without even returning to the table. He spent most of the set glued to his chair, helpless, as Cicero methodically sank

ball after ball. "That man out there just outshot me a little," Danny told a
friend afterwards The final tally: Murphy 11. Jones 6.

And Jersey Red, who lost to Cicero Murphy and Ronnie Allen early in the
second round, lost no more. He beat Handsome Dan, Big Train Stevens, U.
J. Puckett, Richie Florence, Cowboy Jimmy Moore. And when he got up to
play Lassiter, the great and almighty but always suffering Wimpy, he beat him
too. It all came together somehow, rack after rack, and Wimpy couldn't quite
fall into a groove. And Red—through two weeks of high humidity, late-night
gambling, jail time, and cold soup—compiled the best record. He won
thirteen matches in all, losing only three. And Lassiter, who won ten and lost
six, came in second.

And so Jack "Jersey Red" Breit, finally and undeniably, had won.

Dottie said the tournament format gave Jack's victory added resonance. A
double round-robin, she said, measures not just shot-making ability, but
shooting consistency. "When you have to play everybody twice," she said,
"it's a better test of who's good and who's not." The tournament also proved,
once and for all, that Red could beat anyone, *anyone*, in just about any
game. Back in that summer of '69, playing through Houston's mean cops
and foul humidity, Red plowed through every big-time player in big-time pool,
including the king, the great Wimpy Lassiter himself, at the game he loved
best. And this, said Dottie, beaming, was nine-ball. "Wimpy rarely ever got
beat at it."

For placing second—after losing *twice* to Red—Lassiter received $1,250.
Cicero Murphy and Richie Florence tied for third (both had 9-7 records); and
Stevens, despite the pills or because of them, came in fifth. Puckett and
Allen tied for sixth, Handsome Danny came in eighth, and Cowboy Moore
came in last, but still earned $400.

And then Jack and Dottie took to the road again, driving without pause to Phoenix, Arizona, for a Billiards Congress of America event, a straight-pool tournament that Jack needed to win on order to qualify for the big televised U.S. Open held that December. "I drove all night long to get to Phoenix in time," recalled Dottie. Jack won the Phoenix qualifier, with Boston Shorty coming in second, and so he got to the straight-pool nationals, televised on ABC's *Wide World of Sports*. Cameras. Crowds. Nationwide audience. Big time under hot lights.

Las Vegas.

Red ran balls like he was meant too, never missing, never stopping. He beat them all, one after another, just as he had in Houston, demolishing the field in front of him, flush with confidence. He had done it all before, and in front of him, for the taking, stood his destiny: the real and true big time. The cameras and smoke. But also before him stood Mr. Wimpy Fucking Lassiter, blocking his path, as he had so many times before. Always shuffling and hacking into Red's life; always standing between Red and his glory.

With the whispering in his soul and his mournful wife watching from the bleachers, Jersey Red made it to the finals of the Fourth Annual U.S. Open Pocket Billiards Championship, held in Las Vegas, Nevada, and televised nationwide. And it was there that Red got beat: 150-114, 150-120. Set and match. Before the cameras and the lights and millions of Americans watching on black-and-whites, Jack "Jersey Red" Breit showed he really was just second best.

Jack and Dottie would soon retire from the road. Jersey Red's great tournament days were over.

EPILOGUE
WINNERS & LOSERS

"I ain't going to play in no coat, Willie!"

—Minnesota Fats, Valentine's Day, 1978

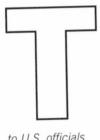

HE SHOW BAR WAS THE SCENE OF A RAID BY 30 SPECIAL AGENTS OF THE INTERNAL REVENUE SERVICE AT ABOUT 1 A.M. THURSDAY. *Money and gambling paraphernalia were seized, according to U.S. officials.*

The IRS had the bar and adjacent Cue Club, where a national pool tournament was in progress, under surveillance for about two weeks. U.S. Atty. Henry Schwarz said the agents observed large-scale gambling. About 40 persons were subpoenaed to appear for questioning by a grand jury in federal court...

—Southern Illinoisan, October 31, 1972

The relentless beat of Georgie Jansco's great heart set the tempo for America's second great age of pool. It tapped out its melody during the Johnston City jamborees, during the Las Vegas Stardust; it became the thud-thud backbeat of breathless newspaper accounts and TV interviews. Georgie Jansco's great song joined those of Red, Fats, and Wimpy: together they became the thundering symphony of America's hustler days.

But on June 4, 1969, just a few months before that year's U.S. Open, the song of Georgie Jansco's heart came to an abrupt halt. A blood vessel had snapped in Jansco's head; his face went horrifically, suffocatingly white; he dropped to his knees. A few hours later, Georgie would be dead. The end came at Union Hospital in nearby Frankfort, where he was connected to long plastic tubes and beeping machines. He never regained consciousness. He never said another word. "We had just gotten home—maybe a week—and it was very unexpected," recalled daughter JoAnn. "It was a terrible shock."

Georgie was just fifty-three years old and still in the process of making himself rich. Just that year he had taken his proceeds from the Stardust and from Johnston City and from a hundred other good bets and opened the Stardust nine-hole golf course. He had the crazy notion to build it over the Johnston City garbage dump. Despite frequent floods and an economic downturn, his daughter JoAnn and her husband David would continue to operate the golf course three decades later.

After Georgie's death, the Las Vegas and Johnston City tournaments fell to little brother Paulie—and of course, it didn't take long for him to fuck things up. Paulie never had a head for numbers—not like Georgie, anyway—and many of the players despised him. Some, like Jersey Red, would boycott Paulie's events. ("Paulie put on airs," sniffed Dottie Breit. "He looked down on the hustlers.") Paulie also had another problem: his big, fat mouth.

Both he and George liked to tell a story, to brag about themselves and to brag about others—but Paulie just wasn't any good at it. He lacked the aplomb and good common horse sense of his brother Georgie. No tact. No discretion. So while Georgie might tell a reporter about how he loved them pool hustlers, and how they could run 102 balls in fifteen seconds while standing on their heads, Paulie would tell a bit more. He'd tell a bit too much. And that's how Paulie got his tit in a ringer, back in '72.

Speaking with Charles Chamberlain, a reporter with the Associated Press, Paulie started out with the usual cock-and-bull about Fats, the only pool hustler America cared about. "Fats has been beaten," said Paulie, "but perhaps only seldom and you don't hear about it. Hell, if he never had been beaten you don't think he would get these kind of matches, do you?"

These kind of matches. *These* kind of matches, said Paulie, meaning the high-stakes variety that Fats might take to Ronnie Allen—a series of $500 or $600 games, say, until one or the other had the entire stake of $12,000 to $15,000 in his pocket. And then, bizarrely, Paulie became even more brazen. "I've had as much as a hundred thousand dollars in my safe-deposit box in the Herris Security Bank, about eight miles away," he told the AP writer. "If they win any money, the checks are made out to me—not to them. I see that they are paid off."

And then Paulie let on how the hustlers came loaded with cash, and how that cash remained impossible to track by the Internal Revenue Service. "At least five of the players—and I won't name them—out of the country's top twenty-five have no Social Security numbers. They have no mailing addresses. They don't exist as far as the government is concerned."

And so Chamberlain, recognizing a colorful quote and a good story, put Paulie in his write-up. And the story went up on the AP wire, and out to newspapers large and small. And among those reading the story were agents of the Internal Revenue Service. And during the early morning hours of October 26, shortly after the opening of the 12th Annual Johnston City All-Around Pocket Billiards Tournament, they arrested every pool hustler in sight.

"About thirty or forty IRS agents and state and local officials already in the crowd watching the tournament stood up and announced a raid was in progress," Paulie told Bowlers Journal. "They locked all the doors and proceeded to search everybody in the place. They searched me and confiscated everybody's money. They said it was gambling paraphernalia because we were intending to use it for gambling...

"They're chasing me out," continued Paulie. "I've had it up to here with all this Mickey Mouse stuff. One of the agents even told me the raid should have never taken place. He said they expected to find all sorts of gambling paraphernalia like craps tables and roulette wheels and maybe twenty or thirty phones to call in bets. Hell, they must have thought I was operating some kind of casino here and I don't know where they ever got an idea like that."

But even before the raid, Paulie had found himself fighting local authorities over his liquor license. Not long after the raid he sold out completely. The tournaments never resumed. The jamborees were over, forever.

It would be unfair, however, to say that Paulie Jansco, all by himself, put an end to America's last great hustler days. It would be unfair and untrue to say that any man, all by himself, could bring them to an end. Rather, the renaissance fell victim to the fickle tastes of Americans, and to its own inertia. The forced shutdown of the Johnston City jamborees only marked that end, like a period at the end of a long sentence. If America's hustler revolution began in the autumn, so also did they end, twelve years later.

"THE SCENE SET IS THE STARLIGHT ROOF OF THE WALDORF-ASTORIA, ONE OF THE MOST FAMOUS ROOMS IN THE WORLD FOR GREAT SOCIAL OCCASIONS. We're on Park Avenue, in the heart of New York City. Hello, everyone, I'm Howard Cosell."

The end of Johnston City would not mark the end for Mr. Minnesota Fats. Not by a long shot. The TV appearances continued. The magazine articles. The interviews and endorsement deals. Measured by these standards—by the standards of showbiz—a high point of Fats's career also marked a high point for American pool. For no single match would hold America's attention like that pitting Mr. Minnesota Fats against Mr. Willie Mosconi on Valentine's Day, 1978.

"Hey, Howard. HOWARD!"

Before cable TV, before two hundred channels and the Internet, before ESPN 1 and ESPN 2, the networks ruled the airwaves. Then, *Wide World of Sports* was king.

"Howard!"

And down at the Waldorf Astoria Hotel, New York City, the Starlight Roof, the world's greatest hustler challenged the world's greatest tournament player. Their battle became America's battle. In 1978 only the Ali–Spinks fights garnered higher sports ratings. Fats–Mosconi became the most highly watched pool match in American history. Perhaps in world history. Who would prevail?

"Howard!"

"The noise in the background, ladies and gentleman, is Minnesota Fats." Howard Cosell, elegant in black tuxedo and white bow tie, mouths the hustler's name with mock disdain, almost with irritation. But Cosell nonetheless recognizes the potential of the moment: this is pure showbiz—not sports, but *showbiz*. Crystal chandeliers, fine wine, beautiful mahogany—and the egg-like Minnesota Fats in an ill-fitting polyester jersey. "This is one of the most fascinating segments we've ever had."

"I never lost one for money in my *life*, beat everyone that ever lived. Never lost in my life." And so Fats begins. "I'm known the world over for that. You can go to any country, any city on earth, and ask Mahatma Gandhi's wife, his mother or his daughter, say, 'You know Minnesota?' 'I know him, known him all his life, he played here when I was a baby. 'What happened?' 'He robbed everybody, that's what happened.' Tell you what happened."

"Where is the chalk?" asks Mosconi. "Did he steal it?"

"Antarctica, I been there. One twenty-six below, played cards aboard ship, never got out of the dining room. I hustle cards and everything; I'm an expert, world champion card player, beat everybody living playing cards. I'm a high-rolling gambler, highest-rolling gambler on earth. Never lost one for money in my life. Whenever I played somebody for money, they got broke. That's the only way you can survive in this business."

"Will you just hit the balls, Fats?"

"Gotta to have *fans*, Willie, or you can't play."

Mosconi, quite predictably, would demolish Fats—as he would in subsequent rematches over the years. Mosconi, enveloped in a quiet fury, methodically and relentlessly pocketed balls. Fats yammered. But it didn't matter. It couldn't matter. Fats had learned that lesson many years ago, a lifetime ago, when old Cowboy Weston lost the match but won the crowd. Pocketing balls was totally beside the point.

"Gotta have *fans* Willie…"

LUTHER "WIMPY" LASSITER OFFICIALLY RETIRED IN 1975, SPENDING MORE AND MORE TIME IN ELIZABETH CITY, WHERE HE SHARED THE OLD FAMILY HOME ON PEARL STREET WITH HIS BROTHER CHARLES, ALSO A LIFELONG BACHELOR. Family members said Wimpy may have had a girlfriend or two, but none that lasted. In 1983 the Billiards Congress inducted Wimpy into their Hall of Fame. By then oilman Walter Davis had taken up Wimpy's bills. Davis, the old childhood chum, never forgot Wimpy's generosity in the schoolyard—the shared candy, the dollar here and there. And so he returned the favor by providing a pension of several hundred dollars each month. It was a greater pension than most lifelong hustlers deserve or expect.

Brother Charles broke his back and went to live with a sister. And so Wimpy, fighting against a horrible dogging solitude, spent more time in the company of his younger brother Clarence, Clarence's wife Barbara, and their five children. Barbara grew especially close to Wimpy, whom she called "Bud"—although she also admitted that she "just wanted to choke him sometimes" because of the endless hours spent at their house. "He was lonely, real lonely," she recalled.

"The night he died, he had been at our house. We lived just a couple of blocks away and he was living in the old homestead...It was probably eight at night, and he rode his bicycle home. He rode that bicycle all the time, and he went home, and he was fine as far as we knew. Nothing was wrong. Someone said they saw him walking down across the street that night—at about eleven.

"The next morning my two sons—who would always go by there, just to go, because he was like a second daddy to them—my two sons, they called and couldn't get no response. So they ended up climbing through the window, and found him dead. He had just twelve dollars and some change in his pocket.

"I knew two or three people in my life who I thought would go to heaven—with no doubt—and he was one of them. He treated everybody like they was supposed to be treated."

IT STARTED WITH A BROKEN RIB. At least, that's what Jack thought he had, with that soreness down his left side, sort of below his shoulder. It has been growing for months, that pain, gnawing at him, and so Red finally mentioned it to Duke. The two were drinking coffee down at Houston's Cue & Cushion. It was the spring of 1996. "I got this pain in my back," Duke remembered Red saying through a pained grimace. "I think I cracked a rib back there. I must have fallen."

By then Jack was sixty-one years old and had been off the road for years. He lived a quiet life in a two-room efficiency with Dottie and their two parakeets. Most days he spent hawking his instructional book, *Winning One-Pocket*, or just shooting the shit with Duke or Texas Bob or Bill Lee out in front of the Cue & Cushion's horseshoe-shaped bar. Or sometimes he made it out to the horse track, and there, wearing a dark Hawaiian shirt and white sneakers, he'd handicap the ponies.

His wavy auburn locks had mostly vanished and his little patch of remaining hair had turned the color of ash. Tiny crevices, formed by the years, ran like rivulets around his mouth and beneath his green eyes. Old age approached—anyone could see it—but still, somehow, Jersey Red had not become old. His boyish charm was still there. His obnoxious boastful arrogance was still there. And he still had the preening strut of a man who had once been the king of 7-11 hustlers (and in Houston's Cue & Cushion still was). It all remained part of Jack. And so on most days, Jersey Red came home a winner.

Except for that damn rib.

"What that was," said Duke, "was a tumor in his lung. And when they extracted it, the doctors said, 'Hey, man, this is big.' Red had noticed that rib acting like that for seven or eight months, but he didn't find out for sure until July or August of that year. And then they tried the treatments, you know, for a couple or three months—until about Christmastime. And that's when they said that they would try a couple of little experimental jobs on him, but that didn't have any effect either."

When Red learned that the pain in his back, that cracked rib, was really a giant tumor growing on his lung, it was already too late. The doctors said the cancer was on the march: spreading through his chest to other internal organs, impossible to completely extract. Neither would the chemotherapy work, although it still made Jack feel like shit. He'd vomit, and cramp, and he lost weight. He also took to wearing a cap, perhaps feeling sheepish that what little hair the years had left him now had been robbed by the murderous chemo. Yet Red kept smiling, kept laughing, kept living. He spent his entire life willfully ignoring an uncertain future, and that willful ignorance would not end now. Especially not now, not when his future was certain.

The certainty of death brought into relief a central contradiction of Jersey Red's life. He was, and always had been, both gregarious and somehow taciturn. He boasted and back-slapped, even as he set up no-win games with the poolroom sheep, as if to ease the pain of their impending fleecing. He'd hang with the drunks, leaning against the bar and yakking it up, discussing who shot John and how the score went. But when it came to things about himself—his secret shames and his secret fears (and for Jack, they were probably the same)—he withdrew. He could not talk about the things that mattered: not with Duke, not with Dottie. And so he never much complained, never said he was scared, never gave any indication that his life was ending. He refused to show weakness.

Like his lifelong rivalry with Wimpy Lassiter and his drive for a world championship, Red probably was driven in part by his love for Dottie. He did not want to upset his beautiful, loving, faithful Texas bride. The lessons learned on the big green and from fifty years of gambling also ensured his silence. Against any adversary—even one given a gargantuan spot—one cannot show fear. He learned through the years that survival depends on one's ability to remain bigger, better, stronger. A boastful gambler can brook no weakness, even when the stakes become astronomical.

CONCERNED FRIENDS SPONSORED A BENEFIT TOURNAMENT FOR JACK AND DOTTIE AT A POOL HALL ABOUT TWENTY MILES SOUTH OF HOUSTON, ON THE HIGHWAY TO GALVESTON. It attracted hundreds of well-wishers, including C. J. Wiley, the young pool hustler from Dallas, and letters and donations from across the country, including books and tapes from Jack's old nemesis, Steve Mizerak, Jr. By then Red had grown gaunt and pale and had begun wearing a dark windbreaker, which protected him from the chill and covered his now bowed shoulders. He had finally become an old man.

"You should have seen the crowd," said Red. "All the cue companies sent cues to auction off. Bloodworth. Viking. It did real good. Real good. And there were so many people you couldn't move around in there.

"At the end, though, I was real tired, but they wanted me to do the double-kiss shot and I made it on the second try. You know, I was so weak that first time that it didn't reach. I was just so weak."

Jersey Red had first made that stunning kiss-kick shot against James Evans, way back in 1957, at the 7-11. On Sunday, November 3, 1997, at that benefit tournament, Red managed it for the last time. It became a final gift from Red—a gift for those who had come out, for those who had wished him well, and for those to whom he remained a hero. And perhaps it was also a sort of payback. Much of the roughly $8,000 raised that day paid for his burial.

The transplanted Yankee hustler had poured his entire life—his entire identity—into a single, maddening endeavor: becoming the best. And yet he died without a sanctioned national title, without money, without fame. He sunk away into obscurity.

But Dottie Breit stuck with her man. *She stuck with him.*

In his failed conquest of America's great bachelor sport, Jersey Red instead won a wife's respect. No more missed meals, no more sleeping beneath the tables. "He became," said Dottie, "the man he wanted to become." And she loved him something fierce. On a cool day in February, they laid to rest the king of the 7-11 hustlers, a poolroom bum no longer.

IN 1984—SIXTEEN YEARS AFTER SO HONORING WILLIE MOSCONI (AND A YEAR AFTER INDUCTING WIMPY)—THE BILLIARDS CONGRESS OF AMERICA INDUCTED MINNESOTA FATS INTO THEIR HALL OF FAME. Fats had once called the organization "the biggest joke in the world." The BCA stood, quite simply, for everything Fats did not: straight pool, clean living, *tuxedos.* And Fats never won a single significant, legitimate tournament—BCA or otherwise. "I'm the one that saved pool—they helped bury it," Fats would say of the BCA. "All them play in tuxedos,…eight, ten, twelve, fifteen jack-offs playing in tuxedos. That's like…wouldn't it be nice to play *golf* in a tuxedo? Wouldn't it be nice to play tennis in a tuxedo? Wouldn't it be nice to play *polo* in a tuxedo? I mean, ain't that ridiculous?"

And yet, there he was, Minnesota Fats, receiving his plaque and the handshake. Men in dark suits applauded. The BCA honored Fats not as a great player, but as a great promoter. *Billiards Digest* proclaimed Fats the greatest draw for pocket billiards since Ralph Greenleaf. One could perhaps take that argument a step further: no player had *ever* brought such attention to the sport. Greenleaf, after all, never got top ratings on *Wide World of Sports*.

Not everyone was happy about this turn of events. "In no other sport could he possibly fool the public like that," billiards pro Danny DiLiberto once said of the Fatman. "Wouldn't I sound foolish if I publicly announced that I could kick one-hundred-yard field goals, or drive a golf ball five hundred yards, or do a seven-hundred-and-twenty-degree dunk? The first person to pay attention to me at all would simply say, 'Prove it,' and that would be that.

"But pool has a public that knows nothing, plus the *media* who know nothing; nobody knows what good pool really is, or what a really good player can do. So he's free to tell them anything he pleases, anything at all. He couldn't play; he *wouldn't* play anybody good. And all the pro players used to stand around helpless with laughter while he told his dumb stories about winning millions in India or the Depression or wherever or whenever. I told every one of them, 'You keep giving him that credibility that he doesn't deserve, and you'll help the con man artist make a name for himself while you, as genuine players, will get zero recognition. That's all that can possibly happen.' And I was right."

In 1984, when the Billiards Congress of America inducted Minnesota Fats into their Hall of Fame, the stuffy organization gave Fats what Mosconi had also conferred some twenty years earlier: legitimacy. Fats proclaimed to the world that he was king.

And finally, it seemed, the world agreed.

Nineteen eighty-four was fateful for other reasons. It was the year Minnesota Fats abandoned both Little Egypt and his wife Eva-line. The portly one simply packed his bags, loaded up one of his long Caddys, and drove south. He ended up in Nashville. The divorce became final a year later.

The couple would not exchange words for ten long years. Evelyn said affection deserted the marriage long before Fats did. She blamed not another flesh-and-blood woman, but Dame Fame, the only mistress for which the gingham girl from Little Egypt could not compete. Fats, it seemed, had become swallowed up by his own greatness. "We were married forty-four years, and I'd say for the last third of those years Fats was overloaded with his business and his publicity—all of it out for himself," said Evelyn, back in 1994. "He'd come back from the trips and find fault with everything. His mouth ran away with him. It was obvious I didn't figure very strongly in his life anymore."

Fats took a room at the Hermitage Hotel, in downtown Nashville, and from 1985 to 1991 held forth on a small couch in the lobby. His years there reaffirmed his startling ability to bend reality to his will. He boasted a sultan's life—nothing but first fucking class for Minnesota Fats, you understand—but without all the unpleasantness of work. At the historic Hermitage he found it: velvet draperies, marble floors, burnished brass fixtures. The hotel gave Fats a $100-a-night room for $400 a month. In exchange, the great and worldly Minnesota Fats had to do the things he did best: talk, spread his bullshit, sign autographs. After a while, even signing autographs demanded too much effort. He used a rubber stamp instead.

"Most mornings about eleven, he'd gather up some leftover rolls from the hotel kitchen and go outside to feed the pigeons," wrote journalist Mark McDonald in 1995. "Most evenings, after his lobby-sitting and a nap, he'd catch a ride to the famous Stock-Yard Steak House, where he'd sneak into the kitchen for a free meal. He'd usually end up downstairs, in the Bull Pen Lounge, where manager Mickey Goodall always kept a table reserved for him. Fats would dance, whistle along with the country bands, and hand out rubber-stamped autographs to the tourists."

In 1985 Fats was fined for shoplifting a $1.99 box of Ex-Lax. In 1987 the IRS charged him for $48,402 in back taxes, fines, and penalties. It remains unclear if he could then raise so much cash. In 1992, at age seventy-eight, he fell and hurt his knee while dancing at the Bull Pen. A year later, while undergoing surgery for that injury, Fats suffered a massive heart attack.

And just then, just as health and happiness finally abandoned Minnesota Fats, Theresa Ward Bell walked into his life. Half Fats's age and knowing not much about pool, the former waitress nonetheless possessed all the qualities of a good woman: she owned her own house. Theresa married Minnesota Fats on March 26, 1993, in a sixty-five-dollar walk-up ceremony at the Bridal Path Wedding Chapel. A skeptical Baptist minister asked the old hustler whether he really wanted to go through with it. "I survived Pearl Harbor," said Fats. "I guess I can get through this."

And so in a back room of Theresa Ward Bell's home, Fats played out his final hustle. The lies and truth had become all scrambled in his mind; the crazy claims real, reality a lost myth. He spoke less, quickly became agitated, withdrew from others. He'd become "a very private man, very shy," Bell would say, shooing away the press and well-wishers. He was even committed briefly to a Tennessee mental ward. On January 18, 1996, alone in that back room of Theresa Bell's House, Fats's heart stopped beating.

MINNESOTA FATS LIVED AN IMPOSSIBLE LIFE—AND IT WAS THE VERY IMPOSSIBILITY OF IT THAT FUELED A REVOLUTION. His myth made magic for millions. The story of America's 1960s pool renaissance was a hustling story, with all its deceit, its hyperbole, its romance. Fats, by the force of his own will, by his arrogance, by his pomposity and his foolishness, created truth. It was a pure-Minnesota Fats-bullshit sort of truth…but the only truth most Americans now remember about that magical era.

Luther Lassiter won Johnston City five times, including five division titles in nine-ball, five in straight pool, and one (against Ronnie Allen) in one-pocket. He dominated pool during the 1960s renaissance.

And yet Lassiter could not conquer his own loneliness. The man who had once said he'd walk a thousand miles for the companionship of a single friend would in the end walk those miles alone. He had swapped the straight life for the gambling life, companionship for greatness. The Faustian bargain devoured him whole.

And Jersey Red, the loudmouthed and preternaturally talented Jersey Red—he too would touch upon greatness. And then Red's great southpaw grasp failed him. He became the era's most celebrated also-ran. But he had a good woman. And she loved him to the end.

So who wins? Who loses?

Life and pocket billiards pose no greater questions.

GLOSSARY

ACTION: The presence of wagers, or people willing to place wagers.

ANGLED: Said of a shot when the lip of the pocket prevents a straight shot from the *cue ball* to an *object ball*.

ARMY: Betting money ("I've got an *army* with me").

BACKER: A person who provides financial support for a pool player. He funds wagers and expenses and in return receives a percentage of the winnings.

BALL IN HAND: The placement of a *cue ball* anywhere inside a specified area of the table after a *scratch* or *foul*.

BIG ACTION: The exchange of large wagers.

BIRD DOG: A person who arranges matches and hustles for a cut of the *action*.

BITE ARTIST: Moocher.

BREAK: The initial shot of any pool game, usually with the *cue ball* placed behind the *string*, or in the *kitchen*.

C-NOTE: One-hundred-dollar bill.

CALL SHOT: A shot that requires the player to tell others which ball he intends to shoot into which pocket.

CUE BALL: The white ball, used for targeting other balls. See *whitey*.

DEAD NUTS: Extreme skill. See *nuts*.

DIAMONDS: The markings, generally placed about a foot apart, on the end *rails* of a table. These are used in various targeting systems and for judging the placement of the *cue ball* after a *foul*.

DUMPING: Intentionally and fraudulently losing a game, so as to divvy up a *backer's* money with the other player.

EASY ACTION: Relative ease in finding pool players with whom to gamble.

ENGLISH: Left or right spin on a pool ball.

FAST ACTION: The frequent exchange of wagers of any size.

FOUL: Any illegal move on the pool table, such as pocketing the *cue ball,* hitting the cue ball twice with the cue stick, or failing to hit a *rail* with the *object ball* or *cue ball* in *one-pocket*. Generally results in loss of turn and the *spotting* of a ball. See also *scratch*.

FUN PLAYER: Amateur. Tournament player.

G: One thousand dollars.

HEAVYWEIGHT: A topflight player.

HIGH RUN: The number of balls pocketed consecutively, without missing, in one game or tournament.

JARRING: Placing a mickey in the drink of an opponent to foul his game.

JAW: The sides of the pocket (a *jawed* ball is an *object* ball that hits the sides of the pocket and bounces back and forth without dropping).

KELLY POOL: A game that makes use of fifteen numbered counters, or pills, corresponding to each of the fifteen numbered balls. The counters allow players to make a secret selection of an *object ball*.

KICK: A shot in which the *cue ball* strikes a rail before contacting the *object ball*.

KITCHEN: The area on the far end of the table behind the *string*, that is, the imaginary line running between the end diamonds on the table. This is the traditional placement area for *break* shots after a *scratch*.

KNIFE AND FORK: A hustler's eating and sleeping money, that is, money required for basic survival.

LEMONING: A hustler's custom of not playing up to his full *speed*, or ability. This is done in order to fool a *mark* into increasing the wager. Also referred to as *playing on the lemon.*

LOCK (also lock-up): A game that can't be lost, due to an inferior opponent or an insurmountable *spot.*

LOCKSMITH: A hustler who specializes in playing lock-up games.

MAKING GAMES: 1. Convincing someone to gamble. 2. Negotiating a wager, the form of pool, and any handicap.

MARK: A pool hustler's potential victim. See also *sucker, pigeon.*

MASSE: Extreme *English* on a *cue ball,* requiring that the cue stick be held in an almost vertical fashion.

MATCHING UP: Negotiating the form of pool and any handicap, on any *money game.*

MISCUE: A *scratch* or missed shot, caused by the cue tip making inadequate contact with the *cue ball.*

MONEY GAME: A game of pool in which a wager has been set by the players.

NATURAL: A simple shot.

NINE-BALL: A rotation game with nine object balls and the *cue ball.* The only permissible object ball in any inning is the lowest numbered ball on the table. The first to pocket the nine balls wins.

NUTS: Skill (He had the *nuts* to win.)

OPM: Other People's Money. That which pool players try to win during money matches.

OBJECT BALL: The targeted ball, as opposed to the *cue ball.*

ONE HOLE: When a player owes a ball in *one-pocket,* or any other game where a *foul* requires a player to *spot* a ball. This generally occurs when the fouling player has not yet pocketed a ball.(Okay, I scratched, now you have me in the *one hole.*)

ONE-POCKET: A game in which an opponent must sink eight balls, of any number, stripe, or color, in order to win. Each ball, however, must be pocketed into a predetermined pocket at the end of the table. Each player shoots for separate pockets, making one-pocket more defensive than other sorts of pool. Also known as *one-hole* or *pocket apiece.*

PIGEON: A pool hustler's potential victim. See also *mark, sucker.*

POOLROOM DETECTIVE: A person who can spot potential hustlers, or *marks.*

RAIL: The cushioned edges of the pool table. Often referred to as the banks.

RAILBIRD: A spectator during a money game. See also *sweator.*

ROLL: 1. A roll of money, often bound by a rubber band, held loose in the pocket of a gambler. Gamblers typically don't use wallets, preferring to keep their money loose for the quick disposal of debts. 2. The trajectory of the *cue ball* or *object ball.* (You got a lucky *roll* on that shot.)

SAFETY: A defensive shot designed not to pocket a ball, but to leave your opponent without an easy shot.

SCRATCH: A *foul,* or illegal shot, in which the cue ball falls into a pocket. Generally results in the loss of turn and the *spotting* of a ball.

SELLING OUT: Leaving an opponent an open table, allowing him to make balls at will. Usually used in reference to poor safety play in one-pocket.

SETUP: An easy shot. See *natural.*

SHORTSTOP: A player who can be beaten only by a top player.

SIDE ACTION: Betting between *railbirds,* or *sweators.* See *side bet.*

SIDE BET: A bet between *railbirds,* or *sweators.* See *side action.*

SPEED: A player's ability.

SPOT: A handicap.

SPOTTING: Placing a ball on the spot on one end of the table after any *foul*.

STRING: An imaginary line on the far end of the table from which the *cue ball* must be shot after *fouls* in certain games. In most games, the *cue ball* must be placed behind the string for the opening break.

STAKEHORSE: A person who provides financial support for a pool player. He funds bets and expenses and in return receives a percentage of winnings. See *backer*.

STALLING: Occasionally losing a game to keep an opponent betting. See *lemoning*.

STRAIGHT POOL: A game in which any ball on the table can be pocketed. A player is awarded a point for each ball pocketed.

SUCKER: A pool hustler's potential victim. See also *mark, pigeon*.

SWEATOR: A spectator during a money game. The term refers to the sweat that may form on the spectator's brow as he frets about the outcome. As noted in *The New Illustrated Encyclopedia of Billiards* (Mike Shamos, The Lyons Press, 1999), the word is spelled with "or" rather than "er" to distinguish it from apparel. See also *railbird*.

TAKEDOWN: The amount of money won at the tables.

WEIGHT: A handicap. See *spot*.

WHITEY: The *cue ball*.

WHO SHOT JOHN: A pool player's unverifiable boast.

APPENDIX I
THE TOURNAMENTS

1960

National Nine-Ball Championship, Macon, Georgia
U. J. Puckett

1961

First Annual World's One-Pocket Billiards Tournament at Johnston City, Illinois
First Place: Johnny Vevis
Second Place: Jimmy Moore
Third Place: Hubert Cokes
Fourth Place: Rudolf Wanderone

1962

Johnston City
One-Pocket: Marshall Carpenter
Nine-Ball: Luther Lassiter
Straight Pool: Luther Lassiter
All Around: Luther Lassiter

1963

New York City World's Invitational 14.1 Championship (Billiard Room Proprietor Association of America)
Luther Lassiter

Johnston City
One-Pocket: Eddie Taylor
Nine-Ball: Luther Lassiter (Second Place: Jack Breit)
Straight Pool: Luther Lassiter
All Around: Luther Lassiter

1964

New York City World's Invitational 14.1 Championship (Billiard Room Proprietor Association of America)

Luther Lassiter

Johnston City

One-Pocket: Eddie Taylor
Nine-Ball: Luther Lassiter
Straight Pool: Luther Lassiter
All Around: Luther Lassiter

1965

New York City World's Invitational 14.1 Championship (Billiard Room Proprietor Association of America)

Joe Balsis

Johnston City

One-Pocket: Larry Johnson
Nine-Ball: Harold Worst
Straight Pool: Harold Worst
(Second Place: Jack Breit)
All Around: Harold Worst

1966

New York City World's Invitational 14.1 Championship (Billiard Room Proprietor Association of America)

Luther Lassiter

Billiards Congress of America U.S. Open Tournament (straight pool), Chicago, Illinois

Joe Balsis

1966 *(continued)*

Johnston City
One-Pocket: Eddie Kelly
Nine-Ball: Eddie Kelly
Straight Pool: Joe Balsis
All Around: Joe Balsis

1967

New York City World's Invitational 14.1 Championship (Billiard Room Proprietor Association of America)
Luther Lassiter
Second Place: Jack Breit

Billiards Congress of America U.S. Open (straight pool), St. Louis, Missouri
Jimmy Caras

California International Open, Long Beach, California
One-Pocket: Ed Kelly (Second Place: Jack Breit)
Nine-Ball: Joe Balsis
Straight Pool: Luther Lassiter
All Around: Luther Lassiter
(Breit was the top money winner after three titlists.)

Stardust Hotel Open, Las Vegas, Nevada
One-Pocket: Eddie Taylor
Nine-Ball: Danny Jones
Straight Pool: Mike Eufemia
All Around: Eddie Taylor

Johnston City
One-Pocket: Larry Johnson
Nine-Ball: Luther Lassiter
Straight Pool: Irving Crane
All Around: Luther Lassiter

1968

New York City World's Invitational 14.1 Championship (Billiard Room Proprietor Association of America)
Irving Crane

Johnston City
One-Pocket: Larry Johnson
Nine-Ball: Danny Jones (Second Place: Jack Breit)
Straight Pool: Al Coslosky
All Around: Danny Jones

1969

Houston Invitational Nine-Ball Tournament of Champions
Jack Breit
Second Place: Luther Lassiter

United States Open Pocket Billiards Championship
Luther Lassiter
Second Place: Jack Breit

World Pocket Billiards Championship
Ed Kelly

Johnston City
One-Pocket: Luther Lassiter
Nine-Ball: Luther Lassiter
Straight Pool: Joe Russo
All Around: Luther Lassiter

1970

World Pocket Billiards Championship
Irving Crane

Johnston City
One-Pocket: Ronnie Allen
Nine-Ball: Keith Thompson
Straight Pool: Luther Lassiter
All Around: Keith Thompson

1971

World Pocket Billiards Championship
Ray Martin

Johnston City
One-Pocket: Jim Rempe
Nine-Ball: Jimmy Marino
Straight Pool: Luther Lassiter
All Around: Jimmy Marino

1972

World Pocket Billiards Championship
Irving Crane

Johnston City
One-Pocket: Larry Johnson
Nine-Ball: Billy Incardona
Straight Pool: Danny DiLiberto
All Around: Danny DiLiberto

OTHER PLAYERS

DON WILLIS

They saunter in, the two egg-shaped strangers, and they could be brothers. They've both got great long faces, big droopy eyes, thick lips. Neither stands taller than five-foot, ten inches tall; each probably weighs 170 or 180 pounds. Their age remains a mystery. Could be mid-thirties. Could be older. Both show gray, but both also have that ageless, wrinkleless skin that comes with fat.

The strangers order whisky. One likes it straight up; the other gets it mixed into an old-fashioned or a sour or something equally revolting. They sip slowly, languorously, and they eye the poolroom. Amid the click-clacking of ivory on ivory and the horrible wheezing nicotine hacks of old men and the horrible, godless spewing profanity—the strangers take a solemn inventory.

Here, in all their hunching and cursing and spitting wretchedness, have herded plump sheep. Here men sport thick gaudy gold watches, sparkling pinkie rings. Some pull cash in loose wads from their front pants pocket. Some shoot quietly, resolutely, with brow-furled intensity. Others seem unable to remain silent. The strangers identify the plumpest—the boastful ones, the ones with cash and attitude—for their fleecing will be the richest of all.

And so it begins. The big hustle, the big hoorah. Dogs, sheep, and men. Here it goes.

You shoulda seen me last week, one stranger says to the other—but with a voice that seems somehow too loud. *Couldn't miss a damn ball. Hell, I think I ran a twenty and a thirty. It was something to see. It went like that all night.*

Well, Lawdy, came the other's wild response. *I run out playing nine-ball twice. Remember that ol' boy from Nixonton? I declare I beat him eight or nine times running. What a look on the ol' boy's face!*

On and on it went, progressively louder, more aggressive, more obnoxious, the volume rising with every downed whisky: *I'm better. No, I'm better. No, I'm better!* And then they'd ask the bartender for his opinion, or they'd interrupt the pinkie-ring guy leaning down over a shot, and they'd shout over to some dude mining for cash in his front pants pocket. They'd deliver their cash-on-delivery soliloquies to anybody who cared to listen. And even those who cared not to. Hell, the strangers agreed, they probably could whup the ass of just about anybody in the whole damn room. Fact is, they probably could whup anybody in the whole damn town.

And when it all came together, and the whisky was flowing just right, and the crowd was big enough, the strangers didn't even ask for a game. It came to them. And always, the challenge came from the biggest, most high-rolling, most self-assured chump present. It came from the sheep in wolf's clothing.

Like a never-ending circus, Luther Lassiter and road partner Don Willis staged nightly performances all across America. They brought their big hoorah to Dee-Troit and Philly and Pittsburgh. They took it to Chicago, to Charleston and Boston. By 1961, just as Fats and Georgie Jansco came together for America's first explosive hustlers' jamboree, Wimpy Lassiter and Don Willis had been doing their thing for a dozen years. As the hustler revolution overtook America, both had become old veterans.

"Lassiter and I were all over together," Willis recalled. "He never came close to losing to anybody. Come to think of it, I didn't either...Lassiter was what you call a comfortable player. When you're betting on him, you can sit in the chair and watch without wiggling endlessly. Also, you can eat and know that you will win. Some of the players that I've been on the road with, I was afraid to go to the toilet, for fear that I would be broke when I came out."

In 1948, shortly after the collapse of the Norfolk scene, Wimpy Lassiter and Don Willis formed what became arguably the most formidable road team in American pool history. Lassiter eventually won eighteen world championships. America has produced no greater nine-ball player. Willis, by contrast, never won a major tournament. But most of the greats acknowledged gambling losses to the Ohio-born hustler. Playing straights, Willis busted straight-pool champ Jimmy Moore. He beat Ralph Greenleaf and Willie Mosconi. And in 1948, when the egg-shaped Willis first waddled into Elizabeth City, North Carolina, he beat the world's greatest nine-ball player ever: Luther Lassiter.

It was the very talent of Don Willis that sealed the partnership—for *nobody* beat Lassiter at nine-ball—and sure as shit not on his home turf, on his own tables, with all his friends watching. The North Carolinian found the loss so astounding, so unprecedented, so downright odd, that he immediately befriended Willis.

In the traveling roadman, it seemed, Lassiter had found an equal. He also found a pure hustler, a quintessential con man, a survivor of cheap whisky, cold bologna, and late-night suckers. Willis never won tournaments because he never played them. He feared not defeat (always the rap on Minnesota Fats), but rather exposure. He wanted no pictures in the paper. He pledged his oath to the cold-hearted back rooms of America. In that arena, Don Willis would prove his greatness.

Willis was born on May 1, 1909, and lived much of his life in Canton, Ohio, where he attended Canton Timken High School. He played semipro football in the late twenties, but also excelled at baseball and basketball. And reminiscent of golf hustler Titanic Thompson, Willis mastered a variety of odd traits:

he could beat any man alive in backward-running races, he could hit wing shot after wing shot (as many as forty-two in a row), he could juggle three pool balls and the chalk.

"I've even won bets on the proposition that I can't name in order the hundred and thirty largest cities in the U.S.," Willis told writer Thomas Fensch for his 1970 book *The Lions and the Lambs*. "There are a hundred and thirty cities over a hundred thousand population. It's easy."

Willis began hustling pool during the Depression. Although Lassiter also began shooting pool during that same era, the two would not join forces until after World War II. Quoted in a 1977 edition of the *Evansville Press*, Willis recalled the beginning of his long, famous partnership with the king of nine-ball.

"I broke Lassiter one night playing nine ball, in Elizabeth City, North Carolina. He suggested that we become road partners. That is what Lassiter wanted to do then. We split everything we made—sometimes as much as $5,000 or $10,000 over a period of several days.

"We never lost. We'd go into a town and ask for their best. We didn't care who they sent. We'd beat him. It helped that he was a good player. A lot of players want to play the worst players; but you couldn't make any money that way..."

Willis challenged the best. Or the best might challenge him. Somebody might interrupt a one-pocket game, or someone might call the local top dog from a nearby phone booth. Or the bartender might let on that, *you know*, he plays some. Somebody, somebody was going to step up. *Hey, buddy, why don't you just shut the fuck up?* Willis & Lassiter had it down to an art, down to a few downed drinks and tuned-up, turned-up, loudmouthed brag-gadocio. Just keep it up, keep it up, and somebody, eventually, would get pissed. Up to the bar, all red-faced and ornery, marched the unwitting victim. He'd come to call the stranger's bluff—*Unscrew your cue, goddamnit! Let's go!*—and at that point, of course, the trap was sprung, the game already over.

Willis, the more obnoxious of the two, often went first. He never feared defeat. The word hardly existed for him. Rather, he feared the paltry wager. And so victory became not the principal challenge, but *action*. Willis needed to stoke it up hot like a boiler room fire; he had to get the action both big and quick. The pigeon must keep reaching, keep the bills coming, and if the pigeon had a backer, so much the better.

As so Don always began slow, playing the lemon, and like all great hustlers, he seemed beatable. But somehow he always dropped just one more ball than the other guy, or he lucked in the nine. And sometimes he'd miss— he'd dog an easy shot, a shot anyone would sink—but somehow *whitey* get lodged behind the cluster. And he'd leave a ball hanging, but with no way for the sucker to come back, to shoot. *Sorry 'bout that buddy.* Somehow Willis seemed to just play lucky.

The wagers stacked up, with Willis winning game after game—he'd lose a few, but not many—until the local quit him. And then it came, like it always came, during those bleary-eyed unending nights, with the booze and the cash still flowing.

Well, shit, buddy, Willis might say. *Maybe you'd have more luck with my friend here. We both can't play this lucky.*

And then Wimpy Lassiter, one of the greatest pool players the world has ever seen, would step from his high stool, unscrew his cue, and go to work.

Lawdy.

RONNIE ALLEN

Those who sweated the Red & Ronnie show at Le Cue—down in Houston—spent years debating which player really was king. Ask five different old-timers and get five different answers: Ronnie Allen was more aggressive, but sold out by risking too much; Jersey Red managed games better, but got shaky when the stakes got high; Ronnie was the better gambler, Red the better tournament player.

Grady Mathews, for one, characterized Ronnie Allen as the world's best one-pocket player. This made Allen only slightly better than Red, said Mathews—surely not more than a half-ball better. Not enough to create a meaningful spot.

"He created power one-pocket," Mathews said of Allen. "He was a risk taker and he moved multiple balls all the time. Ronnie's game is to make two or three moves, and then he'd run out on you. He was very aggressive. When I saw Red and Ronnie playing, it was close."

But Bill Lee, another veteran player, saw Red win plenty of the shoot-outs. "Red was the better player," he said simply—although he acknowledged Allen may have been the more unflappable gambler. "I saw him and Ronnie Allen play for like a week, man; two of the best players in the world just going at it. Ronnie would want to like play three hundred dollars a game, while Red would want to play a thousand a set. Red was the better player, you could see it, but sometimes when it got down to that six-hundred-dollar game ball, and he'd be thinking about Dottie and everything, and how he had to live, sometimes he'd miss. Ronnie would just come when the money was on the line."

Allen began the road trips to Houston in the mid-sixties and became a fixture at Le Cue at about the time Mathews and Handsome Danny played there. Before taking up pool full-time, Allen worked for a while as a salesman and subscription manager for the *Saturday Evening Post*. He also married—

it was around 1959—and he and his wife Fey remained together for thirty-five years. They had two children: Reyna and Tracey.

Although Allen spent his entire life on the road (at the end of the century, Allen remained a road player), he insisted on keeping a home in Burbank, California. This, he said years later, came in reaction to his own childhood—when his father, Jimmy Allen, operated a small carnival, and his family moved from town to town like gypsies. The different schools, the different towns, the different people along the way—he can't remember them all.

"From the first grade through the seventh grade, I was in a different town and a different school every week," Allen told author David McCumber in a 1998 issue of *Billiards Digest.* "Every week, man. Finally we were in southeastern Oklahoma, and my mother threw up her hands and said, 'We have to winter here. I can't move these kids again.' Then the next year my dad got killed and we moved again.

"I always swore if I ever had kids, they'd start school and finish school in the same place, and I did that. Yeah, I went on the road and played pool for a living, but my kids went from preschool through college in Burbank, California. I did that. And I put my kids through college. These pool players, they don't know the choices I made."

After the death of his old man—Allen was then about eleven years old—a family friend with a pool hall in Oklahoma City invited the boy to drop by anytime. And Ronnie did, learning there the secret calculus of bank shots, kicks, and safeties. This strange new education paid off at age twenty when Allen won his first tournament…and $1,250.

At the time of Houston's 1969 Le Cue tournament, Allen was of medium build, with dark hair pushed back over a high forehead and tiny blue eyes. Ronnie also possessed high cheekbones that on any other man would bestow nobility. But on the moon-faced Allen—known for his lifelong love affair with booze, pool, and hell-raising—those high cheeks simply buried his tiny blue eyes deeper into his skull, making them seem more ominously recessed, more mysteriously menacing, especially when he got down under the hot overhead table lights and focused on the money.

Allen racked up a fairly impressive list of tournament wins: first place in the 1966 Las Vegas Stardust Open and second in several of the Johnston City meets. Allen, however, always considered himself more of a gambler (his best game was one-pocket; he despised straight pool), and often commented upon the rigors of tournament play.

"In the tournaments," Allen, in his soft Oklahoma twang, told author Thomas Fensch in the late 1960s, "you start shooting and it's tough, just as tough or perhaps tougher than playing for the cash. I have known guys like Fats who think that hustling is enough because your money or other people's money—OPM—is riding on your shots. To some guys, the idea of money on them makes them sick—actually physically sick. But as far as I'm concerned, the tournaments are tougher."

U. J. PUCKETT

If many called Allen the world's greatest one-pocket player (other candidates: Red, Boston Shorty, and Marshall "Tuscaloosa Squirrel" Carpenter), Allen himself might have bestowed that distinction on his old pal and mentor, U. J. Puckett, of Fort Worth. Allen said it was Puckett who taught him the game—not necessarily how to shoot, but how to *play*—during their wild-assed road years.

The story of 1960s hustling in many ways is the story of road teams. Among the most famous were Wimpy & Willis, Red & Shorty, Fats & the Squirrel.

To that pantheon, one certainly must add Ronnie Allen and U. J. Puckett. On March 19, 1960, during a tournament in Macon, Georgia, Puckett became the nation's nine-ball champion. He was then fifty-one years old, Allen less than half that. And when the two took to the road—like murderous father-and-son outlaws—they went as two bona fide champions, two bona fide gamblers, two bona fide players. They went knowing this: a good loser is still a loser. Working together, they left the pigeons stuck on the rail, shot after god-awful shot, until finally: the run-out. Allen & Puckett—a monstrous Godzilla–King Kong tag team, coming to crush the unwary.

Utley John Puckett (later dubbed "Mr. One Pocket" by author Thomas Fensch; others knew him as "Ugly Puckett") came screaming into this world on April 17, 1911, in Prattsville, Arkansas. His father, a logging train engineer, died from a broken neck. Puckett said a busted chain on a railroad car released an entire load of timber and crushed his father with great violence. Puckett was then five years old.

"After that, we still lived in Arkansas and we were hungry a lot of the time," Puckett told a reporter for the *Fort Worth Star-Telegram* in 1984. "If you never been hungry and not had a way to get food, you've missed something, that's the way I feel. And when I say we were hungry, I'm not just sayin' it. We were.

"I moved to Fort Worth with my mother later on…Ninety percent of the kids I went to school with were Mexican-Americans, and most of the others were black. I learned a lot from them. They were my friends. First pool I ever played for money was against black friends for twenty-five cents." Puckett attended Fort Worth's Vocational High School (later named Trimble Technical), where he gained fame on the basketball court. "First game I played in, we won twenty-six to twenty-five and I scored twenty-five points. Right at the last, I made my team's twenty-five points and the other team had already made theirs. We had a guy named Leland Smalling and he got fouled and made the free throw.

"I remember I went up to him and said, 'Thanks for winning the game. All I could do was tie 'em.' I didn't miss a shot the whole game."

Puckett was a man of many talents. Besides shooting basketball, the towering U. J. could also box, act, and, of course, play pool—a vice he picked up at Fort Worth's Panther's Boys Club. After dazzling his peers (and often robbing them), Puckett quit school so he could hustle full-time.

If he had stayed at Vocational High for just one more month, he would have received a diploma. Instead, Puckett chose the pool hustlers' cliché: piss-poor kid finds easy money, drops out of school, spends the rest of his life cursing over crooked nine-ball racks. U. J.'s cliché, however, was interrupted by both a foray into Hollywood, where he worked as a body double, and the boxing ring, where he racked up a 32-8 pro record.

"I fought forty times and all of them ended in knockouts," he told journalist Christopher Evans in 1984. "I knocked the other guy out thirty-two times. The other times—when I couldn't knock the other guy out—I just sat down and got knocked out myself. Didn't want to spoil a perfect record."

Puckett also claimed to have been hired, in 1936, to play actor Wayne Morris's double in the original version of the film *Kid Galahad*, which also starred Bette Davis and featured Humphrey Bogart in a small role. "Warner Brothers had a big cafeteria with one table where all the big stars ate," recalled Puckett. "Me, I didn't know where to sit, so I just sat down at the big table with Bette Davis and Wayne Morris. They treated me like I was a big star, too."

Puckett, though, gained real stardom playing pool. After returning to the sport, full-time, at age thirty, he posted a surprising victory in a Pittsburgh poolroom against hustler Detroit Slim. Recognizing his own potential, Puckett took to the serious study of spin, squirt, and English. An instructional book by Willie Mosconi improved his game another 40 percent. "In 1935, I beat Mosconi for the first time," he said. "And then pretty soon I beat Luther Lassiter while he was the world nine-ball champ." Puckett then took his game, his good looks (he was about six foot, two inches tall, with dark wavy hair), and his specialized line of bullshit—all quite indispensable in the hustling business—on the road.

Sometimes he'd shuffle into strange poolrooms, wearing a grease-stained old Texaco shirt, and aw shucks his way into hundred-dollar action. Puckett said he never lied about his speed, never said he couldn't play some; he just didn't go around advertising it.

"I'd walk in a poolroom and ask if anybody wanted to play for money. When nobody wanted to play, I'd ask where the closest beanery was, then go there for something to eat. Pretty soon, somebody from the poolroom would come over and say he'd found somebody who wanted to play. Then I'd make out like I really didn't want to play, make 'em convince me that I wasn't gonna get taken by no hustler. Then I'd go ahead and play. Sometimes, I'd win."

Even though Puckett's pool-playing prime came late in life, real fame came even later. About a decade after the Houston nine-ball tournament, he received a mention in *Texas Monthly*, and then much more than a mere mention by Harry Reasoner, whose *60 Minutes* news team came to Texas for a feature story on Puckett. "I loved the guy from the first time I met him," recalled Reasoner. "But Puckett is more than a pool hustler. He's one of those rare people who lives his own life on his own terms. That's rare nowadays. It was a unique experience for me and, since then, we've become good friends."

A year or so after the *60 Minutes* appearance, Puckett became a regular on ESPN's *Legends of Pocket Billiards*, which also featured Mosconi, Cowboy

Jimmy Moore, Joe "the Meatman" Balsis, and Wimpy. He later retired to Fort Worth, where he lived out his last years with his wife Helen and his daughter. He went blind in 1989 and died three years later. One of his old haunts, Fast Freddy's, maintained a U. J. Puckett room in his honor for many years.

JOHNNY ERVOLINO

Although never quite of Jersey Red's caliber, Ervolino also spent his entire life looking for games, traveling the countryside, winning tournaments. Born in 1935, Ervolino learned to play pool at a boys' club a few blocks from his home in Brooklyn. During those days, Ervolino would help with his dad's produce business, but then sneak off during the weekends and play for hours.

He soon realized that gambling with buddies and robbing suckers beat stocking vegetables. "My dad, he was from Italy, and he used to make eighty-five dollars a week and had to support ten kids," croaked Ervolino. "But, you know, I was walking around with three or four hundred in my pocket, and I was practically still in elementary school. I used to have to hide it from him. If my father knew I was a pool player, he would have killed me."

In 1947, at age twelve, Ervolino won a national junior championship. By age sixteen he had dropped out of school and rented his own apartment a few blocks from the 7-11. He'd stay there when he had money, sleep where he could when he was broke. It was also about then that he befriended Jersey Red, and the two began making rounds to McGirr's, Ames, and other Manhattan pool halls.

"And then we'd end up going together to have breakfast, at the nickel places," recalled Ervolino years later. "At the time, it was a big deal. You'd put your money in this slot, and out came your food. It was like a ritual—we'd go every morning, 'cause it was right down the street.

"I remember one day we went to sleep in the theater and Red had started out with thirteen dollars in his pocket. And then we got up and walked around, you know, to get a slice of pizza. And he went to pay and somebody had cut out his pocket. He didn't have a dime to eat the pizza."

Ervolino continued to make games there even after becoming a military cop in 1954. Stationed at Times Square, Ervolino would check his gun with manager Abe Rosen and begin the nightly pigeon hunt. After 1961, with the onslaught of America's pool renaissance inspired by *The Hustler*, Brooklyn Johnny began entering tournaments. In 1971 he won the one-pocket title at the Stardust National in Las Vegas.

THE BIG TRAIN

If there was anybody out of Houston who could almost keep up with Jersey Red, it was Greg "Big Train" Stevens. He hardly ever played tournaments, never took home a trophy. But Big Train, everybody knew, could play some pool. He was a big guy—he weighed maybe 220 or 230 pounds—and seemed to be part Lebanese. John "Duke" Dowell, a Houston poolroom regular, said Big Train didn't seem fat—just sort of "fleshy, you know"—and he had dark hair and dark eyes, which became all the more intense when he started popping pills.

Big Train generally made it into the poolroom on Thursdays, and that's where he'd stay for the next four days. The players were then hanging out at TJ Parker's—a room that never closed. Big Train would come in neat as could be, well dressed, good to go, and start playing. And then after a day or so he'd start popping amphetamines, which would keep him hopped up, shooting pool for hours and days, working, working, working, shooting until he was nearly blind. And then, after four days and typically going broke, Big Train would go home again and sleep. The self-inflicted damage was incredible, recalled Duke:

just eating, sleeping, popping pills, and playing pool. And when he got back to the poolroom and someone busted him (which was often), Greg "Big Train" Stevens would show his other great talent: that of bite artist. He would pick a local player, and then begin to whine and moan and plead to him about needing to borrow a hundred dollars to get a game. Or maybe he'd borrow someone's pool cue, and he'd gamble it away.

Eventually Big Train cleaned himself up, went off to his hometown of Wichita, Kansas, and opened a couple of poolrooms. He was sixty-two or sixty-three years old when he died.

"He'd take pills to stay up," said Bill Lee, a Houston old-timer who died in 2002. "I'd see him take two uppers to stay up and a downer to take off the edge. He'd have the pills in his hand, mixing them up. And he'd be up three or four days, playing pool, and then go back and sleep for like twelve hours and come back. When he would first start playing, he couldn't make a ball for like, twelve hours. And then the next twenty-four to forty-eight hours, he couldn't miss a ball. I remember watching him once and I noticed he wasn't missing, so I figured I'd count. I watched and he didn't miss in thirty-seven racks! I mean, he played safety sometimes, or he wouldn't get something on the break. But whatever ball he was shooting, he'd make. He finally missed and then I started counting again and he went another eighteen racks.

"He could beat five guys in a row, I mean *beat* them, and he'd be playing for days, and he'd win maybe thousands of dollars, and then he'd play the sixth guy, and he'd lose everything. He didn't know when to stop. It'd be too much of everything. He'd be up too long, and he'd give away too much, and he'd lose. He was a gambler. But it didn't matter to him. All he cared about was playing pool. All he wanted to do was play pool."

Duke said he played Big Train Stevens plenty, but because he didn't do speed, Duke claimed, he could only keep up for ten or fifteen hours. And then Duke would quit. He said he couldn't beat Greg straight up, no way, but could hit him just right—after he'd been up for two or three days—get a giant spot, and then beat him like an ugly child. Just beat on him until Stevens was wandering dazed, his pockets turned out, staggering.

"Greg was liable to come in dead broke, and win three or four thousand in the first two or three days," said Duke. "That's when you couldn't mess with Greg. He wasn't liable to miss too many balls at all hardly. But on that fourth day, people who knew him knew how to time him just right; they knew how to bust him, and they'd send him on home broke. It went on over and over, for a long time.

"But that was part of the poolroom, you know, the drugs and the drinking. Them guys came in on those speed pills. And when those diet pills came out in the early sixties and late fifties, them pool players started getting into them things…And so if a guy comes into a poolroom with money in his pocket, and he's been eating speed, he's going to get him a game—whether it's a good game or not, he's going to get him a game. And a lot of guys kinda depended on it."

Duke said you had to be wary about pill-popping hustlers like Greg "Big Train" Stevens. Not because they might fly off the handle, or get into a fight, but because they just might beat your ass playing one-pocket. The pills, at least at first, provided an edge. Speed made men alert.

"They were aware of everything that was going on," said Duke. "You don't overlook too much. If you're in a one-pocket game with somebody, you're subject to overlook something. But if you're eating those pills, you wouldn't overlook nothing. If it [the drug] was hitting you real good, you'd play real good behind it."

AUTHOR'S NOTES

Hustler Days is based upon a review of published material, interviews, and the author's personal observations. Direct quotes are noted with quotation marks. Otherwise, the author uses italics to approximate dialogue that has been described to him, or to capture the mood of certain events. The author used some license when reconstructing early pool matches in order to facilitate the narrative's flow.

INTRODUCTION

Besides his personal recollections, the author included material from *Hustlers, Beats and Others* by Ned Polsky (Lyons Press, 1998), and from *The New Illustrated Encyclopedia of Billiards* by Mike Shamos (Lyons Press, 1999). For inspiration regarding the nature of gamblers and gambling, the author looked to *The Crossroader* by N.M. Moore Jr. and Walt Darring (Regency Press, 1992).

CHAPTER 1: SHOOTING DOWN THE COWBOY

Chapter 1 is drawn largely from *The Bank Shot and Other Great Robberies* (World Publishing, 1966), written with Tom Fox. The author also included material from a July 27, 1978, article in *Rolling Stone* magazine by Robbert Sabbag and material from several interviews with Arthur "Babe" Cranfield and sociologist Ned Polsky. Also included is material from the book *Only Yesterday: An Informal History of the 1920s* by Frederick Lewis Allen (John Wiley & Sons, Inc., 1997). The author obtained some material about Ralph Greenleaf from a January 2000 *Billiards Digest* article by Mike Shamos.

CHAPTER 2: UNDER THE LEMONADE SUN

Some of the author's observations of Elizabeth City are drawn from his travels there and his interviews with local residents. Information about the Great Dismal Swamp, including Colonel William Byrd's description of it as "a vast body of dirt and nastiness," comes from the North Carolina Department of Cultural Resources. Other historical material comes from *The Year Book of the Pasquotank Historical Society* (1983), edited by Edna M. Shannonhouse.

Documents obtained from National Archives (and graciously provided to the author by the Lassiter family) revealed details about the Lassiter family's participation in the Civil War. Regarding Wimpy Lassiter's early home life, the author drew from the recollections of his younger brother, Clarence, and from Walter Davis, a childhood friend.

For this chapter the author also drew from interviews in a February 27, 1977, article in the *Charlotte News and Observer* by David Zucchino; in a March 1982 article in *Commonwealth Magazine* by Mike D'Orso; in an October 16, 1967, article in *Sports Illustrated* by Bob Ottum; in a May 29, 1977, article in the Virginia Pilot; and with Jim Rempe in *Billiards, Hustlers & Heroes: Legends & Lies and the Search for Higher Truth on the Green Felt* by John Grissim (St. Martin's Press, 1979).

The book *The Big Change: America Transforms Itself: 1900—1950* by Frederick Lewis Allen (Transaction Publishers, 1993) and Fats's autobiography also proved useful. Another of Lassiter's friends, Ed Tarkington, gave crucial assistance.

CHAPTER 3: THE RING GAME

Details relating to the family heritage of Jack "Jersey Red" Breitkopf came from interviews with Red's extended family, including Ann Webb, Art Breitkopf,

Herman Breitkopf, and Bonnie Bobbitt. Bonnie Bobbitt's genealogy work also proved invaluable.

Through multiple interviews, Jersey Red's brother, Marty Breitkopf, gave a firsthand account of the hustler's early family life in Newark. Cousin Art Breitkopf also provided insight. Red's widow, Dottie Breit, as well as Red's good friend John "Duke" Dowell, passed on childhood stories they heard from Red.

Other sources include the County of Essex (Red's birth certificate) and Red himself. Stories regarding his first hustle and his treatment by the city's black players, for instance, come directly from the author's interviews before Red's death. Red repeated some of those stories in other published works.

CHAPTER 4: THE BIG LIE OF LITTLE EGYPT

Fats's apocryphal story related to his arrival in Little Egypt comes from his autobiography. It was also repeated to the author, in various forms, by residents of Du Quoin, Dowell, and Johnston City, Illinois. Descriptions of 1940s Du Quoin, and Fats's early years there were taken from interviews with various residents, including Jess Kennedy, Ronnie Stroud, Mike Lively, John Ogolini, and Dowell mayor Luciano Lencini. The author also drew from his own observations of the area, including observations of the St. Nicholas Hotel in downtown Du Quoin. Joe Scoffic, owner of the St. Nicholas and one of Fats's first friends in Little Egypt, described Fats's arrival and the subsequent holdup of a high-dollar poker game at the St. Nicholas.

Fats's autobiography, a January 2, 1994 article in the *San Francisco Examiner,* and Evelyn Wanderone—during two interviews before she died—provided crucial details regarding their courtship and Fats's early years in Little Egypt.

CHAPTER 5: THE KING OF NORFOLK

Details regarding Wimpy Lassiter's Coast Guard career come from Lassiter's Coast Guard record, obtained from the National Archives. Those records—including his medical record—also provide a physical description of the then-twenty-two-year-old hustler. Jane Thompson, wife of one of Lassiter's commanding officers, provided further detail. More help came from Lassiter's brother Clarence and Lassiter's friend Ed Tarkington.

Lassiter himself spoke often of his experiences in Norfolk. Some of Lassiter's relevant interviews include those in *Commonwealth Magazine*, March 1982; the *Florida Accent*, August 25, 1968; *Sports Illustrated*, March 23, 1964, and October 16, 1967; a Bob Joyce article in the *The Daily Advance*, date unknown; and a *Virginia Pilot* article by Bob Lipper, May 29, 1977.

Some material also came from Fats's autobiography and Fats's first wife, Evelyn (who recounted to the author the bit about Fats's rejection by U.S. Army recruiters).

Details related to the 1953 tournament in San Francisco's Downtown Bowl can be found in Willie Mosconi's autobiography, *Willie's Game*, written with Stanley Cohen (Macmillan Publishing Company, 1993) and in various editions of the *San Francisco Chronicle* between March 2, 1953, and March 13, 1953.

CHAPTER 6: THE DEATH OF POOL

This chapter draws largely from Professor Polsky's work, *Hustlers, Beats and Others*. It also draws from interviews with Clarence Lassiter, Wimpy's brother, and from both Mosconi's and Fats's autobiographies. The author also included information from *Pool: History, Strategy and Legends* by Mike Shamos (Michael Friedman Publishing Group, Inc., 1994) The *Philadelphia Inquirer* provided information about the 1954 tournament at the Allinger

Billiard Academy. *Legends of Billiards* by George Fels (Billiards Digest, 1993) provided insight on pool player Irving Crane. This chapter also drew information from the *Philadelphia Daily News*, including an article from April 30, 1966.

CHAPTER 7: RED'S LAST REFUGE

Much of this chapter was drawn from interviews with Jersey Red, his brother Marty Breitkopf, and his friends Johnny Ervolino and John "Duke" Dowell. Billiards writers Eddie Robin and George Fels, as well as Professor Polsky, graciously provided further insight.

Dale Shaw's article "Anatomy of a Pool Hustler," from the November 1961 edition of *Saga Magazine,* provided a backdrop for this chapter. Other published sources include June 1967 and July 1968 editions of *Bowlers Journal and Billiard Revue*; the August 25, 1968, edition of the *Florida Accent*, and the fine work of Thomas C. Shaw, managing editor of *Pool & Billiard Magazine*. His March 1997 profile of Jersey Red proved particularly useful. The author also included information from various *Billiards Digest* columns by Fels, and details about the first appearance of the so-called "Jersey Red shot" from the book *Winning One-Pocket* by Robin (Billiard World Publishing, 1996).

CHAPTER 8: CROSSROADS

The author drew some of his observations about Johnston City and Little Egypt from his travels there. He also interviewed JoAnn and David McNeal (in their Johnston City home); Jan Jansco (grandson of George Jansco); Marshall "Tuscaloosa Squirrel" Carpenter, and Mike Shamos. Dottie Breit, widow of Jersey Red, provided additional recollections of George Jansco.

Karen Fox, widow of *Philadelphia Inquirer* writer Tom Fox, provided insight regarding the first Johnston City jamboree and her husband's initial article about it for *Sports Illustrated.*

Major published sources include Shamos' *Pool: History, Strategy and Legends;* Polsky's *Hustlers, Beats and Others; Willie's Game* by Mosconi and Cohen; and *The Lions and the Lambs* by Thomas Fensch (A. S. Barnes and Co., 1970).

Besides numerous editions of the *Marion Daily Republican* and the *Southern Illinoisan,* newspaper and magazine sources include a 1963 edition of the *Fort Worth Star-Telegram;* a December 4, 1966, edition of *Sports Illustrated;* a 1961 edition of the Long Beach Independent-Press-Telegram; a 1987 edition of the *Los Angeles Times,* a March 24, 1995, dispatch by United Press International, and a February 23, 1983, article for Knight-Ridder Newspapers.

CHAPTER 9: WORLD'S GREATEST ROADHOUSE

Regarding Red's arrival in Houston, the author drew from numerous interviews with Red's widow, Dottie Breit, and Red's friends: Duke Dowell, Bill Lee, and Reeves Smith. Billiards writer George Fels also helped. The author likewise interviewed pool pro Grady Mathews for this chapter.

Chapter 9 also depends in large part on various interviews with JoAnn and Dave McNeal in Johnston City, Illinois. The author obtained additional details related to the early Johnston City events from the *Marion Daily Republican* and *Southern Illinoisan.* Also included is information from *Bowlers Journal* and a November 19, 1962, edition of *Newsweek.*

CHAPTER 10: 1965

The author drew descriptions of the first Stardust event from his interviews with JoAnn McNeal, as well as from various articles in the *Las Vegas Sun* and

Bowlers Journal. Additional information comes from the *National Billiards News* and the *Billiard Review.*

Arthur Cranfield provided details of the 1965 world's straight pool tournament in New York. An April 9, 1965, edition of *Time Magazine* and a March 26, 1965, edition of the *New York Times* also proved useful. This chapter includes information from the *Marion Daily Republican.*

Information related to Wimpy Lassiter came from Lassiter's friend Ed Tarkington; Red's widow Dottie Breit; a 1970 article in *Playboy* magazine; and *Bowlers Journal*—including a 1966 article by Tom Fox.

Information related to Minnesota Fats came from Dottie Breit, Fats's autobiography, Sabbag's 1970 article for *Rolling Stone*, and articles in *Esquire* and *Life* magazines.

Descriptions of Jersey Red and Dottie Breit's road trips come from interviews with Dottie Breit and include some license by the author.

CHAPTER 11: THE WOLF

This chapter includes information drawn from interviews with Karen Fox, widow of Fats's biographer Tom Fox. The author also interviewed JoAnn McNeal and pool pros Nick Varner and Jimmy Moore. Dowell mayor Luciano Lencini and other friends of Fats graciously provided extra help.

Craig Vetter's 1970 article in *Playboy* magazine proved invaluable for its description of the 1969 matchup between Wimpy Lassiter and Ronnie Allen. Fox's May 1967 article in *Bowlers Journal* ("Another Win for Wimpy") about that year's World's Straight Pool tournament provided a plethora of details related to Lassiter's character and that year's BRPAA championship. More detail came from the *New York Times* and the Associated Press.

Coverage in the *Los Angeles Times*, including a January 22, 1967, article, detailed that year's Long Beach tournament. The chapter also includes information from the *Billiards Review*.

CHAPTER 12: THE HUSTLER KING

The recollections of John "Duke" Dowell and Dottie Breit proved useful for chapter 12. Breit also provided the author with copies of tournament charts from her collection of personal memorabilia. The Houston Police Department helped put the 1969 gambling raid into context (it was the largest such Houston raid in memory).

Others interviewed for this chapter include pool pro Grady Mathews and Red's friends Bill Lee, Reeves Smith, Willie Elder, and Denny Glenn.

Published sources include the Associated Press, the *Houston Post*, and the *Houston Chronicle*. From the *Houston Post*, the author drew material from a September 13, 1969, article by Tommy West. From the *Houston Chronicle*, the author drew information from a January 5, 1969, article by Zarco Franks, an August 10, 1969, article by Bob Rippy, an October 26, 1969, article by Martin Dreyer, and an unbylined article that appeared on September 12, 1969.

Various longtime journalists at the *Houston Chronicle*, a former employer of the author, also provided recollections of Zarco Franks.

Regarding the 1969 U.S. Open, the author drew material from the *New York Times*, recollections by John "Duke" Dowell and Ed Tarkington, and a videotape of the ABC *Wide World of Sports* that featured the matchup.

EPILOGUE: WINNERS & LOSERS

JoAnn McNeal graciously related details of her father's death. Clarence, Barbara, and Mike Lassiter spoke of the passing of Wimpy Lassiter. Dottie

Breit and John "Duke" Dowell spoke of Red's difficult battle with cancer. Jersey Red himself told the author about the benefit tournament held on his behalf. The author also attended Red's funeral.

For this chapter, the author also interviewed Red's friends Duke Dowell, Denny Glenn and Bill Lee.

Dottie Breit spoke about the character of Paulie Jansco, as did JoAnn and Dave McNeal. Other sources were a July 1969 edition of *Bowlers Journal and Billiard Revue*; a July 31, 1972, Associated Press dispatch by Charles Chamberlain; July and December 1972 editions of *Bowlers Journal and Billiard Review*, and two editions of the *Southern Illinoisan*, one from October 17, 1972, and the other from January 9, 1974.

The July 28, 1978, article in *Rolling Stone* magazine by Sabbag detailed Fats's matchup with Willie Mosconi at New York's Waldorf-Astoria. Quotes for this section were drawn from that article. According to billiards columnist George Fels, only the Spinks/Ali fight that year would have garnered higher television sports ratings.

Fels also provided information about Lassiter's and Fats's inductions into the Billiards Congress Hall of Fame—in 1983 and 1984, respectively.

The author also drew information about Fats from a February 11, 1968, nationally syndicated newspaper article by Mike McGrady. A piece by Mark McDonald that appeared in the *St. Louis Post Dispatch* on January 9, 1994, spoke of Fats's divorce, move to Nashville, and second marriage.

Evelyn Wanderone also spoke to the author about her breakup with Fats. Several friends of Fats in Du Quoin—John Ogolini and Dowell mayor Luciano Lencini among them—provided further detail.

The observations of renowned billiards writer Robert Byrne also proved invaluable.

Finally, material related to Fats's visit to the Nashville psychiatric ward and his fines for shoplifting and unpaid back taxes come from the Associated Press. Those articles appeared on September 15, 1993; September 14, 1985; and May 7, 1987, respectively.

APPENDIX II, THE PLAYERS:

Descriptions of the Big Hoorah hustle were taken from various published accounts, including an April 1965 edition of the *Canton Repository*. Published works include an Aug. 20, 1977, edition of the *Evansville Press*, Robert Byrne's *Wonderful World of Pocket Billiards* (Harcourt, 1996), John Grissim's *Billiards, Hustlers & Heroes, Legends & Lies and the Search for Higher Truth on the Green Felt* (Book Sales, 1982) and Fench's *The Lions and The Lambs*. The author also interviewed Willis' friend Dean Chance of Wooster, Ohio; and Dick Moecia, of Canton, Ohio.

The author drew details about poolroom legend Johnny Ervolino through various interviews with Ervolino between June and October 1998.

For stories of Greg "Big Train" Stevens, the author spoke to Bill Lee, John "Duke" Dowell and Dottie Breit in Houston.

Bill Lee, Dowell and Grady Mathews also spoke to the author about Ronnie Allen. A 1998 article by David McCumber in Billiards Digest, as well as a May 1968 article in *Bowlers Journal and Billiards Revue*, also shed light on Allen's character. The author reviewed relevant material in Fensch's book, *The Lions and the Lambs*.

Again, Fensch's book proved useful with regards to the section about U.J. Puckett. The author also reviewed various articles in the *Fort Worth Star-Telegram*, including Puckett's June 24, 1992 obituary in that newspaper. A Nov. 1968 edition of *Bowlers Journal and Billiards Revue* proved useful.

ACKNOWLEDGMENTS

I would like to thank a few people—they deserve more credit than I can express. Claudia Kolker, my good friend from Houston, encouraged me from the beginning. My sister, Mary Catherine Johnston, selflessly read half-baked early drafts of both the book and the proposal. My agent Dan Mandel stuck with me; my editor at Lyons, Ann Treistman, created order from chaos. Jon Resh, the very talented graphic design artist in Chicago, volunteered both his time and his apartment couch. Mike Panozzo graciously allowed me access to archives and photos at *Billiards Digest*. I also want to thank my parents, Alec and Aida Dyer, for their constant support. Several others also lent a hand, including JoAnn and Dave McNeal in Johnston City, Clarence and Barbara Lassiter in Elizabeth City, and Dottie Breit in Houston. Others who provided encouragement or assistance include Steve Campbell, Dery Dyer, John "Duke" Dowell, Devon and Andrea Fletcher, John Gravois, Stephanie Elizondo Griest, Steve Jetton, Julie Mason, John Moritz, Ned Pickler, Doug and Debbie Posso, and Jay Root. For inspiration, I must thank the first pool hustler I ever knew—my Uncle Rob—as well as those I met later in life: Miguel Solano, Julio Granados, and Luis "Pichitas" Calderon. Giants all.

Again, Thanks.

INDEX

Brazeltown, Dottie. *See* Breit,
    Dottie Thorpe
Breit, Dottie Thorpe, 142–46, 155
    Houston Invitational, 193, 204,
        206
    1965 Hustlers' Jamboree,
        171–72
    on Jersey Red, 111, 150, 151,
        218
    on the road, 151–52, 155–56
    1967 World Championship,
        181, 183
Breit, Jack. *See also* Breitkopf,
    Jack; Jersey Red, 3, 6–7,
        152, 167, 190
    Winning One-Pocket, 215
Breitkopf, Arthur, 39, 40
Breitkopf, Eda Weinstein, 38, 39
Breitkopf, Jack; *See also* Breit,
    Jack; Jersey Red
    early years of, 40–42
    family of, 38–40
    pool training of, 42–48
Breitkopf, Jake, 39–40
Breitkopf, Louis Jacob, 38
Breitkopf, Marty, 39, 42, 44,
    104
Breitkopf, Max, 39
Broadway Fats. *See* Minnesota
    Fats
Brock's Billiards, 29
Brooklyn Johnny. *See* Ervolino,
    Johnny

Brunswick Billiards, 100, 119,
    127
Bums, 33
Byrd, William, 6, 19, 20n4

C

Camp, Marcel, 73
Canton, Joe, 94
Caras, Jimmy, 79, 81, 82
Carpenter, Marshall "Tuscaloosa
    Squirrel," 7, 242
    1961 Hustlers' Jamboree,
        114–17, 126, 129
    1962 Hustlers' Jamboree, 137
    1963 Hustlers' Jamboree, 139
Carson, Johnny, 133, 162,
    162n22
Case, George, 41
Castras, Jimmy, 16, 49–56,
    58–59
CBS, and 1963 tournament,
    139
Central Cue, 142
Chamberlain, Charles, 210
Channels, Roy, 184
Cheek, Nubby, 178–79
The Chinese, 42–43
Cincinnati Kid. *See* Willis, Don
City Billiards, 25–26, 29
Clay, Cassius, 162
Cobb, Ty, 153
Cohen, Stanley, 80
Cohn, Rachel (Ray), 39–40

Hustlers Holiday in the Lion's Den
(Fox), 127–29
Hustlers' Jamboree
1961, 114–17, 124–33
1962, 134–36
1963, 138–40
1964, 152–53
1965, 169–73
1969, 185–89
Hustling, nature of,
111–13

I

Ives, Speedy, 29, 30, 34

J

Jacobson, Paul, 91
Jaffey, Milt, 164
James, Etta, 3n1
Jansco, George
death of, 208–9
1961 Hustlers' Jamboree,
114–17, 132
1962 Hustlers' Jamboree,
134–35
1963 Hustlers' Jamboree,
138–40
1964 Hustlers' Jamboree,
152–53
1965 Hustler's Jamboree,
169–73
and Minnesota Fats, 120–21,
183–84

and Stardust Invitational,
163–64
on World's Invitation
tournament, 138
Jansco, JoAnn. *See* McNeal,
JoAnn Jansco
Jansco, Paulie, 116, 120–21,
134, 152, 165–66, 185
Cue Club raid, 209–11
Jersey Red. *See also* Breit, Jack;
Breitkopf, Jack, 38, 154,
242
at the 7-11, 101–3, 104–5
and baseball, 103–4
and Dottie Thorpe, 141–46,
222
in Houston, 146–51
Houston Invitational, 190,
196–98, 203–6
1963 Hustlers' Jamboree,
139–41
1964 Hustlers' Jamboree,
152
1965 Hustlers' Jamboree,
169–73
"Jersey Red shot," 107
and Johnny Ervolino, 246–247
last years of, 215–18
1967 Long Beach Invitational,
175–77
and Minnesota Fats, 57, 108
on the road, 155–57
and Ronnie Allen, 240

1965 Stardust Invitational,
166–69
1965 straight-pool tournament,
157–61
style of, 109–13
temper of, 108–9
1966 U. S. Invitational Pocket
Billiards, 174
1969 U. S. Open Pocket Billiard
Championship, 190–92,
207
1967 World Championship,
178, 181–83
1963 World's Invitation
tournament, 137–38
Jimmy the Greek. *See* Castras,
Jimmy
Joey with Glasses, 105, 168
Johnny Irish. *See* Lineen, Johnnie
Johnson, Harold, 142, 143
Johnson, Larry "Boston Shorty,"
7, 128, 141, 166, 190,
207, 242
1965 Hustlers' Jamboree,
171, 173
style of, 106
Johnston City (IL), 52, 69, 114
1961 Hustlers' Jamboree,
124–33, 132–33
1962 Hustlers' Jamboree,
135–37
1963 Hustlers' Jamboree,
138–40

1964 Hustlers' Jamboree,
152–53
1965 Hustlers' Jamboree,
169–73
1969 Hustlers' Jamboree,
185–89
Jones, Handsome Danny, 7, 167,
171, 190, 240
Houston Invitational, 194, 196,
198, 202, 203, 205
1961 Hustlers' Jamboree, 117,
129–32
1962 Hustlers' Jamboree,
135–36
Jones, Jimmy, 34

K

Kefauver, Estes, 88
Kelly, Ed, 175, 175n24
Kelly, Eddy, 167
Kennedy, Jess, 52
Kennedy, John F., 141
Keogh, Jerome, 15
Kid Galahad, 244
Knoxville Bear. *See* Taylor, Eddie
"Knoxville Bear"
Kupcinet, Irv, 162

L

Laden, Beefy, 30–31, 35
Lake Drummond Hotel, 20,
20n5
Lassiter, Charles, 24, 213, 214

M

Maples, hardwood, 6

Marion Daily Republican, 172

Marketing, emergence of, 17–18

Marriage rate, and pool, 91–92

Massey, Mike, 195, 201

Mathews, Grady, 195, 240

McCumber, David, 241

McDonald, Mark, 220

McGehean, Eddie, 167

McGirr's (poolhall), 105, 105n9, 112, 117, 246

McGown, Frank, 178

McMullen, Bill, 30, 31

McNeal, David, 121, 209

McNeal, JoAnn Jansco, 121, 134, 164–66, 170, 209

Miller, Al, 172

Minnesota Fats, 3, 4–5, 6, 8, 87

at the 7-11, 108

adopting identity as, 121–24

appetite of, 55–56, 61

Bank Shot and Other Great Robberies, The, 34, 53–54, 184

and Billiards Hall of Fame, 218–19

at Cranfield's, 13–16

early years of, 11–12

and Evelyn Inez Grass, 58–61, 63, 219–20

exhibition with Cowboy Weston, 12–13

fame of in 1960s, 161–63, 183–85

family of, 8–11

and George Jansco, 120, 183–84

The Hustler character, 1, 117, 121–22

1961 Hustlers' Jamboree, 116, 127–28, 129–33

1962 Hustlers' Jamboree, 135–36

1965 Hustler's Jamboree, 169–73

impact of, 221–22

last years of, 220–21

in Little Egypt, 49–63

and one-pocket, 57–58

other nicknames of, 13

semiretirement of, 88, 93, 94

and Willie Mosconi, 121–22, 122n13, 212–13

and Wimpy Lassiter, 34–37, 70–73

and World War II, 70–71

Mizerak, Steve, Jr., 141, 190, 217

Moore, Cowboy Jimmy, 7, 167, 175, 190, 237, 245–246

1953 championship, 82, 86

1954 championship, 94, 95–96, 100

Houston Invitational, 196, 198, 206